Overture To
Victoria

Fortune
from Aunt Sylvia.
Feb: 24ᵗ '63.

Overture
to
Victoria

by McKenzie Porter

Longmans Green
& Company Toronto

*Longmans Green & Company
20 Cranfield Road, Toronto 16
First Edition 1961*

*Printed and bound in Canada
by the
T. H. Best Printing Company*

ACKNOWLEDGEMENT
of Copyright Material

*Quotations from the following books
are made with the kind permission of
the publishers*

*Royal Dukes, by Roger Fulford.
Gerald Duckworth & Co. Ltd.*

*Castle of Quebec, by Joan E.
Morgan. J. M. Dent & Sons (Canada)
Limited*

*Gibraltar and the Mediterranean,
by G. T. Garratt. Jonathan Cape
Limited*

*The Royal Family, by Pierre Berton.
Alfred A. Knopf Incorporated*

ACKNOWLEDGEMENTS

Hector Bolitho gave me from his own collection much unpublished material on the Duke of Kent and Julie de St. Laurent. He also introduced me to one of their descendants in England, who augmented the verbal information I had acquired from other descendants in Canada.

Luis Carrier of Montreal, a historian and an intimate of the Kent descendants in Canada, was another excellent source of enlightenment.

Sir Owen Morshead, Librarian at Windsor Castle, was friendly and helpful.

In Martinique, *E. Goyheneche*, Archiviste-en-Chef; *A. Michaud*, secretary to the Bishop; and *F. Boucly*, Procureur Général, went to considerable trouble on my behalf.

The library staffs of the University of Toronto, the University of British Columbia, McGill University in Montreal, and the British Museum co-operated with kindness and efficiency.

My father, *John M. Porter*, of St. Anne's-on-the-Sea, England, and my brother, *F. E. S. Porter*, of the same town, provided assistance of an important nature.

My wife *Kathleen* typed my notes and my fair copy and gave me constant encouragement.

In making use of published material I leaned heavily in parts upon *W. J. Anderson, David Duff, Roger Fulford, Thomas Raddall, B. Dufebvre, G. M. Trevelyan,* and *Gaston de Lessert*, whose works are listed in the bibliography.

To all these people, living and dead, I offer my sincere thanks.

to my wife
KATHLEEN

Chapter I

IF YOU ask the average British subject to name Queen Victoria's father, it is highly likely that you'll confound him. Historians, of course, know that he was Prince Edward, Duke of Kent, fourth son of George III. But people whose knowledge of the Georgian era is limited to high-school books generally look blank at mention of his name.

The reason Edward has been forgotten is simple: Queen Victoria didn't wish him to be remembered. There were aspects of his background that conflicted with her stern moral code. For twenty-seven years before he married Victoria's mother, Edward lived with a beautiful French countess who concealed her identity under the romantic pseudonym of Julie de St. Laurent. This liaison, which was probably strengthened by a morganatic marriage, produced two sons, the first of whom grew up in Canada and the second in Australia.

Had Julie de St. Laurent been a Protestant, it is possible that the elder of these boys would have been acceptable to the British Government as a king of England. But Julie was a Roman Catholic, and so her union with Edward, under the terms of the Royal Marriage Act, was invalid. There was never the slightest risk of the obscure half-brother in Canada challenging Victoria's right to the throne; but his very existence irked and unsettled the Queen. He constituted a standing reminder of the barn-yard manoeuvres that had preceded her own birth.

After the death in 1817 of Princess Charlotte, daughter of the Prince Regent, it was necessary for three sons of George III to marry for the specific purpose of begetting another heir to the throne. Included in this trio of conscripted bridegrooms was the fifty-year-old Edward. He had to part from the delightful woman he'd adored for more than a quarter of a century and walk to the altar with that plump, energetic, and amorous little chatterbox, the Princess Victoria of Saxe-Saalfeld-Coburg. Queen Victoria, the fruit of this marriage, winced at the thought of its expedience. Although she once insisted that she was proud of her soldier father, she rarely mentioned him. And she detested her mother.

At Victoria's court the subject of her father's association with Julie de St. Laurent was taboo. Throughout her reign it was always politely pretended that Julie had never existed. After the letters between Edward and Julie passed into Queen Victoria's hands, they were never seen again. Nineteenth-century biographers were too fearful of Victoria's displeasure to explore her father's life in detail. As a result Edward is one of the most shadowy figures on the Georgian tapestry. He flits like a wraith through Regency biography, manifesting himself here and there in a few brief, vivid scenes and then sinking back into the shadows.

Edward held no happier a place in his family's esteem than he did in his daughter's memory. His half-witted father disliked him from the day he broke a clock. Because he was sexually constant, temperate in his use of alcohol, opposed to gambling, and conservative in his dress, he was mocked by his licentious, drunken, prodigal and foppish brothers. The Prince Regent dubbed him "Simon Pure". Even the royal princesses thought him stuffy and nicknamed him "Joseph Surface".

He was a fine soldier, valiant in the field and meticulous in the garrison, and for this reason he incurred the professional jealousy of his brother the Duke of York, the Commander-in-Chief of the British Army. York deliberately deprived Edward of a fighting command during the Homeric days that led up to Waterloo. In the military sphere Edward also encountered a formidable enemy in the shape of the Duke of Wellington. The Iron Duke despised Edward and called him "the Corporal", because Edward believed that soldiers should be taught to read and write. Furthermore, for reasons of War Office politics, the severity of Edward's discipline was grossly exaggerated and he was often represented as a tyrant and sadist.

The aristocracy looked upon Edward as a dangerous eccentric because he was years ahead of his time in political theory. He championed Robert Owen, the father of British socialism, and Joseph Lancaster, the pioneer of universal education. Edward was the patron of scores of charities. Although he was a stalwart monarchist, he absorbed many of the democratic ideas of Louis Philippe,

2

the "Citizen King" of France. While he had a right royal sense of his own dignity, he once consented gallantly to dance with a poor old woman; and he was not ashamed, when hamstrung by poverty, to drive his own coach and pair. He was a burly man, more than six feet tall, and in the street one day he knocked out a political brawler.

Edward had many weaknesses, of course, including a certain pomposity, a tendency to dabble too deeply in the private affairs of other people, an appalling inability to handle money, and an incurable urge to whine about his penury. But he bridged the great gulf between the eighteenth and nineteenth centuries, and founded many traditions upon which the twentieth-century concept of monarchy is based. He inaugurated the trend that changed the throne from a hierarchical into a popular institution. Queen Victoria was unreasonably ashamed of her father. It is hoped that this biography will show that she owed more of her greatness to Edward's genes than she did to Albert's brains.

Chapter II

WHEN Prince Edward Augustus was born on November 2, 1767, his father George III was twenty-nine years old and in the seventh year of his sixty-year reign. His mother Charlotte was twenty-three. Two-thirds of Britain's nine million population could remember—many with wistfulness—the romantic Stuart risings of 1715 and 1745. The courts of Europe were still full of exiled Scots who dreamed of a third rebellion. But the House of Hanover, despite its unpopular Teutonic temperament, was now impregnable. It had been fortified by conquest and prosperity, while the Stuart dynasty had been discredited by the notorious crapulence in Naples of the Young Pretender. Although George III smarted under the gibes of John Wilkes, who accused him of despotic ambitions, the crown sat squarely on his head.

Under the aggressive ministries of William Pitt the Elder, recently ennobled as Lord Chatham, Britain had risen toward the zenith of her power. During the Seven Years War France had been defeated in the colonial battles of West and East. Canada had fallen to General James Wolfe at Quebec. Nearly all the settled terrain of North America was now within the British Empire. The wealth of the West Indies poured into London, Bristol and Liverpool. Robert Clive, now Baron Clive of Plassey, had just returned from India for the last time, leaving that rich and exotic domain safe in British hands. Captain James Cook was about to sail once more, and to pick up, in the easiest and cheapest act of territorial accretion on record, the continent of Australia. There wasn't a nation on earth that dared to twist the lion's tail.

Arts and letters flourished. Doctor Samuel Johnson was expounding his philosophy in the Mitre Tavern. Edward Gibbon was writing *The Decline and Fall of the Roman Empire*. Sir Joshua Reynolds was founding the Royal Academy. At Drury Lane David Garrick was playing King Lear. All over the country crescents of houses were rising in the style known as Georgian, and they represented the most graceful architecture England had seen since the Roman occupation.

Gentlemen still wore a wig, a three-cornered hat, brocaded coats, knee breeches of satin or velvet, hose to match, and buckled shoes. Ladies wore big feathered hats, full-skirted silk and muslin dresses in pastel shades, and spike-heel pumps. The middle and lower classes copied these fashions in wool and fustian. Food was plentiful, and never was England more carnivorous. The affluent ate prodigious meals of beef, lamb, duck, chicken, and game, washed down with French wines. The poor devoured tripes, cow-heels, pigs' knuckles, cheese, and home-brewed beer. In the cities hundreds of steam-filled eating-houses thrived.

The heavy diet of the age stimulated the lustiness of the sexes. In an era of flagrant sensuality, noblewomen rode in sedan chairs through the muddy streets of London to rendezvous with noble lovers, and bore a bewildering confusion of blue-blooded bastards. In dark corners of the Strand, servant girls were tipped sixpence or a shilling for pleasuring men of James Boswell's tastes. The illegitimacy and disease arising from wide-spread carnal exercise prompted a certain Dr. Condom to invent a druggists' commodity that became the object of civilization's most furtive industry.

But on the whole life was worth living and prospects were serene. Napoleon wasn't born yet. The American Revolution was nine years off. The French Revolution was not due for twenty-two years. In the nation's side the sharpest thorn was the highwayman, and on its reputation the blackest blot was the slave trade.

At first thought it seems incredible that Edward, born in such an epoch, should eventually sire Victoria, who would reign on into the days of automobiles, telephones, machine-guns, submarines, and radio telegraphy. But when it is remembered that the Industrial Revolution was already gaining momentum, the two-generation span between such contrasting eras does not seem so fantastic. Before Edward was three years old Richard Arkwright's spinning jenny and James Watt's steam engine had been patented. Coal had been matched to iron. Steel, for centuries exclusive to the sword and the ploughshare, was now in demand for cog-wheels and pistons. Peasants from Scotland, Ireland, Wales, and the southern English shires, robbed of common land by the spread of enclosure, were trickling toward the potteries, mines, factories, and foundries of

Staffordshire, Lancashire, Yorkshire, and Durham. The trickle would become a freshet and the freshet a flood.

Most of these toilers would suffer the abysmal poverty and awful rigours of the world's first industrial class. A few, however, would become rich. The new magnates would smother the classical traditions of the eighteenth century under a blanket of nineteenth-century materialism and vulgarity. They would build miles of mean streets for their workers within earshot of the peremptory factory whistles. Partly because they were to become contemptuous of the frills and fancies of inherited privilege, and partly because the fox-hunting clergy had no stomach for life among the "dark Satanic mills", they would turn their backs on the ancient ceremony and pomp of the Church of England, heed the passionate apostles of dissent, and in many cases make a cult of nonconformity.

Steeped in statistics, devoted to detail, and mated to machines, they would buckle a belt of grime around England's green waist. Dull dogs they might have been in southern English eyes, but within a generation these northern masters of the mills were to become in-directly the masters of the earth. Edward would be among the first of royal blood to recognize their achievements, to sympathize with their finer sentiments, and to perceive the Golden Fleece that lay beyond the muck, sweat and tyranny of their course.

His parents, George III and Queen Charlotte, were lumpish. They displayed the temperamental mediocrity of the petty German line-age from which they both sprang. They shrank self-consciously from the brilliance of London society. Buckingham House saw less and less of them after the King reached his thirties, and they divided most of their time between Windsor Castle and Kew Palace.

George III's dislike of the English nobility probably stemmed from his humiliation by Lady Sarah Lennox, the beautiful daughter of the Duke of Richmond. As a youth he had been captivated by Lady Sarah, but he had been much too solemn to please so mettle-some a woman. After sending a proposal of marriage to Lady Sarah by an intermediary, he met her soon afterwards and asked: "What do you think of it? Tell me, for my happiness depends on it." Lady Sarah tossed her head and replied, "Nothing, sir." Whereupon George cried pettishly, "Nothing comes of nothing," and stamped out of the room.

It is doubtful whether George III would have been allowed to wed Lady Sarah in any event, for his Hanoverian mother, the Princess of Wales, indifferent to the fact that Stuarts, Tudors and Plantagenets had taken brides from the English peerage, believed that only the tiny German states nurtured Protestant girls whose pedigrees fitted them to become a queen of England. Largely as a result of her machinations, George III was matched with the Princess Charlotte of Mecklenburg-Strelitz, a German duchy of small landowners and compliant serfs. Brought up in an atmosphere of frugality, needlework, music, ten o'clock bed, and best clothes on Sunday, Charlotte had once asked: "Who will ever marry a poor little Princess like me?" Her brother, Duke Adolphus Frederick, the ruler of Mecklenburg-Strelitz, was chiefly remarkable for his skill at embroidering beautiful dressing-gowns.

The crusty homespun character of George III dovetailed nicely into Charlotte's prim personality, and they were in accord when they eschewed the masked balls, routs and banquets then in vogue. The King behaved like a suspicious peasant, not only in society but in the affairs of state. When Chatham claimed for the office of Prime Minister powers superior to those of the monarch, George III was filled with astonishment, bewilderment and hate. When Chatham urged greater legislative freedom for the American colonies, George III became almost apoplectic and got rid of him.

To George the colonies were but a collection of sharecroppers huddled on the perimeter of his holdings. He never showed any sensibility of their problems, and it is doubtful whether he had more than a schoolboy's knowledge of their geography, climate, economy, progress, or aspirations. They were no more than tithe-payers, there to do the bidding of his stewards, the governors.

George's insistence that the American colonies should share the cost of the Seven Years War was not unreasonable, for, after all, they had been saved from the possibilities of French dominion. But the bull-headed manner in which, through the medium of his new and most malleable Prime Minister, Lord North, he specified what sort of taxes they should pay cost England dear. The effect of the Boston Tea Party on George III's thinking was negligible. The significance of the American Revolution never penetrated his skull. Burgoyne's defeat at Saratoga in 1778 was to George a mere reverse, for in his Teutonic eyes Europe was still the power-house of the earth and a colony here or there mattered little. He plodded through his early reign as stuffily and blindly as a bucolic village squire, as if the peoples who owed him allegiance were no more numerous or important than the forelock-tugging vassals of his tinpot dukedom in Hanover.

When Queen Charlotte was delivered of Edward in Buckingham House, a red-brick residence which stood on the site of the present Buckingham Palace, he proved to be the biggest baby she ever had. His three older brothers, subsequently George IV, Frederick, Duke of York, and William IV, were aged five, four, and two respectively, and his sister Charlotte, the Princess Royal, was an infant of twelve months. Within the next twenty-four years George III and Queen Charlotte were to beget ten more children. All would survive to maturity save the youngest sons, Octavius and Alfred, who were to die in infancy.

Spiritually, Edward was a son of the nineteenth century. On the night he was born the royal family mourned a typical son of the eighteenth century. Over the way in St. James's Palace the body of another Edward—George III's favourite brother, the then Duke of York—was lying in state. York's sudden end, at the age of twenty-five, had resulted from a chill sustained through exposing his perspiring body to the night air after a romp with a company of trollops in Monte Carlo. The royal homes were draped in crêpe. Courtiers spoke in whispers. Years later the infant born in this hour of mourning told his chaplain: "My arrival was somewhat mala-propos. Sometimes the thought has crossed me whether my in-opportune appearance was not ominous of the life of gloom and struggle that awaited me."

George III named his fourth son after his deceased brother. Al-though Edward, Duke of Kent, grew up to be a gallant, he was in a different class from his late uncle Edward, Duke of York. In his attitude to women he was as courtly as his uncle had been lascivious. The reason for his distinctive sexual fastidiousness is not easy to perceive in the early records of his youth. Up to the age of seventeen he was educated under conditions which depraved his six brothers.

George III reared his sons with ambivalence. In one respect he treated them like Little Lord Fauntleroys, in another like boisterous young animals. At Kew, thirteen miles up the Thames from West-minster, visitors may still see around the Green the houses George built as a royal colony. Most of them were inhabited by physicians, governesses, tutors, ushers, pages, and maids. There were few courtiers of noble blood in attendance, another pointer to the theory that the King and Queen were at ease only in the company of England's humbler classes.

The famous Kew Gardens, nearby, had been laid out by George III's widowed mother in collaboration with her reputed lover, Lord Bute. Later George III built his mock-Gothic mansion at Kew but his residence was the old Palace. The Kew Palace servants were poorly paid. Most of them were boarded out around the Green and had to provide their own meals from their wages. Some stigma was attached by the upper classes to this form of domestic economy. Charlotte also took an unqueenly close interest in the private affairs of her servants, punishing by dismissal the most trivial acts of impropriety. There was a certain stinginess, too, at her table. Horace Walpole, the essayist, who lived in an ugly mansion stuffed with curios at nearby Twickenham, was invited over to dinner one night. He complained, with a wealthy bachelor's petulance, that the Queen's hairdresser waited at table and that not enough beef was allowed for the soup.

The Queen brought up her daughters as she had been reared herself. They were schooled on narrow, crimping lines and imprisoned within the family circle. It is not surprising to read in some accounts a hint of unorthodox relationships with their brothers. Princess Sophia was so repressed that she was eventually seduced by an elderly royal attendant named General Garth.

The Queen's ideas of medicine were eccentric even for those days. She raised no objections when Sir George Baker, an old-fashioned physician, prescribed a strong emetic for whooping cough. When they had measles the children were bled and blistered. Even a fall from a horse was followed by being bled. But in spite of these enfeebling therapies, most of them grew up strong.

Some thanks for their health were due to the King. He was fanatical about the simple diet and fresh air recommended by the Duke of Buckingham, whose own handsome sons were much admired. For breakfast at eight o'clock the royal children had dry bread, with a basin of warm milk, or a mixture of two-thirds milk and one-third tea, with a little sugar. Dinner, at two in the afternoon, consisted of meat without fat, clear gravy, and greens. Sometimes they were allowed fish. They were especially fond of

9

shrimps, which at that time were nearly always served cold in a congealed butter sauce. Before the Princes and Princesses were permitted to eat such shrimps, however, the butter sauce was always warmed and strained away.

As a dessert they enjoyed fruit tart, but were always ordered to eat it "without the crust". The Princes were given one glass of wine a day. Twice a week all the children were allowed coffee. At suppertime they received more tea and bread. For some obscure reason the children went without supper every Monday. It could be that this day was set aside for social calls. In their memoirs several women comment with amusement on the appetite displayed by the Princes and Princesses when out visiting.

The children's bedrooms were spare and draughty in the extreme. The floors were devoid of carpets, and no curtains were permitted around their four-posters. Queen Charlotte ordered that once every fortnight the children should have a bath "whether they need it or not".

Every Thursday Kew Gardens was open to the public. Crowds came up from London and in the distance were able to see the Princes at work on a model farm run by Arthur Young, the famed agronomist, or playing single-wicket cricket. Once a week the royal family walked two miles through Kew Gardens to Richmond, the Princes and Princesses following their parents in couples.

We get our first glimpse of Edward at a noble gathering summoned by George III for the purpose of inspecting the royal progeny. On a dais before the braided throng stood George, Prince of Wales, aged seven, in scarlet and gold. He already wore the highest decoration the Sovereign of England may bestow—the Order of the Garter. Prince Frederick, the favourite, aged five, was equipped with a child's-size mitre, crosier and cope to signify his rank of Bishop of Osnaburg, a see over which his father, as Elector of Hanover, held power of appointment. Prince William, aged four, Princess Charlotte, aged three, and Prince Edward, aged two, still deemed a trifle young for honours, were dressed more modestly in Roman togas.

The astonished peers, who hated having to drag themselves to King George's tedious court, whispered malicious descriptions of the scene to journalists, and the outcome was a press cartoon depicting the nation's leaders kneeling to one Prince who was riding a hobby-horse, to another who was flying a kite, and to a Princess who was suckling at the breast of a wet-nurse. Public ridicule helped to drive the King and Queen deeper into that reclusive bourgeois life which alienated them from the affections of a people who have always preferred their monarchs to be splendid, sophisticated, and manifest.

In *Mrs. Delany's Correspondence* there is a vivid account of a lugubrious family outing from Windsor Castle to Bulstrode Park, the ten-miles-distant home of the Dowager Duchess of Portland. "Farmer George", as the King was then nicknamed, drove the Queen himself in a phaeton, a light two-horse carriage with four high wheels which appeared on the improved turnpike roads and inspired the North American buggy. Following them, in a column that might have been going to a rustic fair, were the Prince of Wales and Prince Frederick, aged sixteen and fifteen, on horseback. A post-chaise came next, carrying Princess Charlotte, aged twelve, who dandled on her knee four-year-old Prince Adolphus. In a coach and six bringing up the rear were Princess Augusta, aged ten, Princess Elizabeth, aged eight, Prince William, aged thirteen, and Prince Edward, aged eleven.

Arrived at Bulstrode Park, the family filed into the house, and the King asked the Dowager Duchess of Portland if he might show her pictures to his pet son the Bishop. While this was being done the Queen talked to Mrs. Delany, a friend of the Duchess, about chenille work. Then the whole family inspected the china cabinet. The boys, including the Bishop, kicked their heels impatiently and stood about whistling. The girls skipped around asking questions. Afterwards they all sat down to a meal. "The Royals," Mrs. Delany recalled, "ate abundantly."

Soon afterwards Mrs. Delaney was invited to pay a return visit to Windsor Castle. She was received by the Queen and five Princesses. At seven in the evening the King appeared, followed by the seven Princes. Music was played and the children danced together. The Prince of Wales danced a minuet with the Princess Royal. Mrs. Delaney was charmed. But if on some other evening she had stumbled into the older boys' quarters at Kew, she might have been shocked.

Among three houses on the Green, George III divided his seven sons. The Prince of Wales and Prince Frederick shared one, Prince

William and Prince Edward a second, and the Princes Ernest, Augustus, and Adolphus a third. The houses were adequately furnished and well staffed. The King, however, visited the Princes' houses only at six o'clock in the morning, when he went around knocking at his sons' bedroom doors and inquiring gravely how they had passed the night.

The Prince of Wales and Frederick spent most of their time with their pages. These youths, in order to curry favour with the Princes, admitted raffish visitors to the house during the late evenings. It was through this custom that the Prince of Wales got embroiled at the age of eighteen with the actress Perdita Robinson.

Throughout his teens the Prince of Wales angered the King by his precociousness. Once, for example, he put his mouth to the keyhole of the King's bedroom door and shouted "Wilkes for Liberty!" This, no less than the Prince of Wales's physical cowardice, infuriated the King. In a sense Frederick, Duke of York, was even worse. In his teens he was a most unbishop-like bawd and bully. But craftily he managed to conceal his more serious misdemeanors, and remained for life the apple of the paternal eye.

The house of William and Edward must have been affected to some extent by the atmosphere in that of their older brothers. After the Perdita Robinson scandal, George III bundled the fourteen-year-old William off to sea, evidently to save him from further contamination. But the damage had been done. Within a few years William was an incorrigible tippler and wencher. Meanwhile Edward, from the age of twelve to seventeen, was kept alone in his Kew house and guarded by a porter, a night watchman, a page, three maids, and a housekeeper. He received a new suit every two months and a pair of new shoes every fortnight. His household was allowed two thousand pounds a year for food. His tutor was John Fisher, who subsequently became the Bishop of Salisbury. Although Fisher was nicknamed "The Kingfisher", on account of his sycophantic predilection for royal employment, he appears to have done his duty by Edward, for the boy grew up intelligent, well read, and sober. Unlike his brothers, he was no liar. Fisher has recorded that Edward's love of truth "was paramount to every other consideration".

Although the most dutiful and upright of the Princes, Edward, oddly enough, was the most unpopular with his father. Some writers have attributed this to the fact that as a small boy in Kew Palace he deliberately smashed a clock that had belonged to the Duke of Gloucester, Queen Anne's son. The Kingfisher thought little of the clock. In mitigation of Edward's offense he said it was "old-fashioned and clumsy". Even so, Edward's destruction of it aroused the King's rage. The remorse Edward suffered during a period of harsh punishment may explain his later mania for collecting clocks of all descriptions.

The sight of Edward always irritated the King. Whether the King's feelings dated from the clock incident is of little account. What emerges clearly from records of the father-and-son relationship is an illustration of that widely held theory that in judging others, man is inclined to be most critical of those weaknesses to which he himself is prone. The King saw in Edward signs of the same gravity and stolidity that were responsible for his own exclusion from the affections of the lovely, witty Lady Sarah Lennox, and from the effervescence of London's aristocratic life. George protected himself from these disagreeable reminders by keeping Edward at a distance.

The further he was pushed away, the more wistful Edward became for affection. There was a poignant moment one day when Fisher read to Edward the story of what the Duke of Ormonde said on the death of his son. Ormonde said he would not change his dead son Ossory "for the best living son in Europe". Edward began to weep, and when Fisher asked why, Edward said he wondered if his own father would express the same sentiments if he should die. But before Fisher could think of a reply, Edward said: "As I am a child I suppose not. But if I live to grow up perhaps he would say the same."

At seventeen, after five years of loneliness, Edward was sent for military training to Luneburg, in Hanover. This flat, foggy Lutheran province on Germany's North Sea coast shared Britain's monarch from the day its Elector became George I of England in 1714 until the day the Hanoverian dynasty died with William IV in 1837. Throughout all these years consideration for Hanover played an important part in British foreign policy.

Hanover's military traditions were almost as stiff as those of neighbouring Prussia. Troops were drilled into the precision of machines; and, while they lacked resourcefulness, they were steady. Hanoverian officers were once described by the Duke of Wellington as "splendid". At the Battle of Waterloo, Wellington was thankful for the Hanoverian column that helped him to crumple Napoleon. Edward's subsequent reputation as a military martinet stemmed from his harsh Hanoverian training.

During two years at Luneburg, Edward grew into a hefty young man more than six feet tall, as athletic as he was scholarly, and as energetic on the barracks square as he was polite in the ducal drawing-rooms of Germany. He had dark auburn hair, a round head and face, slightly protuberant blue eyes—and that little nose like a bird's beak, that small cupid's-bow mouth, which were to be his daughter's most dominant features.

Edward took beer and wine with the other cadets, but never got drunk. He liked a game of whist but didn't gamble at dice. He was a good dancer but no Lothario. He had an exaggerated regard, in fact, for all that is implicit in that well-worn term, "conduct becoming of an officer and gentleman". And so, of course, he was regarded as a bit of a prig. His sisters later called him Joseph Surface, after the unctuous character in Sheridan's *School for Scandal*.

In 1787, when he was nineteen, Edward was transferred to Geneva to take a post-graduate course under a liverish old warrior named Baron Wangenheim. George III allowed Wangenheim six thousand pounds a year for both their expenses. Wangenheim, who was a sybarite and a gourmet, spent most of the money on comfortable quarters and a succulent cuisine. All Edward received in the way of pocket-money was 31s. 6d. a week, a pittance for a man of his rank. Edward later described Wangenheim as "an arbitrary and inflexible governor" and as "a mercenary tyrant".

Edward's lifelong incompetence at finance was the result of being deprived during his formative years of any opportunity to handle an adequate allowance. The manner of his upbringing at Kew had imbued him with a sense of princely importance, and being proud of his rank, it was only natural that as a young socialite in foreign parts he should wish to keep up appearances. On a weekly handful of shillings, this was plainly impossible. He wrote to his father asking that a bigger part of the six thousand pounds remittance to Wangenheim should be set aside for his personal use. Wagenheim, fearing he would have to forego his ample quarters and exquisite sauces, intercepted the letter. Though the absence of a reply was in this case no fault of the King's several of Edward's subsequent solicitations which did get through were disregarded. In consequence Edward sank into a mood that prompted the remark: "I have so seldom found a gracious answer to any of the trifling requests that I have made to the King that I am now very shy of asking."

In Geneva, Edward was hedged about with a thousand temptations to spend. He made a modest pretence of remaining incognito, by assuming the name Le Comte de Hoya. But his true identity was known to everybody in the city. From the moment the news of his impending arrival reached the local dignitaries in Geneva, feverish preparations were made for his participation in ceremonies of all kinds. His progress down the road from Luneburg to Geneva was reported daily by couriers to the Syndics, or members of the Swiss legislature.

When it appeared that Edward would arrive after dark, a Syndic named Cayla ordered an unprecedented breach of custom. For centuries the gates of the walled city of Geneva had been closed from sunset to dawn, and anybody arriving too late to enter had to rest overnight in an inn outside. Under the date of December 14, 1787, however, we find this entry in the *Registre du Conseil de Genève:* "M. le Syndic says that he has been informed that Prince Edward of England, who comes to Geneva on a visit under the name of Le Comte de Hoya, is on the point of arriving, and that he will stay in the home of a certain citizen of this town, which he has rented. The Noble Cayla says that he has left orders at the Gate of Cornavin that it is to be opened in the event of the Prince arriving after it has been closed."

A few days after he reached Geneva, Edward made his first public appearance. The occasion could hardly have been more solemn. He sat in a special enclosure, surrounded by Swiss aristocrats, to hear a public eulogy of a recently deceased Noble named Buisson, and a reading of that departed gentleman's will.

More cheerful events, however, lay ahead of Edward. Geneva was then a most fashionable city. There was a large international colony of wealthy parents, who rented mansions for the duration of their sons' studies at the famous university. Almost every evening Edward broke away from Wangenheim and attended theatres, suppers and balls.

He found two companions in the young Princes of Hesse. With

them he was present at a Grand Revue of the Swiss Guard at the Plainpalais in May 1788. Two Swiss Nobles, de la Rive and Rigaud, formed part of his suite. Edward was accorded high military honours during the march past.

Edward was seized upon by the Syndics as a means of affording them a flattering link with the mighty Crown of England. On the occasion of George III's recovery from his first bout of madness, the Geneva Archives record: "The Noble F. A. Neville was commissioned yesterday to carry the felicitations of the council to M. le Comte de Hoya on the return to health of His Majesty the King, his father, which event has filled us with the keenest joy, and to assure him of our regard for His Majesty, and of our devotion to his Crown, and of our desire to render agreeable unto His Royal Highness the sojourn which he continues to make in our city."

Edward took youthful pleasure in the importance he was accorded, and on several occasions responded to it with acts of generosity which he could ill afford. In *The Diary of Events at Geneva from 1782 to 1811,* by M. Dunant-Martin, there is a reference to a visit Edward paid to a charity performance for the Geneva Hospital at the Comedy Theatre. Dunant-Martin wrote that the performance "brought in only thirty louis, of which Prince Edward contributed six". Another item in the diary speaks of Edward's munificence when he appeared at a reception for the benefactors of the Arts Society in Room 200 at the Town Hall. There is a further note in the Swiss State Archives about Edward's gift of a thousand French livres to the Geneva General Hospital. Thanks for this were sent by a Syndic to Edward in a letter addressed to Wangenheim. The old Baron must have been highly perplexed as to where Edward got the money.

Whenever Edward wrote to the King asking for money, Wagenheim destroyed the letter. The old despot kept himself acquainted with his pupil's private habits and sentiments through the medium of Edward's valet, a disloyal character named Rymer. Instead of mailing Edward's letters immediately, Rymer took them first to Wangenheim, who steamed them open. Any which displeased him he destroyed. The resulting paucity of correspondence from Edward aggravated the King's animosity. The King was also angered by continual letters from Wangenheim complaining of Edward's extravagance. Edward, blind to what was going on behind his back, was hurt and bewildered by the coldness of his father's return correspondence.

It was, of course, easy for a Prince of England to borrow money, and it is not surprising that Edward discovered this means of relieving his embarrassment. Much has been made by some writers of the "extravagance" which followed his success at raising a loan. But as Ernest Hartley Coleridge discovered when he was writing the life of Thomas Coutts, Edward's banker and stalwart friend, there was "no evidence of the riotous living or profligate expenditure of his elder brothers". In fact the debts Edward incurred at Geneva were so reasonable, in view of Wangenheim's perfidy, that the King in a fit of contrition acknowledged responsibility for them.

Had the King kept his promise to pay off Edward's Geneva debts, the Prince's story might have been happier. But George left the debts unpaid, and so set on Edward's heels a pack of creditors who hounded him into the desperate resort of fresh borrowings to stay their pursuit. The borrowing habit persisted as Edward found out that sources of funds were plentiful. In consequence his interest load increased, his creditors multiplied, and he was dogged by pecuniary difficulties to the end of his days.

Certainly he should have cut his coat according to his cloth; but he was born to the cloth of gold. Thomas Coutts held that Edward's spending "did not exceed the obligations of his rank". In a letter about his Geneva debts, written years later to the Prince Regent, Edward offered the fairly reasonable explanation that at Geneva he was "incapacitated from enjoying those indulgences which not only princes but private gentlemen expect at a certain age, and I borrowed money to procure them."

His only dubious indulgence at Geneva was an affair with an actress named La Dulaque, who starred at the Comedy Theatre. Edward was introduced to this artist by an eighteen-year-old youngster named Audeoud, the son of a prominent government accountant. Subsequent events suggested that Audeoud's motive in serving as intermediary was not entirely selfless. He used his association with the English Prince to enhance his own glitter and importance in La Dulaque's eyes, and then sought a share of her caresses. Though Edward had earned a reputation for drawing-room graces, he must still have been inexperienced in boudoir techniques, for he could not keep La Dulaque to himself.

17

In a letter from F. J. Butin to Leonard Bordier, quoted by J. P. Ferrier in his *Legal Dramas and Comedies of Old Geneva,* it is stated: "La Dulaque, an actress pretty and frivolous rather than clever, has become the mistress of Prince Edward . . . who has been here some time with his tutor. She ruined his health, she ruined his purse, and she was furthermore unfaithful to him. Audeoud got the upper hand of Edward as far as she was concerned. Audeoud, . . . who considers himself to be of high rank, distinguished, and of polished manners, brought ruin upon himself in every way by also enjoying the favours of the celebrated La Dulaque."

The youthful *maison-à-trois* did not last long. Butin's letter goes on to say that Audeoud's father and mother "discovered the affair, and managed so well that La Dulaque went off one day and left Geneva without so much as a farewell to her illustrious friends."

The manner in which Audeoud's father and mother "managed" was to appeal to the Syndics and to Baron Wangenheim to get rid of her. Dunant-Martin's diary for December 1, 1788, says: "The Syndics have forbidden this young woman to entice Audeoud. But she has refused to obey. Prince Edward's tutor has already asked that she should be sent away from the town because he considers her corrupt and dangerous. Although the Prince is over twenty years old, and officially of age, it has been agreed to overlook this fact. This will assist the tutor to keep La Dulaque in her place."

In the end La Dulaque was persuaded to leave town for a sum of twenty louis. Edward and Audeoud were evidently not alone in regretting her banishment. Butin wrote: "She had a trick of making herself agreeable and her departure spread sorrow in all hearts." A man named St. Gerand, the manager of the Comedy Theatre, also had to be recompensed for his "loss of considerable custom".

If Edward pined for La Dulaque, his yearning was brief. The image of the fickle actress had hardly begun to fade in his memory when it was abruptly erased completely by the reality of lovelier features. They belonged to a woman who for twenty-seven years occupied alone and undisputedly the romantic division of Edward's bulldog heart. She will remain in the shadows of history until somewhere, some time, more of her correspondence is discovered and the long grey blanks in the record are filled. Yet she is not altogether a mystery woman. Like an unknown member of the *corps de ballet,* she sometimes makes, from the furthermost recesses of a darkened stage, a sudden explosive leap into that spotlit pool where the principles are poised; and though in a second she is gone again, her impact leaves an indelible impression on the mind of the audience.

She adorned Edward and adored him. In consequence he displayed her in public with pride and cared for her in private with tenderness. Light-heartedly she shared the endless exiles into which he was driven by his hostile father and jealous brothers, and the perpetual humiliation of his financial difficulties. Her congenial disposition and her impeccable social talents made Edward's formal life pleasurable and strengthened the bonds of his many informal friendships. The tiny fount of humour that had survived Edward's stodgy upbringing often spouted joyously in response to her animation and wit. When finally the British Crown demanded an heir of Edward, she yielded him up to a German Princess with grace and dignity.

Even those chartered libertines, his brothers, came to speak of her respectfully as "Edward's French lady". The love of Edward and this woman was little short of an idyll. It has been described as "one of the few fair flowers that blossomed on the family tree of the Hanoverian Georges". Her name was Alphonsine Thérèse Bernadine Julie de Montgenet, Baronne de Fortisson.

Chapter III

EARLY in the memorable year of 1789, the clothing of European women underwent a dramatic change in style. The fantastic eighteen-inch head-dresses and long silver-knobbed walking-sticks popularized by Madame de Pompadour, and in vogue for more than twenty years after her death, were suddenly abandoned. Women now let their own hair fall naturally about their shoulders, and walked without support. Many wore broad-brimmed beaver hats of a mannish cut. Low necklines vanished under modest jackets. The filmy flounces of taffeta petticoats gave place to full, concealing skirts of wool. Heels were lower than at any time during the eighteenth-century.

Men's garb was also transformed. Brilliant colours were superseded by sober blues, browns, and greys. Long double-breasted coats with brass buttons and hammer-claw tails hinted faintly at modern man's full evening dress. Only waistcoats remained fancy. The first ankle-length trousers made their appearance, though knee breeches were as yet more common. Silver-buckled shoes were replaced by simple laced footwear or stout riding boots. None save officers in uniform carried the sword.

Increasing severity in dress reflected the deepening gravity of the age. The new power implicit in steam-driven machinery filled men's minds with uncertainty and foreboding. The elementary economics of landowner and peasant, and of merchant and craftsman, were ripped apart by the swift, erratic shift of speculative industrial funds. All classes were preoccupied by growing financial complexities. The rich tended to get richer and the poor to get poorer; but between them lay an ever expanding band of shopkeepers, professional men, and manufacturers, who were envied by those below and feared by those above. This burgeoning bourgeoisie was disgruntled by its inadequate representation in affairs of state, for even the most liberal politicians still came largely from aristocratic homes. Class warfare was in the offing. Europe seethed with discontent and rang with the cries of reformers.

Ten years had passed since Chatham, a dying man, had staggered into the House of Lords and made his final passionate appeal for a reasonable compromise with the American revolutionaries. For six years the United States had been recognized diplomatically as a republic. The Old World, marvelling at the New World's audacity and spirit of independence, was afire with the democratic ideas that had been carried back across the Atlantic by returning soldiers. Of all the cities in Europe, London was the most stable and Paris the most agitated.

In France, out of twenty-three million people, a million beggars had been counted. The peasantry was paying four-fifths of its income in various taxes. Harvests had been poor and many town dwellers, without realizing that they were inaugurating a new delicacy, had been reduced to eating frogs. The currency was debased.

Yet luxury and license among the nobility had never been more flagrant. The rule of Louis XVI and Marie Antoinette was absolute. The States General, France's nearest approach to a parliament, had not been convened since 1614. Voltaire had been dead for eleven years, but his radical precepts were now widely espoused by the middle class and even by some of the aristocracy. The Marquis de Lafayette, the French general who had helped the American rebels defeat the British, was dreaming of emerging from the impending cataclysm as France's George Washington. Down in the South of France, however, a young ensign named Bonaparte was racked by wilder ambitions.

Meanwhile French army discipline was disintegrating and officers never knew whether their troops would subdue the marching mobs or join them. Nervously, Louis XVI made concessions, but his change of heart came too late. The rumble of approaching revolution grew louder every day. The hour of the tumbril and the guillotine was at hand.

In the sophisticated salons of Paris a brittle gaiety masked the apprehensions of the nobility. *Les grandes dames* were at home as usual to princes, ambassadors, statesmen, celebrities and amusing popinjays, and to the motley procession of perfumed wives, concubines, actresses and adventuresses who frothed and sparkled in their wake. Beyond the gilt and the plush and the flowers, and above the strains of the string orchestras, few failed to hear the mur- murings of hatred outside. Though the nobility affected not to notice it, one problem was uppermost in their minds: to flee or not to flee?

Among those distressed by this pregnant question were a young couple named the Baron and Baronne de Fortisson. Their efforts to reach a decision were rendered no easier by the existence between them of a carefully concealed but fast widening estrangement. Al- though they were parents of an infant daughter named Mélanie, they had never been genuinely happy. They were first cousins on their mothers' sides and victims of the old French custom of mar- riage by family arrangement. Both could trace their lineage back to the Dukes of Normandy. Julie, Baronne de Fortisson, was also the Comtesse de Montgenet in her own right. If the revolutionaries gained control of France, the de Fortissons would be among the first to lose their heads.

Yet Jean Charles André de Mestre, Baron de Fortisson, was not entirely opposed to insurrectionist aims. He was a professional artil- lery colonel, a good field officer who had been embittered by the demoralizing effect on the troops of corruption and neglect among the general staff. At this critical moment for France he was torn, as were so many other officers, between his devotion to the nation and his allegiance to the King whose weakness and blindness were responsible for its sorry state. In fact he had been driven to the point of insanity by his riven loyalties, and treated in a mental hospital. Long ago he would have taken Julie and the child to safety had he not loved France more than either of them. As things were, he hung on to the remnants of his crumbling regiment, hoping against hope for a break in the louring political skies and a contrite return of his many deserters.

Julie de Montgenet was born in the late seventeen-sixties on a small family estate at St. Laurent-Sur-Mer in the Norman department of Calvados. As a girl she was taken out to Martinique in the French West Indies, where her parents owned sugar plantations. At Trois Ilets in Martinique she was a day girl at a convent named La Maison d'Education pour les Jeunes Personnes. One of her fellow-pupils there was Marie Josephine Rose Tascher de la Pagerie, daughter of a French colonel, and afterwards wife of Napoleon and Empress of France.

Though Josephine was several years older than Julie, the two were playmates. They liked to loll in hammocks surrounded by admiring negro girls from their parents' estates. Josephine played the guitar and Julie sang. The girls learned little but singing, dancing, embroidery, languages, and the social graces; but, to be fair to the convent, it should be added that these were all the talents then required of upper-class women.

The convent depended largely on school fees, catered frankly to the pretentions of the colonial upper crust. The nuns made no bones about their resolution to turn out girls who were pleasing to men. In this respect Josephine and Julie were among their triumphs. The girls bloomed early in the sultry climate, and were not short of practice in the art of flirtation. Both were pursued ardently by the young officers of the French garrison and by the scions of the rich planting families. But both were set apart by their ambitious mothers for men of rank in France. In their late teens, well polished and gift-wrapped, the girls were shipped home—Josephine for the Marquis de Beauharnais, and Julie for her cousin, the Baron de Fortisson.

An oil portrait shows that Julie was a rare beauty, with huge sloe eyes, a patrician nose, a sensitive mouth, a long slender neck, and an abundant tumble of curls. Her husband, however, was more appreciative of a gun barrel's machining or the mechanism of the new exploding shells. His coldness saddened Julie, his preoccupation with the withering army deprived her for weeks on end of his company, and the reproach in her eyes irritated de Fortisson. A frost set upon their relationship that not even mutual danger could melt.

Meanwhile Julie's sister the Comtesse de Jensac; her brother, a brilliant young engineer; and her close friends—who included Louis Philippe, eventually "the Citizen King of France"—were urging her to leave the country. For the sake of appearances, however, she remained at her husband's side. Putting up a good front was one of Julie's characteristics.

On July 14, 1789, the Paris mob captured the Bastille, the prison that symbolized the tyranny of the Bourbons, and the bloody upheaval began. The only regiments remaining loyal to the King were foreign mercenaries. De Fortisson found himself without a single gunner under his command. In a fit of anguish and despair he decided to abandon France. With Julie, the child Mélanie, and thousands of other high-born refugees, he crossed the Swiss border and entered Geneva. Too stubborn to admit the possibilities of a successful revolution, he had failed to take the precaution of liquidating his property and transmitting funds abroad. In Geneva, therefore, the de Fortissons were penniless.

The international colony of Geneva received the French *émigrés* with compassion, gave them shelter, entertained them lavishly, and in many cases arranged for their onward movement to other countries in Europe and America.

One of the de Fortissons' good Samaritans was Auguste Vasserot, Baron de Vincy, a thirty-five-year-old Swiss who combined military careerism with virtuosity at the harpsichord. De Vincy had commanded a Swiss regiment in the service of France. During the Revolution he had lost much of his income when feudal dues on lands he owned in French territory were abolished. So he had returned to his seat near Geneva and was devoting himself to entertaining French refugees. He had a curious eccentricity. To protect himself from cold in winter and flies in summer he kept in his salon at Vincy the hood of a carriage, and under this frequently received his guests. He was so likeable, however, that the idiosyncrasy amused rather than offended. Among his closest friends was Edward. And Edward was presented at Vincy one night to the de Fortissons.

Without country or money, the de Fortissons were ready to clutch at a straw. In Edward they divined a rock. Was he not a son of George III, a king who was recognized throughout the world as the embodiment of resistance to revolutionary movements? Was he not a prince of the most powerful nation on earth? Where else could the de Fortissons find a stouter champion? In her determination to cement a friendship with Edward, Julie relied heavily on her beauty.

At first, as she flattered him, Julie summed up Edward as a bore. Against the background of debonair French courtiers, he suggested a bull mastiff at a poodle show. He never wore the peruke or used lavender water. His cuffs were without ruffles and his coat was clean of frogging. He spoke intelligently, but rarely affected mannerisms to capture attention or impart distinction to his personality. If he found conversation trivial, he was indulgent, for no malice tinged his remarks. Since malice is the spice of party chit-chat, Edward didn't get much of a hearing. He had a weakness for rolling, sonorous phrases which tended to depress or repel his hosts and fellow guests. Deep down in him lay a pool of wry humour, but it rarely bubbled to his lips on social occasions.

Under normal circumstances a volatile woman like Julie would not have looked twice at Edward. And yet, as she deliberately dazzled him in the hope of receiving favours for herself and her husband, Julie gradually discovered that his lack of guile was attractive and that his stolidity had at least the virtue of honesty. Patently he was a young man of high principles, and this was a quality Julie esteemed. Edward was about her own age, and about ten years younger than her husband. Most important, though, Edward was utterly masculine.

It is not known exactly when Julie, in trying to capture a benefactor, found herself confronted by a lover. But it was certainly very soon after that first meeting in Geneva. To de Fortisson, brooding over his broken world, Julie's infidelity was but a raindrop in a sea of trouble. Cynically, he shrugged his shoulders and became a *mari complaisant.*

Edward's expenses in Geneva were increased by his efforts to impress Julie, and he turned once more to the money-lenders. Julie introduced him to scores of blue-blooded French *émigrés,* and they were naturally glad to escape from their new penury by accepting the hospitality Edward showered upon them. If Edward's entertaining at theatres, suppers and balls was unnecessarily lavish, it was because he felt the need to compensate for his heavy personality. And he profited from his munificence. In the Gallic environment of Julie's circle some of his Teutonic stodginess dissolved, and he acquired what Roger Fulford has described as "a certain deliberate graciousness". Julie's early advances to Edward were undoubtedly meretricious, but after a short time she was reciprocating his love-making with genuine ardour.

In the winter of 1789, when he was twenty-two years old, Edward decided to go to London to confront his father in person and seek more money. He left the house without informing Wangenheim of his intentions, arranged secretly for an open carriage, and made an impetuous seven-hundred-mile gallop to Calais.

He could not have chosen a more unpropitious moment. George III had already suffered his first bout of madness, and his condition had been aggravated by his knowledge of the promiscuity of his three elder sons. The Prince of Wales had defied and insulted his father by contracting a morganatic marriage with Mrs. Fitzherbert. Stories of a recent freebooting tour by the Duke of York through the boudoirs of Germany had sorely grieved the King, since they were a painful denial of the high concept he had always cherished of his favourite son's character. Prince William, after earning national acclaim for his plucky participation as a boy in several naval battles, and basking for years in paternal approval, had lately fallen from favour through settling down in Petersham Lodge, Richmond, with a Miss Polly Finch.

The King wished his children to accept the same rules of royal marriage to which he had himself submitted reluctantly. Royal spouses, he held, even though they might resemble pedigreed heifers, must be selected from the Protestant ducal households of Germany. The persistent attempts of his sons to circumvent this edict, and so preserve themselves from unwanted buxom embraces, provoked the King into rages that constantly shook his precariously balanced mind.

When he set out from Geneva, Edward was well aware of the King's simmering anger over the older Princes' peccadilloes. He must also have realized that Wangenheim had certainly informed the King of his liaison with Julie. To seek an audience with the King in these circumstances was an indication of his continuing ingenuousness. The manner in which he set about his mission revealed that he had learned little yet of diplomacy.

In the middle of a dark January night in 1790, he reached London unheralded and took a room in a hotel off St. James's Street. Next day, instead of informing the King of his arrival, he sent a message to Carlton House, the orgiastic home of the Prince of Wales. Accompanied by the Duke of York, the Prince of Wales came around to the hotel and carried Edward off to Carlton House in high glee. Edward attributed his brothers' warm welcome to fraternal affection; but his appeal to them at that time was political. His daring arrival in London without authority suggested his readiness to flout the King. Thus he appeared to his brothers as a promising ally in their vendetta against their father.

Relations between the King and his two older sons had never been blacker. For months the Prince of Wales and the Duke of York had mimicked and belittled the King in the ruttish, bibulous com-

JULIE

*Baronne de Fortisson
and Comtesse de Mongenet*

*Courtesy Damase Potvin from his
"La Dame Francaise du Duc de Kent".*

EDWARD

*H. R. H. Duke of Kent and
Strathearn, Earl of Dublin*

*Hector Bolitho Victoriana Collection.
Toronto Public Libraries.*

PRINCE EDWARD
as Colonel of the 7th Royal Fusiliers, Quebec, 1790.

John Ross Robertson Collection,
Toronto Public Libraries.

pany of Charles Fox and other opposition Whigs who were their regular companions. During the King's recent insanity the Prince of Wales had hatched an unsuccessful plot to establish himself as Regent. The King was aware of his older sons' disloyalty, and when he discovered that Edward was with them at Carlton House he jumped to the conclusion, in his shock and wrath, that Edward had joined their cause.

To the irritability that Edward had always aroused in the King was now added hostility. Without even receiving him, George ordered him enrolled forthwith into the army, in the rank of colonel, and posted to the garrison at Gibraltar. When Edward pleaded for an audience the King granted him ten minutes only, and this was to take place on the morning of his departure for the Rock.

What was said at the interview has never been recorded, but it is certain that Edward's hopes of a better allowance were shattered. It is also likely that he was informed in peremptory terms that the matter of his elevation to a royal dukedom, and the parliamentary grant such a title would entail, had been postponed indefinitely. If Edward had the temerity to raise the question of his Geneva debts then, this could have evoked nothing more than vituperation. And so, on the bleak morning of February 1, 1790, Edward sailed for Gibraltar with debts of twenty thousand pounds hanging around his neck and no income to count upon but a colonel's pay. He must have been a somewhat puzzled and mortified young man.

It would have been easy for him to desert Julie at this time, but his love for her was deep. Through the influence of William, his brother in the navy, Edward managed to smuggle the de Fortissons and baby Mélanie out of Switzerland. The family travelled on forged papers to the French Mediterranean port of Toulon, where a small British warship awaited them. Aboard this they were carried to Gibraltar. There the Baron de Fortisson became a member of the Corps de Noblesse Emigrés, and with an air of icy resignation one of Edward's aides-de-camp. Though Edward was often seen in Julie's company, her husband was always coldly but discreetly in the offing. This gave a semblance of respectability to the affair. Not that it mattered. Many other French refugees were in Gibraltar. The social life was promiscuous. If anybody suspected that Julie and Edward were lovers, few cared.

Edward was posted to the command of the Queen's Royal Regiment. When dealing with this stage of his career, it has been customary to draw attention to his severity as an officer. Roger Fulford in his *Royal Dukes* describes how "all day long there were men in motion, obedient to Edward's orders, deploying over the scorched acreage of the Rock." Fulford adds: "Soldiers on parade always drove him slightly mad, in much the same way as donkeys on the green affected Miss Betsy Trotwood." Some writers have even described Edward as sadistic. He cannot be seen clearly as a soldier, however, unless the general military customs of his day are also brought into focus. These conditions are often blurred by writers, who exaggerate the dimensions of the gulf that separated officers and men during the late eighteenth and early nineteenth centuries. In many histories and biographies of these times the officers are depicted as high-born, whip-cracking tyrants and the men as low-born, long-suffering sheep.

The custom of buying commissions undoubtedly resulted in the gazetting of scores of wealthy officers who were also despotic and inept, but on the whole the system worked well. It vested military authority in men who had a stake in the nation's constitution, kept the higher ranks free of fortune-hunting adventurers like Napoleon, and protected the Government from the threat of overthrow by an army cabal. For every vicious, venal or idle officer there were ten who did their duty well.

In the memoirs of William Cobbett and Private Wheeler, which picture candidly conditions in the ranks during the days that led up to Waterloo, many tributes are paid to gallant and kindly officers. One of the most common terms employed by the men when speaking of a company commander was "father". The men expected, and in most cases received, paternal treatment. After all, they were not unlike children.

The troops were all volunteers, drawn largely from the illiterate peasantry and city slums. For many the army was an escape from uncongenial families, dire poverty, and even the law. In action they were courageous and obedient. Out of the line they were dissolute and mulish. The reason generally advanced for their drunken, intractable habits was their miserable rate of pay. A private, for instance, received only a penny a day, out of which he had to buy his own food and pay for his own washing, mending, shoes, shirts, socks, gaiters, hair-powder, and pipeclay for cleaning his white web equipment. But it is often forgotten that it was customary for privates to supplement their income by doing odd jobs for civilians, working as officers' servants, selling the proceeds of loot, and engaging in that notoriously ambiguous military pursuit known as foraging.

During periods of peace they had plenty of opportunity for these extramural earnings. Cobbett wrote: "My leisure time, which was a very considerable portion of the twenty-four hours, was spent not in the dissipation common to such a way of life but in reading and study." While Cobbett swotted and within a few months soared up to the rank of sergeant-major, most of his comrades were content to booze, brawl, and fornicate. As a private Cobbett had been able to get by on the financial resources open to him. Less prudent men, however, disported themselves and often deprived themselves of food in order to pay for their excesses. With pity Cobbett looked on some men who were "crying on account of their hunger".

Alcohol and empty stomachs are rarely reconcilable with discipline. Too much free time, too much drink, and lack of official rations were responsible for 90 per cent of the peace-time army crime sheets. The intellect of the average soldier was low and there was little use appealing to his reason. Flogging was the standard deterrent to defaulters, yet we may infer from the bland way Private Wheeler talked about it that the men looked on it with no more horror than the soldier of today looks upon field punishment. Though hundreds of lashes were often ordered, the full sentence was rarely carried out. A man suffering to the full the common sentence of 999 lashes would obviously be flayed to ribbons. So it was customary for an officer standing by to stop the punishment when he thought the man had enough to make him think twice before committing the same offence again.

Many statements have been made to the effect that in Edward's army days it was impossible for a private to rise to a commissioned rank. This is untrue. Listen to Cobbett: "There is no situation where merit is so sure to meet with reward as in a well disciplined army. Those who command are obliged to reward it for their own ease and credit. I was soon raised to the rank of corporal, a rank which however contemptible it may appear to some peoples' eyes, brought me in a clear twopence a day and put a very clever worsted knot on my shoulder too."

Before Cobbett left the army in the rank of sergeant-major, he had been tempted to accept the offer of promotion to the commissioned rank of ensign. During Cobbett's army career he noted that Adjutant-General Sir William Fawcett; a General Slater, who commanded the Household Guards; and a Colonel Picton, commanding officer of the 12th Regiment, had all risen from the rank of private. In Cobbett's own regiment the adjutant, the quartermaster, and one captain had been promoted from the ranks.

Edward has been tagged as a martinet partly because of twentieth-century misconceptions about eighteenth-century military life, and partly because he arrived at Gibraltar at an unpropitious moment. The seven years that had gone by since the Rock had withstood gloriously a three-year siege had been a prolonged furlough. The Governor of the Rock and commander of the garrison was a Major-General Charles O'Hara, who had taken advantage of the tranquility to spend all his time building an enormous tower. Ostensibly the tower was for the purpose of observing Spanish troop movements as far away as Cadiz, but in reality O'Hara intended it to stand as a memorial to himself. From a military point of view the tower proved so useless that the British Government refused to foot the bill, and O'Hara had to pay for it out of his own pocket. Until its demolition in relatively recent times, it was known as O'Hara's Folly.

While O'Hara was occupied with his architectural futility, the other officers relaxed in the billiard-rooms of the messes and the beds of the local courtesans. The troops rolled around the streets in a perpetual state of intoxication. They filled their bellies with cheap wine and brandy at some ninety taverns—whose license fees, significantly enough, were a perquisite of the Governor and provided O'Hara with an income of seven thousand pounds a year on top of his pay.

Edward, fresh from military school, his brain teeming with stern but proven principles, and his heart full of youthful zeal and optimism, had expected the Queen's Royal Regiment to be a magnificent body of warriors. Their sloppiness shocked him and he resolved to smarten them up at once. A more mature man would have set about this task slowly and cautiously. But twenty-three-year-old Edward advanced like a Turk in a bayonet charge.

He arose himself at five in the morning to watch parades he

30

ordered for six. He bristled at the sight of a dull button or a dirty gaiter. The slightest fault in drill caught his eye, and sergeants were ordered to repeat the movements until they were executed perfectly. He paid frequent visits to his men's billets, running his finger along the window-sills to draw attention to dust, pointing sternly at offending pieces of orange peel, and upturning boots in a ceaseless hunt for missing studs. At dinner in the mess, his conversation consisted almost entirely of speeches about his determination to improve discipline and morale. But was this sadism?

The manner in which he jerked subordinate officers out of their lethargy filled them with a bitter mixture of remorse, resentment, and jealousy. We can imagine the complaints in their letters home to titled relatives about the way Edward dragged them from their beds at the crack of dawn to inspect weapons, tore them from their dice and billiards to give lectures on tactics, and kept them from the arms of their mistresses to participate in less agreeable night exercises. Obviously Edward's reputation developed from this kind of correspondence.

His rigorous regimen inevitably produced a heavy crop of defaulters. In recording the fact that Edward ordered floggings, some writers have expressed such pain and surprise that one might imagine he was the inventor and sole practitioner of this form of correction. In point of fact, according to the *Dictionary of National Biography,* he was one of the first general officers in the British Army to abandon flogging. He was also the first officer in the British Army to open a regimental school for the improvement of the men's education.

The reason usually put forward for Edward's first expulsion from Gibraltar after little more than a year of service there was his unpopularity with the rank and file. No doubt this was true in the case of those who tasted his punishments. But there is no evidence to support the theory that hatred of Edward was wide-spread. Other reasons for his posting away from the Rock appear far more acceptable.

The rapidity with which he restored order in the Queen's Royal Regiment showed up the commanding officers of other units and stigmatized the entire O'Hara régime. Furthermore, Edward encouraged his troops to drink wholesome beer. This brought to O'Hara's headquarters a procession of protesting wine vendors, who doubtless reminded the Governor that he stood to lose his license fees if their tavern profits turned to losses. Another pin-prick suffered by O'Hara was his social eclipse. As the King's son, Edward outshone the King's representative at garrison ceremonials. With the vivacious Julie at his side, Edward was the central attraction in both military and civilian drawing-rooms. After a year on the Rock, Edward's association with Julie was no secret, and O'Hara doubtless saw in it an opportunity to get rid of the young Prince. He wrote to the King, and the King at once ordered Edward posted to Quebec.

The Baron de Fortisson could stand the humiliation of his position no longer. He refused to accompany the lovers over the Atlantic. Furthermore, he had heard that the new régime in France was offering an amnesty or a pardon to *émigré* officers who would return to the newly constituted army. He bade Edward and Julie a bleak farewell and returned to his own country. As we shall see, he was to meet his death, some years later, under conditions of fantastic coincidence.

To Edward, posting to Quebec amounted almost to banishment. Europe was still the centre of the world, and Quebec was generally looked upon as a snowy waste or as a convenient receptacle for black sheep, political incompetents, and military failures.

In his twelve months on Gibraltar Edward had earned the esteem of many officers who had deplored the conditions which prevailed before he arrived. One group of them subscribed to a memorial of his stay. It was a portal cut into one of the bastions, and it is known to this day as Prince Edward's gate. A Captain Fryer of the Royal Engineers organized a rousing send-off, consisting of a supper in the Europa Hotel, which stood on the site now occupied by the New Mole House, or the Admiralty Workmen's Building. This was followed by an open-air ball amid the ruins of an ancient Moorish fort. Minuets and quadrilles were danced under the light of the moon and a thousand paper lanterns.

Edward and Julie, heralded by a fanfare, walked slowly to their seat, bowing to the files of guests as fifty musicians played a grand march. They sat under a canopy of pink silk flanked by two statues. The first of these was of Minerva; and this statue pointed to a bigger one labelled Fame. Behind Edward's chair was an enormous rising sun made of velvet. Though the prediction implicit in this symbolism was never fulfilled, the motif showed that Edward's virtues had not passed unnoticed.

Nor, despite his reputation for extravagance, had Edward's credit expired. He decided to pay off his Geneva debts of twenty thousand pounds by issuing bonds for this amount, repayable at the end of five years with 5 per cent interest. All the money was put up by civilians on the Rock. To pay his Gibraltar debts Edward sold his equipment.

In May of 1791, Edward, Julie, and Julie's small daughter Mélanie embarked in a British warship for Quebec, as the troops sang a song composed in honour of the occasion:

> For Royal Edward leaves us now!
> 'Twas he who taught us how to bear
> The soldier's toil, the leader's care,
> Yet cheered fatigue with festive hours
> And strewed life's rugged path with flowers.
> Ye breezes softly waft him o'er
> To brave the cold Canadian shore
> To spread afar his rising fame
> And make his own a glorious name.

Ahead were the ten most fruitful years of Edward's life.

Chapter IV

THIRTY-TWO years had passed since General James Wolfe had defeated General Joseph Montcalm in that battle on the Plains of Abraham which had cost both their lives. Though the *Québecois* had remained wholly French in temperament, only a handful still cherished a secret allegiance to France. The great majority were now loyal to the King of England. Thus, in that terraced huddle of quaint granite houses on the rock that rears almost vertically for 335 feet above the St. Lawrence, Britons and French had achieved in a generation what their kinsmen over the Atlantic had failed to accomplish in a thousand years—the art of peaceful coexistence. To this early concord the bilingual nation of Canada owes her independence today.

The reasons for the good relationship, which has resisted many keen corrosives, are not difficult to isolate. For a century before Wolfe's attack Quebec was a neglected French colony, and the love of the settlers for the motherland had withered. Sweating in summer temperatures of ninety degrees, shivering in winter temperatures of forty degrees below zero, and surrounded by hostile Indians and trackless bush, the 150,000 *Québecois* endured a more rigorous existence than any other white men on earth. Before the British conquest they suffered these hardships primarily for the purpose of providing Paris with luxurious furs. The knowledge of their servitude rankled and aggravated their resentment of France's failure to provide adequate funds for development, exploration, and military protection.

Like most unwanted or unheeded children, the *Québecois* grew up self-reliant, acquisitive, opportunist, and worldly. When a *Québecois* thought of the French King, he pictured in his mind's eye the notorious silkiness of the court at Versailles and its susceptibility to the oily art of flattery. His attitude to the impotent legislature in Paris was one of cynical reproach or downright contempt. Time and distance, too, helped to wear the ties thin.

Most of the *Québecois* were third- or fourth-generation Canadians. Few could afford to visit France. Deepening and spreading ignorance of the way of life in France resulted in waning concern for her welfare. The great disparity between living conditions in France and in Quebec left the inhabitants of both countries with few interests in common. Yet the grievances of the *Québecois* were never expressed in revolutionary movements. Patient, devout, and conservative, they submitted dutifully to the patriarchal rule of the great landowning colonial seigneurs, and if wronged without redress practised the resignation they derived from their Roman Catholic faith.

When Montcalm struggled to build up the defences of Quebec, it was patent to all the citizens that he was handicapped by the corruption of French colonial officials and by the indifference of the overseas Government. Wolfe's victory neither surprised nor pained the *Québecois*. They accepted it with a phlegm born of the conviction that the new rule could not possibly be worse than the old.

Any lingering regard for France was dissipated by news from Paris that Louis XV had given a sumptuous banquet to celebrate Quebec's loss as a release from "an alarming drain on the treasury", and that Voltaire, at a feast in his home at Ferney, had congratulated his royal master on having "rid himself of those fifteen thousand *arpents* of snow".

When the *Québecois* were given by the British one of the most generous peace treaties in history—a treaty which included the right to retain their own language, civil laws, and religion—they began to look with respect upon their conquerors.

The policy of the redcoats toward the *Québecois* was well summed up in a letter written by General Thomas Gage, Governor of Montreal, to the British Secretary of State three years after the battle. It said of the *Québecois:* "No invasion of their property or insult to their persons has gone unpunished. All reproaches to their subjection to the fate of arms, reviling on their customs or country, and all reflections on their religion have been discountenanced and forbid. No distinction has been made betwixt the Briton and the Canadian, but equally regarded are all as the subjects of the same Prince. The soldiers live peaceably with the inhabitants and they reciprocally acquire an affection for each other."

The policy bore fruit. When in 1775 the colonies to the south began their struggle for independence, many leaders expected Canada to join them. George Washington addressed the following letter to the inhabitants of Canada: "Friends and Brethren: The unnatural contest between the English colonies and Great Britain has now risen to such a height that arms alone must decide it .... Above all we rejoice that our enemies have been deceived with regard to you. They have even dared to say that the Canadians are not capable of distinguishing between the blessings of liberty and the wretchedness of slavery ... but they have been deceived. ... Come then my brethren, unite with us in an indissoluble union, let us run together to the same goal. ... Come then, ye generous citizens, raise yourselves under the standard of general liberty, against which all the forces and artifices of tyranny will never be able to prevail."

Washington's exhortation, however, met with shot and shell. Britons and *Québecois* stood shoulder to shoulder at the walls of the Quebec Citadel in 1775. In this year General Richard Montgomery was killed and General Benedict Arnold was wounded as their American revolutionary column tried without success to reduce the garrison and persuade French Canada to join the Thirteen Colonies.

The subsequent revolution in France, with its repudiation of the Church and the feudal order that Quebec still honoured, served only to strengthen that first welding of Gauls, Anglo-Saxons and Celts into the biracial fulcrum on which Canada has balanced ever since.

The real moulder of the fraternity was the soldier-statesman Guy Carleton, Governor of Quebec, later Lord Dorchester. Wounded himself in the Battle of the Plains of Abraham, Dorchester stood by in silent grief as Wolfe died in the field from a French musket shot. On taking over Wolfe's command, Dorchester's first act of gallantry toward the *Québecois* was to order a funeral with full military honours for their own fallen General Montcalm.

The American attack led by Montgomery confronted Dorchester with a highly painful coincidence. Years before he had been Montgomery's friend, neighbour, and comrade-in-arms in Ulster. Though he regarded Montgomery as a British traitor, Dorchester ordered that he should be buried decently and took care to have the fallen general's watch returned to his widow.

Then for thirty years Dorchester ruled Quebec with a felicitous blend of justice, discipline, high ceremonial, and gaiety. The droll and gallant manner in which he acquired his child bride—who was to exercise considerable influence on the history of Canada—appealed to the French sense of romance.

Dorchester went to England to woo Lady Anne Howard, elder daughter of his great friend the Earl of Effingham. Lady Anne, who regarded him as a sort of middle-aged uncle, was astonished at his suit and anguished at having to reject it. To her young sister Lady Maria, then just eighteen, she said with tears: "I have been obliged to refuse the best man on earth." Lady Maria replied: "The more fool you. I only wish he had given me the chance." On hearing this, Dorchester immediately proposed to Maria and was accepted. Though her husband was old enough to be her father when she accompanied him to Canada, Lady Maria was happy with him for the rest of their married life.

She was petite, blue-eyed and fair-haired, but she carried herself erect and with an airy, aristocratic grace that relieved her husband's more majestic dignity. In his biography of Dorchester, *The Father of British Canada,* the late Colonel William Wood painted a word picture of Lady Dorchester which well explains her appeal to the formal *Québecois:*

> To her dying day she kept up a prodigious stateliness of manner. Before meals she expected the whole company assembled to remain standing until she had made her royal progress through the room. She was a living anachronism for many years before her death, with her high-heeled, gold-buttoned, scarlet-coloured shoes, her Marie Antoinette coiffure raised high above her head and interlaced with ribbons, her elaborately gorgeous dress, her intricate array of ornaments, and her long, jet-black official-looking cane. But she was no anachronism to herself, for she still lived in the light of other days, in the fondly remembered times when, as the *vicereine* of the Chateau St. Louis, she helped her consort to settle nice points of etiquette and maintain a dignity befitting His Majesty's chosen representative.

Lady Dorchester went to great lengths to find out how the seigneurs ranked among themselves and with the English-speaking aristocrats, and never embarrassed or offended by the manner in which she finally settled ticklish points of precedence. She spent hours deciding who should partner whom in the state minuet. When a bishop entered, would the French prefer dancing to cease? Yes. Then cease it did. Was that de Lotbinier girl's curtesy low enough? No. Then she herself would correct the girl discreetly. For seven years after the fall of the Bastille, Lady Dorchester saw to it that the stately little court of Quebec echoed the court of Windsor, with a few nicely blended undertones from the court of Versailles.

This happy fusion of cultures on high satisfied the humbler *Québecois,* whose social and economic life was affected little by the change of régime. As *les habitants* pushed the bush further and further back from the city, the Anglo-Saxon heretics judiciously refrained from criticizing their custom of building first a fine new church with a tall spire, and only later the surrounding village. The trappers still trapped, though their furs were now diverted to London. The *voyageurs,* the great French-Canadian canoe men, switched from the employ of the French Compagnie des Indes to that of the British North West Fur Company, and they still drove their big shells, singing lusty songs, to the head of the St. Lawrence and onward, for a thousand miles more, through Lake Ontario and Lake Huron, to the westernmost reaches of Lake Superior. On shooting the succession of rapids between Lake Ontario and Quebec City, they would cry exultantly: *"Vive le roi!"*

Two hundred miles of river between Quebec City and Montreal were still plied in summer by the big row-boats and rafts, and in winter by the big horse-drawn sleds of the French-Canadian transport companies. From the farmlands around Levis, on the opposite shore of the St. Lawrence, peasants still brought to Quebec City daily supplies of poultry, eggs, and vegetables, and the meat of deer, caribou, and moose. They used canoes in summer, sleds in winter. When the freeze-up was incomplete in spring and autumn, they crossed surging races of yellow water in a canoe until they reached an ice-floe. Then they hauled the loaded canoe onto the ice, and dragged it across the slippery surface until another channel forced them to take to the water again. It was a precarious journey which cost dozens of lives every year.

In Quebec City horses and oxen pulled huge wagons or sleds up the steep slopes from the Lower Town on the banks of the river, where the merchants and artisans lived, to the Upper Town, on top of the Rock, where aristocrats built their homes. Even dogs were pressed into haulage. Big St. Bernards were harnessed to carts or sleds laden with merchandise, and the smaller Indian huskies, often driven by children, ran between the shafts of little conveyances on wheels or runners. The gentlefolk rode in the cariole, a name given to the high two-wheeled hooded carriage used in summer and also to the sled of similar design used in winter.

Everywhere through this bustling Gallic life, so rapidly adapting itself to extremes of cold and heat, moved the enigmatic Indians, with tomahawks in their hands and feathers in their hair, and sometimes with fire-water in their bellies and hatred in their hearts.

A few Negroes were to be seen, too. Though slavery was not customary in Quebec, there was no law against it, and many United Empire Loyalists had brought their human chattels with them from the United States. An advertisement displayed as late as 1793 read: "To be sold: A likely healthy stout mulatto man, aged 23 years; has been used to housework, speaks both French and English, is fit for any hard labour."

In his *Travels in North America* that peripatetic Swede, Peter Kalm, was especially struck by the beauty of eighteenth-century Quebec women:

> They dress out very fine on Sundays, and though on other days they do not take much pains with other parts of their dress yet they are very fond of adorning their heads, the hair of which is always curled and powdered, and ornamented with glittering bodkins and aigrettes. Every day but Sunday they wear a neat little jacket and a short petticoat which hardly reaches half the leg and in this particular they seem to imitate the Indian women. The heels of their shoes are very high and narrow and it is surprising how they walk on them.
>
> When they go out of doors they wear long cloaks which cover all their other clothes and are either grey, brown or blue. The women may thus have the advantage of being in a *déshabillé* under their cloaks without anybody perceiving it.

Kalm also noted that the rude conditions of Quebec had failed to rob the French women of their traditional sauciness:

> The girls commonly sing songs in which the words *coeur* and *amour* are very frequent. A girl of eighteen is reckoned very

poorly off if she cannot enumerate at least twenty lovers. These young ladies, especially those of the higher rank, get up at seven and dress until nine, drinking their coffee at the same time. When they are dressed they place themselves near a window that opens into the street, take up some needlework and sew a stitch now and then, but turn their eyes to the street most of the time. When a young fellow comes in, whether they are acquainted with him or not, they immediately lay aside their work, sit down by him and begin to chat, laugh, joke and invent *entendres;* and this is reckoned being very witty. In this way they frequently pass the whole day, leaving their mothers to do all the business of the house.

Kalm visited the houses of Quebec and left a piquant description of home life:

They breakfast commonly between seven and eight. Some of the men dip a piece of bread in brandy and eat it, others take a dram of brandy and eat a piece of bread after it. Chocolate is likewise very common for breakfast and many of the ladies drink coffee. Dinner is pretty exactly at noon. People of quality have a great variety of dishes and the first follow their example when they invite strangers. The loaves are oval and baked of wheat flour. For each person they put a plate, napkin, spoon and fork. But knives are generally omitted, all the ladies and gentlemen being provided with their own. Fruit, berries and vegetables in considerable variety are found on the tables. Sometimes they put whole cucumbers on the table and everybody that likes takes one, peels and slices it, and dips the slices into salt, eating them like radishes. In the country it is usual when the husband receives a visit from persons of rank, and dines with them, his wife stands behind and serves him, but in the towns the ladies are more distinguished and would willingly assume an equal if not superior power to their husbands.

The English, Irish, Scots, and Welsh were sleek with prosperity and spent their leisure blithely. According to the French-Canadian writer, Émile Montague, their greatest propensities were for "playing cards, playing at shuttlecock, playing the fool, playing at love, driving in the open cariole, dancing, skating, picnics, berry picking expeditions and much hospitality".

Though many soldiers, sailors, and diplomats in Britain shuddered at the idea of being sent to Quebec, most of those whom fortune brought to the little city were pleasantly surprised. Horatio Nelson, as a young post captain, visited Quebec in 1782 and fell so deeply in love with a local girl that he announced it would be "quite impossible" for him to leave Canada without offering her his hand. When told that such a marriage would ruin his career, the gallant sailor cried: "Then let it follow!" Fortunately for Lady Hamilton and British arms at Trafalgar, Nelson was dragged forcibly aboard the frigate *Albermarle* and removed from the scene of his passion.

A few years later Major Thomas Scott arrived as paymaster of the 70th Regiment. Despite many letters from his brother Sir Walter, the celebrated novelist, warning him that Canada would inevitably be taken over by the United States and that he would lose his British citizenship, Major Scott remained happily in Quebec until his death.

In 1789 Prince William, who had been the last member of the British royal family to visit New York while it was still a colony, was also the first member of the family to visit Quebec. At a merry round of balls he avoided all the duty partners to whom he had been committed by Lady Dorchester and filled a dozen younger, prettier, but more humble and gullible Quebec women with hopes of a permanent alliance and even with dazzling dreams of marriage. One American beauty named Betsy Green, who lived in a house that still stands at the corner of Rue du Tresor and Rue Ste. Anne, was reputed to have surrendered her virginity to him on a promise of matrimony.

Now, two years later, Quebec City was waiting excitedly for the arrival of William's younger brother Prince Edward.

Chapter V

ON THE evening of August 11, 1791, His Majesty's Ships *Ulysses* and *Resolution,* seven weeks out from Gibraltar, rounded Point Levis and sailed into the view of a mighty throng lining the dock. Ashore a band began to play. Out in the river the ships broke flags. A thousand men of the 7th Royal Fusiliers, lining their decks, shouted three cheers. On the quarter-deck of the *Ulysses* stood Edward. He held his hat in his hand. His red hair blew wildly in the breeze. His plump red face swelled and his eyes bulged in mingled pride and astonishment at the scale of the welcome. A little behind him, in the shadow of a companion-way, stood Julie and her daughter Mélanie.

As the ships drew alongside the quay, the martial music rose in a crescendo and streamers fluttered out of tier upon tier of windows. In a roped-off area on the dock stood the Dorchesters, surrounded by a suite dressed in styles that must have suggested to Julie the half-forgotten days of Madame de Pompadour. Beyond were the townspeople, craning their necks for a glimpse of Edward.

There were British merchant families, proud and solid in good Yorkshire woollens; French farmers in homespun, carrying sickles and accompanied by wives who held babies at the breast under their long hooded cloaks; British redcoats clanking in their accoutrements, seemingly top-heavy under their high head-dresses plastered with white paste; French priests, silent but smiling in their black cassocks; leather-clad explorers with abstracted eyes, stout calves, and feet in supple moccasins; trappers in caps of mink and squirrel-tails, and blouses of fringed deerskin; the cheerful, noisy United Empire Loyalists, still wearing the three-cornered hats, buckled shoes, and fancy waistcoats of earlier Georgian days; and the painted aborigines, uttering strange cries and waving tomahawks, green ears of maize, and canoe paddles in response to the emotional vibrations of a stirring if dimly comprehended occasion. These were the elements of which a nation was to be compounded, and the moment Edward stepped ashore he warmed to them.

At a levee in the Chateau St. Louis, the traditional home of French and British viceroys since the days of Champlain—it stood on the site of the present Chateau Frontenac Hotel—Edward said: "Gentlemen, I request that you will be fully convinced how grateful I must feel for the flattering sentiments you have expressed toward my person. I am anxious that during my stay in this country my conduct may prove I am deserving of them. Nothing will give me greater pleasure than if I shall be fortunate enough to find an opportunity of being personally serviceable to you. Till then I hope you will remain fully persuaded of my gratitude and esteem."

The *Gazette de Québec,* a bilingual weekly newspaper, reported:

> On Tuesday the regiment disembarked on the riverside of the Lower Town, where, after it had formed ranks, His Royal Highness, in compliment to the garrison, caused it to perform the customary evolutions, accompanied by a salute on the drums, the band playing "God Save the King". The regiment then mounted to the Place d'Armes, before the Chateau, where, having formed ranks before a vast concourse of spectators, it was reviewed by his Excellency Lord Dorchester and his Honour [the Lieutenant Governor] General Sir Alured Clarke, His Royal Highness commanding in person in a manner that revealed the prince and the soldier. Thence the regiment marched through the Rue St. Louis, deposited its flags at the residence of His Royal Highness, and proceeded to the fortifications at Cap Diamant. It would be unjust to this regiment were it not to state that we do not remember having seen in this country any other of such splendid appearance.

The troops were all over five feet nine inches tall, big men for those days, and Edward contributed heavily out of his own pocket toward the upkeep of their uniforms. He also spent eight hundred pounds a year on his regimental band.

Julie became Edward's chatelaine at 25 Rue St. Louis, a fifteen-room granite house of spare Georgian design. It still stands in the shadow of the Chateau Frontenac, overlooking the crooked streets and staircases and the slate roofs and dormer windows of the Lower Town. Kent House, as it is now called, was rented by Edward from a Judge Adam Mabane, a former army surgeon who had amassed a fortune after settling in Quebec.

Almost before they had had time to unpack, Edward and Julie were caught up in an exhilarating program of receptions, balls, suppers, picnics, and amateur theatricals. Julie was generally reputed to be a widow who had married Edward morganatically in Malta, shortly before reaching Quebec. The Dorchesters and others who doubted this story had no inclination to deny it. In England the Prince of Wales had set a precedent by taking a Roman Catholic to wife morganatically, and for the sake of social harmony it was assumed by some and pretended by others that Edward had so protected Julie's honour. As a result Julie received in Quebec the same respect that Maria Fitzherbert enjoyed in London. She took the name Julie de St. Laurent—after her native town in France—and this was widely regarded as her recognition of the limitations of a morganatic marriage.

The Roman Catholic clergy, believing she was simply Edward's mistress, were uneasy in their attitude toward Julie, but they took their lead from the Dorchesters and refrained from any act or comment that might humiliate her. Julie, after all, was so obviously not a courtesan.

P. B. Casgrain, in the Quebec *Bulletin des Recherches Historiques,* described Julie as "a person of distinction and education, most charming, amiable and kindly. She conversed agreeably, speaking her native French with purity, as she also did the English language, which she wrote perfectly correctly. What charmed most in her was a certain infectious warmth, simple, natural and well bred." After emphasizing that Edward always treated Julie with "the respect and attention of a good husband", Casgrain added: "It is perfectly natural that the Prince, ill-treated by his father from childhood, hated and exiled from court by him, slandered in the eyes of the royal family, among whom he found no sign of affection, should have attached himself to such a superior woman as Madame de St. Laurent. Alone, he concentrated all his affections on this companion, who was worthy of them, and it is not apparent that he ever failed her or indulged in fleeting loves, like the other Princes of the House of Brunswick."

Edward, now twenty-four, was also approved by the *Québecois.* In another issue of the *Bulletin,* Emile Sedilot described Edward as "a handsome and brilliant officer, valiant on the field, gallant with the sex".

Less than two weeks after Edward's arrival in Quebec, the Dorchesters left for a furlough in England. Before their departure, however, Lady Dorchester saw Edward well launched socially. To her great delight, and to the joy of the *Québecois* women, he observed all his duty dances. And he danced well.

Had Edward proved to be as arrogant and smug as his brothers, the notables would not have been surprised. Instead, however, he showed an engaging humility. In the absence of the Dorchesters it would have been simple for him to become the leader of society. Yet, to everybody's admiration, he paid meticulous honours to Sir Alured Clarke, the Lieutenant-Governor, who had assumed Dorchester's responsibilities.

The presence in Quebec of Colonel John Graves Simcoe, during the first nine months of Edward's stay, also tested the Prince's modesty and found it watertight. Simcoe was awaiting a formal proclamation of a new act dividing all Canada north of the St. Lawrence into two provinces, each with a new degree of legislative freedom. They were to be named Lower Canada (French-speaking Quebec) and Upper Canada (English-speaking Ontario). After the division, Simcoe was to proceed to Upper Canada as Governor. Out of consideration for Edward's rank of colonel, Simcoe, a courtly soldier and a stickler for military etiquette, refused to accept promotion to brigadier until such time as he left Quebec for his new office in the west. On the ground of Simcoe's seniority as a colonel, however, Edward insisted on deferring to him in matters of precedent.

Simcoe, whose enlightened reign in Upper Canada is familiar history, won the lasting friendship of Edward. "They seemed by instinct to be drawn to each other," says John Ross Robertson in his notes to *The Diary of Mrs. Simcoe*. Robertson adds: "It was a generous friendship and Prince Edward, then, and after he became Duke of Kent, never forgot to write . . . to Simcoe."

We are indebted to Mrs. Simcoe, a cheerul, gregarious and highly educated woman, for a diary that casts light on Edward's rising gaiety and grace under Julie's influence.

"I was at a very pleasant ball at the Chateau and danced with Prince Edward," she wrote. "The Fusiliers are the best dancers, well dressed, and the best looking figures in a ballroom I ever saw. They are all musical and like dancing and bestow as much money as other regiments usually spend on wine in giving balls and concerts, which makes them very popular." Mrs. Simcoe danced with Edward many times in the Fusiliers barracks, which stood on the site of the present city hall. In addition to the usual minuets, Edward introduced her to such lively Canadian dances as "The Money Musk" and *"Le Jupon Rouge"*.

As winter deepened Mrs. Simcoe went riding in a cariole on the ice of the St. Lawrence—she was nearly "sea-sick" as its runners roller-coasted over the undulating surace—and met Edward, with a hilarious party enjoying the same fun. "The scene on the river is now very gay," she wrote. "Numbers are skating; carioles are driven furiously; and wooden huts are built on the snow where cakes and liquor are sold."

Besides dancing and sleigh-rides, Edward encouraged his officers to join in the French-Canadian enthusiasm for amateur theatricals. A shell-proof chamber in the St. Louis Gate in the walls was made into a theatre by the Fusiliers. At the invitation of the regiment, a French-Canadian amateur company staged Molière's *Le Médecin Malgré Lui* and *La Comtesse d'Escarbagnas*. The Fusiliers, who nostalgically named the theatre The Haymarket, followed up with a play entitled *The Wonder*. Despite his friendship for Edward, Colonel Simcoe was not amused. Ruefully Mrs. Simcoe wrote: "Colonel Simcoe does not like to see officers so employed and does not intend to go to the theatre again."

Mrs. Simcoe never mentions Julie de St. Laurent by name, but in her diary there is a tart comment which probably alludes to Edward's companion: "It is the custom here," she wrote, "to make parties to dine in the country at a distance of ten miles. They often carry a cold dinner and return to a dance in the evening, and this in the severe weather, which seems as much relished by the English as the Canadians. Their partners must be very agreeable indeed or they would never like these parties."

All the *Québecois* were impressed by the quality of the Fusiliers' band, which was Edward's great pride. He made its services available for many dances and charity concerts. It also played every Sunday at the Anglican services. These were held at special hours in the old Roman Catholic Recollect church on whose site stands the present Anglican cathedral. "Prince Edward," reported Mrs. Simcoe, "always goes to church."

While Edward clung to the Church of England, his love of Julie and increasing affection for the French Canadians prompted him to identify himself with many activities of the Church of Rome. He soon went stomping and beaming around the Couvent des Ursulines, a Quebec show-place. Mrs. Simcoe wrote:

> The Superior, La Mère Saint Louis Gonzague, is a very pleasing conversable woman of good address. The nuns appeared cheerful, pleased to see visitors, and disposed to converse and ask questions. Their dress is black with a white hood and some of them look very pretty in it. They carry cleanliness and neatness to perfection and are industrious in managing a large garden. They educate children taking both pensionnaires and day boarders. They make many decorations for their altars and church and gild picture frames. They showed a fine piece of embroidery worked by an English nun, since dead. Some of them made boxes and pin cushions of birchbark worked with dyed hair of the elk. It is so short that it must be put through the needle for every stitch, which makes it tedious. All sorts of cakes and sweetmeats are made here and all the desserts in Quebec are furnished by the nuns. They dry apples in a very peculiar manner. They are like dried apricots. All these things are of use to maintain them, their finances being very moderate.

The annals of the Ursulines contain the following entry:

> On December 20th, 1791, Prince Edward obtained permission to enter the convent to hear the sister Marie de l'Incarnation take her vows. He followed the ceremony closely in company with M. Hubert [the Bishop of Quebec] and many officers of his suite. Afterwards the Mother Superior conducted the Prince through the different departments of the convent. His Royal Highness inquired with graciousness into our way of life. Later he accompanied the Mother Superior to a table on which we had laid some excellent desserts, and he ate with satisfaction. One hour after his departure the Prince sent to our community a gift of two hundred and eighty pounds in return for the three guineas' worth of hospitality we had extended to him.

47

Msgr. Jean François Hubert was one of many high-ranking clergy entertained by Edward and Julie at Kent House and in the officers' mess of the Fusiliers. When Hubert was drowned, after falling through the ice on the St. Lawrence in 1792, Edward sat in an open boat, almost day and night, from May 21st to June 6th, directing a search for the body. The river was dragged systematically and the Fusiliers dived persistently until the body was recovered and buried in consecrated ground. For this and many other chivalrous acts toward the Roman Church, Edward won the clergy's esteem.

Among Edward's favourites was Father P. Félix de Berey, the last Provincial of the Recollects in Canada. De Berey, who had been wounded on the Plains of Abraham administering the last sacraments to a French soldier, was a great wit. Mrs. Simcoe found him "too jocose for his station"; but the Fusiliers, as they rocked with laughter over the port at his humour, loved him.

Edward promoted gatherings in which veterans of both sides in the Battle of the Plains of Abraham were brought together and with music, dancing and good fare encouraged to forget old scores. At these soirées he made much of the ageing Colonel François Dambourges, who had fought *against* the British on the Plains and *with* them during the American attack on Quebec. Dambourges was the hero of the skirmish at Sault au Matelot, where Benedict Arnold almost succeeded in penetrating the defences of the city. It pleased Edward to nickname Dambourges, Capitaine Balafré (Scarface), because he had on his cheek a pronounced cicatrix resulting from a saber wound.

As Dambourges had been born in Bayonne, Edward took pleasure in impressing and hoodwinking young ensigns by introducing him as "the inventor of the bayonet". One ensign looked up his military history and later informed Edward: "You are misled, sire. The bayonet was invented at least fifty years before Colonel Dambourges could have been born." Edward slapped him on the back, laughed, and complimented him on his shrewdness.

Edward was visibly moved on December 17, 1792, at the official opening of Lower Canada's first Parliament. The Parliament was divided into an Upper House, the Legislative Council, composed of distinguished men appointed for life, and a Lower House, the Legislative Assembly, whose members were elected by the people. Half of the Upper House and two-thirds of the Lower House were

French Canadians. Procedure was modelled on that of the Lords and Commons in England.

The scene of the opening was the old Bishop's Palace, which served as the parliamentary buildings for many years. In the absence of Lord Dorchester, Sir Alured Clarke arrived in a gilded coach, accompanied by a mounted escort, and to the strains of "God Save the King" moved through a brilliant throng toward the throne. There, surrounded by officers in red and gold, among whom the burly Edward was prominent, Clarke read the Speech from the Throne. His audience, members of the Upper and Lower Houses, were all in court dress. The ladies of Clarke's suite were "admitted within the railing or body of the house". All were "without hat, cloak or bonnet, having been ordered to leave the same in the Great Committee room previous to their Introduction to the House". A small public gallery was packed with citizens.

The ritual corresponded to the same state occasion in England. There were, for example, the Mace, and the Scarlet Cloth of State. The Lower House was summoned to the presence of the Upper by Black Rod. Gentlemen Ushers, bowing quaintly, saw people to their places. Edward's band played. It was a historic occasion, for it was the first time that legislators of foreign birth, race and language began to shape laws according to British traditions. One in the throng noticed "a tear in Edward's eye".

The warmth of the Anglo-French relations which Edward so carefully fostered arises pleasingly from an account by the French-Canadian writer B. Dufebvre, in his *Cinq Femmes et Nous,* of a party held in the Prince's honour. The host was Judge Thomas Dunn, a senior member of the Legislative Council who frequently took charge of the provincial administration during the absence of the Governor. A tall, strong man in his fifties, Dunn gave the lead to many in the British colony by marrying a French-Canadian woman. Born Henriette Guichaud, she was the widow of a Dr. Fargues. In the two grand salons of Dunn's big stone house at the corner of the Rues St. Louis and Ste. Ursule, some forty French and English guests were gathered to meet Edward for the first time. The older guests of both races spoke French. The younger ones, headed by Dunn's pretty stepdaughter Juliette Fargues, chattered in a mixture of French and English.

Four aged men sitting near the blazing chimney were the doyens of the gathering. One was Joseph Gaspard Chaussegros de Léry, Seigneur de Gentilly, aged seventy, like Dunn a member of the Legislative Council. The tiny man to his right, who shivered a little in spite of the fact that his face was roasted by the flames, was Judge Adam Mabane, who rented Edward the house on St. Louis Street. A great friend of the French Canadians, he was, in the eyes of Governor Dorchester, "a little too democratic". The third member of the group was Colonel Samuel Holland, the Surveyor-General, a tall, heavy soldier, now balding, who had fought with Wolfe and in the American Revolutionary War, and still wore a red tunic of old-fashioned cut. He was married to the former Marie Rolette, a pretty *Canadienne* with whom he had eloped. Rich, intellectual, and influential, Holland was regarded as the city's foremost savant. The last person in the quartet was François-Marie Picote de Bellestre, a sharp-tongued observer of the political scene, venerable but vigorous. He talked volubly, punctuating his phrases with a rapping of his cane on the floor.

Three people chatting on the sofa were Colonel the Honourable François Baby, Madame Baby, and Colonel Henry Caldwell. Baby was the Adjutant-General of Militia in Lower Canada. He spent many years in London after the Battle of the Plains of Abraham, as the representative of French Canadians at the Court of St. James's. Although he did not marry until he was sixty-five, his young bride, Marie-Anne Tarieu de Lanaudière, gave him a dozen children. Baby was one of the first Quebec French to become formally a British subject, but he still remained a fervent Canadian and a devout Catholic. Caldwell, who was assistant Quartermaster-General of Wolfe's invading force, now lived the life of a *grand seigneur,* entertaining lavishly with his wife, a sister of Baron Hamilton, at their magnificent town house in Quebec and their country manor at Belmont. Their only son John was a lively figure among the bilingual youngsters.

A noble-looking man in his sixties, with a faintly cynical smile, was William Smith, born in New York, educated at Yale, and a United Empire Loyalist who became Canada's first Lord Chief Justice. He was talking to William Grant, the Receiver-General, second husband of the Baroness (in her own right) de Longueuil. This ancient title, first bestowed by the kings of France upon the Le Moyne family, was eventually transferred to the British peerage by

Queen Victoria, as a tribute to her father's love of the French Canadians. Its present holders still bear the name Grant.

Others in the group were Madame Elzéar Taschereau, widow of a great French-Canadian statesman and destined to be ancestress of several more; Antoine Juchereau-Duchesnay, Seigneur de Beauport; and Charles Louis de Lanaudière, owner of five seigneuries, proud holder of the nickname *"le beau chevalier"* and for years the favourite aide-de-camp of Dorchester. Here, too, was Major John Stewart, later Lieutenant-Colonel of the Royal Artillery, and founder of a famous Quebec family. They were listening with some embarrassment to Herman Whitsius Ryland, secretary to a long succession of Governors, who was regarded as an *"arriviste qui se donne des airs d'aristocrat"*. Ryland was attempting to be witty, but was boring a group of young listeners with his clerkish fatuities.

Two of the youngest married couples at the party were Louis and Madame Roche de Saint-Ours, and Louis and Madame de Salaberry. Madame de Saint-Ours, a Scot, talked French with a strong English accent that added to the charm of her animated conversation. Louis de Salaberry, Seigneur de Montmorency, a man of taurine build, standing a head above everyone else in the room, was to become the greatest friend and confidant Prince Edward ever had. Twice de Salaberry had been severely wounded fighting on Britain's side against the Americans. During the 1775 attack on Quebec he was badly hit about the body by an American shell which landed in Fort St. John. The following year he was hit in the knee by a musket ball in a border skirmish. He had been retired from the army on full pension in the rank of lieutenant. When Edward arrived in Canada de Salaberry was living quietly at Beauport in the bosom of a large and happy family.

Now trumpeters sounded Edward's personal fanfare. Conversation ceased as the twenty-five-year-old Prince, tall, strong and elegantly attired in a glittering dress uniform, made his entrance. Holding his right hand lightly was Julie, radiant and gorgeously dressed in the Pompadour mode of Quebec. Together the young couple toured both salons, speaking a word to everyone present.

When the formalities were over the minstrels struck up a minuet. Later there was a supper. Tables were piled with pyramids of fruit and bowls steamed with such French-Canadian delicacies as the muffle of a moose, small steaks from a bear, and a pie garnished with roasted cock's-combs.

Mrs. Simcoe found the Dunn house, like many others in Quebec, unbearably hot—she estimated the temperature at ninety degrees— yet dancing proceeded until dawn.

Edward's French was as good as Julie's English. Their personal relationship and their linguistic gifts symbolized the deepening harmony of the two races in Quebec. The Quebec *Bulletin des Recherches Historiques* said: "Full of tact, amiable, light-hearted and speaking French as if it were his native language, Edward quickly became popular among the French Canadians. In fact he seemed to frequent French-Canadian society more than that of the English." The *Québecois* responded warmly to his congenial approaches. On each of his birthdays in Quebec City every householder in town placed lighted candles in the front windows.

In the spring of 1792 Edward and Julie rented as a summer home Montmorency House, a graceful, rambling wooden mansion by the Falls of Montmorency, six miles east of Quebec City. It stands on the edge of a roaring cataract which falls for 280 feet to a backwater of the St. Lawrence. Baroness Riedesel, wife of Baron Frederick Adolph de Riedesel, commander of a corps of Brunswickian mercenaries stationed in Quebec shortly after the American Revolution, described its setting as "sublime". The house was built by General Sir Frederick Haldimand, a Swiss by birth who commanded British troops during the American Revolution, and was for some years British Commander-in-Chief in America. Today the place is a monastery, and though it is lamentably lacking in souvenirs of Edward and Julie, it is a big tourist attraction.

Half-way between Montmorency House and Quebec City lies the suburb of Beauport, where Louis de Salaberry lived. On his daily drives between Montmorency House and the Fusiliers' barracks in the city, Edward got into the habit of calling on de Salaberry. An intimate friendship ripened, and soon de Salaberry and his wife were exchanging visits regularly with Edward and Julie.

The brawny Louis de Salaberry, scion of an old French military family, but born in Canada, had as a boy watched the Battle of the Plains of Abraham from the roof of a house. His father Michel had fought in that battle against Wolfe. After the French defeat the de Salaberrys were one of the first families to transfer their allegiance to the British Crown. Correspondence between Edward and the de Salaberrys, exchanged over a period of many years and preserved in Canada, is one of the richest sources of information on the Prince's life. In the first of these letters, dated March 1, 1792, Edward wrote to de Salaberry, who was ill:

I am in despair, my dear de Salaberry, that we shall not have the pleasure of seeing you here today. I am more pained to know the cause but I hope it will not result in anything serious. Keep yourself cheerful, have a little patience and do not venture out until you are completely recovered. The moment you inform me the roads are passable I will lose no time in repairing to Beauport with Madame de St. Laurent, who joins me in assuring you of those sentiments of distinguished consideration and esteem with which I am always your most devoted and faithful
Edward, Col., R. Fusiliers

Three months later Madame de Salaberry, the former Catherine Hertel, a slight and graceful woman known to her husband and intimates by the pet name Souris, received from Julie a letter of congratulation on the birth of a son. The letter is one of the few of Julie's that survive. By good luck it glows with the spontaneity, affection and merriment that characterized her temperament:

Hurrah! Hurrah! Hurrah! A thousand rounds in honour of the charming Souris and the new-born. In truth my head is full of joy and my hand trembles so much that I can scarcely hold my pen. And it is another boy! How I wish I were one of those powerful fairies who were able to bestow their gifts in such profusion. How the dear child should be endowed! Unfortunately all this is but an illusion. But never mind. Something tells me that the pretty little fellow has been born under a happy star. Kiss him for me, my dear friend, and tell him of this prediction. I was never so happy in my life. I have this moment sent the news to our dear Prince. It is needless to await his reply to assure you how delighted he will be. I know his sentiments too well to have any fear in expressing them. I will go to Beauport today about seven o'clock. Tomorrow I will go again, and every day. Ah, I wish it could be this very instant of my life. I reserve it to myself to congratulate

M. de Salaberry in person on the happy event. And in the meantime I embrace the whole household, without distinction of age or sex.

This child, the youngest de Salaberry son, was named after Edward. Although the subsequent baptism of the child was valid, many French-Canadian Catholics consider that the Church's acceptance of Edward and Julie as godparents was regrettable.

The de Salaberrys were fervent Roman Catholics. Discussing their piety, the French-Canadian author de Gaspé wrote: "The bell sounds the last stroke of the *Agnus Dei.* The father and mother rise and their seven children follow them to partake of the Easter Communion. Some who witnessed this religious act of the whole de Salaberry family said to me that the sight made a vivid impression on the faithful gathered in the church."

According to the discipline of the Roman Catholic Church, heretics and persons of ill repute are not acceptable as godparents. Edward certainly rated as a heretic; and if Julie did not rate as a person of ill repute, her unsanctified relationship with Edward disqualified her from godmotherhood. Why Edward and Julie were given the honour has puzzled generations of Roman Catholics.

The truth is that both the de Salaberrys and the Quebec clergy were bulldozed into the arrangement by Edward's youthful brashness and importunity. This arose out of the ardour of his friendship for the de Salaberrys, though it was hardly, on these grounds, excusable.

In a letter written at the time, the Grand Vicar Gravé contended that Edward boldly asked de Salaberry to make Julie and himself godparents. Prizing and reciprocating Edward's friendship, and perhaps a little dazzled by his rank, de Salaberry could utter only some faint demur about the possible reaction of the clergy. Edward brushed aside his friend's scruples. He followed up with a sentence that amounted to arrogance. "The Roman Catholic clergy should be aware," Edward said, "that their existence in the province is almost entirely the fruit of my father's goodness of heart. It is not as the King's son, but as the son of a sovereign who has taken the Roman Catholic clergy of Canada under his protection, that I wish to be allowed perfect freedom in this matter." Edward then added, with staggering effrontery: "In any case I do not wish to trouble anyone, and my chaplain, a respectable man, can do himself what I wish."

The idea of having a Protestant chaplain baptize his child must have appalled de Salaberry. Instead of quarrelling with Edward, however, he went to the Grand Vicar Gravé and explained his delicate position.

Gravé, like the rest of the Quebec clergy, felt in debt to the Throne of England for the freedom of his Church. He had no wish to bicker with a young Prince who eyed that Church with cordiality if not with deep understanding, and who had sewn so many good seams into Anglo-French relations. Although de Salaberry's account of Edward's high-handed attitude toward the forthcoming baptism pained Gravé, the Grand Vicar excused the Prince on the grounds of his immaturity and Protestant ignorance. In agreement with de Salaberry, Gravé decided on a compromise which would minify the breach in Church rules and satisfy Edward's desire.

The baptism was performed by the Bishop of Capse. At the ceremony the Bishop said: "This child is born a Catholic. He is about to be baptized in order to be brought up in the faith of the Catholic, Apostolic and Roman Church. Monseigneur, what name does Your Royal Highness wish to give this child?" At this point the Prince stepped forward and said "Edouard". But he did not take the child in the usual way; he withdrew and let the Beauport curé, M. Renaud, hold him. The Grand Vicar Gravé explains rather lamely: "So the Prince is not *really* his godfather."

In the parish register at Beauport the baptism is recorded in the following words:

The second day of July, one thousand seven hundred and ninety-two, by us the undersigned Bishop of Capse, in the presence of M. Renaud, Curé of Beauport, was baptized Édouard Alphonse, born the twentieth of June past, of the legitimate marriage of Monsieur Ignace Michel Louis Antoine de Salaberry, Esquire, Seigneur de Montmorency, one of His Majesty's Justices of the Peace, etc., and of Dame Catherine de Hertel; the godfather was His Royal Highness, Monseigneur the Prince Edward of England, Knight of the Most Noble Order of the Garter and of the Most Illustrious Order of St. Patrick, Colonel of the Royal Fusiliers Regiment, Commander at Quebec, etc., etc., etc.; the godmother, Madame Alphonsine Thérèse Bernadine Julie de

Montgenet de St. Laurent, Baronne de Fortisson; who have signed with us. [Signed] Edward, Prince of Great Britain; Montgenet de St. Laurent, Bne. de Fortisson; Fredk. Aug. Wetherall, Captn. 11th Regt.; Renaud, Ptre.; Adelaide de Salaberry; John Hale; Wm. Henry Digby, Lt. Royal Fusiliers; Ch. de Salaberry; Cha. Thomas, C.C.P.

Charles François,
Bishop of Capse

Deprived of love and companionship during the sensitive years between the ages of twelve and seventeen, Edward treasured friendship and displayed exalted notions of its responsibilities. In his championship of those who won his affections he was often impetuous and indiscreet. This was evident when de Salaberry decided to stand as a candidate for the Council for Dorchester County, one of the twenty-one counties into which Lower Canada, or Quebec, had been divided. De Salaberry's opponent was a lawyer named Berthelot d'Artigny. Abandoning the principles of royal and military abstention from political polemics, Edward flung himself with candour into the heat of the election on the side of his friend. At first the notables of Quebec were shocked. Later they were wryly amused at the manner in which Edward conducted himself during a riot that climaxed the campaign.

The *Gazette de Québec* reported that during the counting of the votes de Salaberry led for a long time. Then d'Artigny began to catch up. Edward was clearly excited. A point was reached when it was evident that d'Artigny might outstrip de Salaberry. At this moment de Salaberry's supporters, said the *Gazette,* "hit upon the simple idea of demolishing the hustings". With the ballot boxes destroyed and the counted votes still running in de Salaberry's favour, the returning officer decided he had no alternative but to announce de Salaberry the victor. D'Artigny's supporters howled in protest. There were ugly cries about the patronage de Salaberry derived from his important British connection. Stung by these allusions to himself, or perhaps alert to the chance of effecting a *fait accompli,* Edward sprang onto a stage and held up his arms dramatically.

"Gentlemen," he cried, "is there any among you who does not regard the King as the father of his people?"

There was a short silence. Then somebody shouted *"Vive le roi!"* The cry was taken up by many others.

"Is there any among you," continued the Prince, "who does not regard the new constitution as the best possible to obtain the happiness of His Majesty's subjects and the good government of this country?"

The acclamations were repeated.

"I therefore advise you," the Prince said, "to retire peacefully. I commend you to peace, concord and unanimity. Let me hear no more of these odious distinctions between English and French. You are equally His Britannic Majesty's beloved subjects."

The *Gazette de Québec* concluded: "The tumult ceased and the threats, rage and fury gave place to admiration and applause."

Berthelot d'Artigny suspected, rightly or wrongly, that the destruction of the hustings followed by Edward's appeasement of the mob smacked of conspiracy. He left the scene frostily, without a glance or a word to the Prince. His chief supporter, the judge Pierre Amable de Bonne, also departed without paying royalty the customary respects.

René Boilu, a deputy in the first Legislative Assembly of Lower Canada, has left a memoir of the incident which may be consulted in the library of the Sulpician Order in Quebec. He speaks of the period of remorse suffered by Edward for the injustice he had helped to inflict, by either accident or design, upon d'Artigny and the influential de Bonne. Then Boilu describes the reconciliation. Edward approached de Bonne and d'Artigny at another election at Charlesbourg, and said: "Monsieur de Bonne. If there is coldness between us I beg of you to forget it. For my part it is forgotten entirely." Then, turning to d'Artigny, he said: "And I beg of you sir to pay me the same compliment." The two men held out their hands and the enmity was dissolved. In his biographical essay *La Dame Française du Duc de Kent,* Damas Potvin says: "It was, in effect, the offender who extended the pardon." But Potvin acknowledges the price paid by Edward in pride and dignity.

No sooner was this touching act of peace over than Edward's high spirits erupted again. Seeing two Charlesbourg electors pummelling a third—who happened to be a supporter of the candidate Edward favoured—the Prince dashed to the rescue and floored both with a stunning right and left. One of these men lived to see the arrival in

57

Canada of Edward VII in 1860, when he was Prince of Wales. With great pride and a little illustrative shadow-boxing, the old man told the Prince how the latter's grandfather had knocked him out.

The incident provoked comment, yet Edward's popularity survived. *Québecois* attributed his gaffes to exuberance rather than to malice or despotism. There was something irresistible about Edward in the role of stalwart friend. He was no less attractive as a pillar of public safety.

Edward raised his Fusiliers from their beds one night and led them until dawn in a battle against a great fire that raged in the Lower Town. After this he bought a fire-engine himself, kept it always at the ready in the Fusilier's barracks, and took the reins of the horses whenever the engine clattered out over the cobbles in response to an alarm.

Not many men so young and high-born demonstrated such compassion as Edward for age and penury. He paid a visit once to a poor centenarian woman on the Ile d'Orléans and asked her if there was anything he could do for her. "Sire," she said, "dance a minuet with me so that I may be able to say before I die I have partnered the son of my sovereign." Edward sent for the string section of his regimental band. The music began. Then Edward, in the words of de Gaspé, "danced with the greatest possible grace". Later "he conducted the old woman to her seat and gave her a respectful salute, which she returned with a most profound curtsey".

On realizing that there were few opportunities of education in Quebec City for the poor, the Prince co-operated with a citizen named James Tanswell in the opening of a Sunday free school "for the benefit of those of every description who are desirous of acquiring the necessary and useful branches of education". One of the rules stipulated that reading, writing and arithmetic should be taught in both languages "to render the acquisition of the English language as easy as possible for His Majesty's new subjects".

Sir Brenton Haliburton, who served for several years as an officer under Edward, wrote: "A tale of woe could always interest him deeply and nothing but gross misconduct could ever induce him to abandon any whom he had once befriended." Sir Brenton described Edward as "an affable and polished gentleman", and went on to discuss his talent for hospitality. "At his table everyone felt at his ease. But while it was evidently his object to make them so his dignified manner precluded the possibility of any liberty being taken by the most forward."

Edward's thirst for knowledge of Quebec life flattered and pleased *les habitants*. He enjoyed charging about in a cariole with Julie and studying the customs of the people. Scores of peasants received an unexpected call from him and boasted for years afterwards about how he enjoyed the maple syrup, salmon, lobster, venison, or other local delicacy they served him.

Although Julie was a little weak in the chest and prone to catch cold easily, she braved the most rigorous weather to keep him company on his journeys. She even insisted on travelling with him when, in August 1792, he made the seven-hundred-mile trip through intense heat to Fort Niagara on Lake Ontario, then the headquarters of his old friend Brigadier General Simcoe, Governor of Upper Canada. Before they left Sir Alured Clarke was evidently perturbed about Mrs. Simcoe's reactions. He warned Simcoe by courier that Edward would be accompanied by "a larger suite than I wish attended him from an apprehension that it must occasion some embarrassment".

Like Dorchester, Simoe had worked hard to relieve the monotony of garrison-town life by hospitality and ceremonial. Though Fort Niagara was rougher, smaller, and more English than Quebec City, social life flourished on the same sort of banquets, balls, card parties, and musical evenings. The log town in sight of United States territory, ever ready to defend itself from border attacks, had an exciting atmosphere of its own. The troops dominated the scene, but among them moved Indians, Negroes, half-breeds, adventurers, smugglers, courtesans, and, doubtless, spies. There was tension in the air. Duels over a woman, a card game, or an insult were common. Passions flared easily, but interdependence sustained an over-all sense of unity, civic pride, and loyalty to the constitution Simcoe represented.

Edward and Julie left Quebec City on Saturday, August 12, 1792. They travelled in a newly painted barge, decorated with flags and covered by an awning. It was fitted with comfortable bunks and a tiny dining saloon. Twelve oarsmen rowed it. When the barge came to rapids, the oarsmen climbed out onto the shore with a long rope and pulled it. At Kingston, where the rapids ended, the couple transferred to the armed schooner *Onondaga* and sailed the length of Lake Ontario to Fort Niagara. On the way the *Onondaga* saluted several U.S. warships. When the schooner reached Fort Niagara on August 21st, guns boomed a royal salute.

Edward agreed to review the 5th Regiment on August 23rd, and it was characteristic of him to ask for a parade at six-thirty in the morning. Instead of groaning, the 5th Regiment was delighted. A review in the later-morning temperature of ninety degrees would have been torture. Edward was pleased with the regiment and asked if he could transfer some of its men to his own 7th Royal Fusiliers. Simcoe granted his request. A parade of all men over five feet nine inches was called. They were cautioned to be "perfectly clean". Edward then pointed out the men he would like. He informed them that none was expected to make the transfer "but by his own choice and acquiescence". Every man Edward selected made the move.

Later the same day Edward set off stoutly to see the famous Niagara Falls. There was no settlement on the banks of the gorge at that time. Unbroken forest and slippery rocks made the descent arduous and even, in parts, dangerous. Edward hopped and jumped down at such speed that he left his puffing retinue far behind. For an hour he stood speechless with awe at the base of the thundering cataract, and then he scrambled back up to dine with a Mr. Hamilton at Queenston.

During their stay at Fort Niagara, a ball was held for Edward and Julie at Navy Hall, the Simcoe residence. Gifts of fruit and flowers poured in for them from the residents. The Mohawks, in full war paint and feathers, staged a national dance, gave Edward a gift of wampum, and appointed him Chief of Chiefs. On August 26th Edward sailed away from Fort Niagara in the *Onondaga*. From the deck his newly acquired troops stood at arms and returned the salute of their old comrades in the 5th Regiment.

As a military man, Sir Brenton Haliburton described Edward thus: "His discipline was strict almost to the point of severity. I am sure he acted on principle. But I think he was somewhat mistaken in supposing such undeviating exactitude essential to good order."

Every morning Edward rose in time to be on parade with his beloved Fusiliers at seven o'clock. In the summer, when he had to drive down from Montmorency House, he got up at five o'clock; in the winter, when he lived in Kent House, only a few hundred yards from the barracks, at six. He had an orderly on duty throughout the night in winter to keep a fire going in his room and to rouse him with a cup of coffee. As in Gibraltar, so in Quebec, Edward expected his junior officers to be present at first parade. There was much moaning, of course, and writing home of martyred letters.

But preserving regimental discipline in Quebec was no task for an easy-going officer. Hard drinking was customary among the rank and file. There were many lonely outposts to be manned in the bush, and tedium was added to the stress of climate. Rum was the familiar solace, and excesses were treated with lenity.

The Duc de la Rochefoucauld, a descendant of the seventeenth-century French philosopher, who journeyed from Kingston to Montreal during the time Edward was in Quebec, noted that "the soldiers were without exception as much intoxicated as any I ever saw in the French service." Four soldiers who manned the oars of his boat as it travelled down the St. Lawrence "were drunk to such a degree that we scarcely made fifteen miles on the first day, even though we covered twelve of them under sail."

The troops were unable to do as many odd jobs for civilians as they were in Britain, owing to the plenitude of cheap aboriginal labour. Poverty increased their distress.

At the same time their uniforms and equipment were highly unsuited to the terrain. Sentries stood on trails miles out in the wilderness, surrounded by bears, wolves, and moose, and by treach-erous Indians with scalps in their belts. Yet they wore tight scarlet coats, pipeclayed webbing, powdered hair, and high glistening helmets, as if they had been posted outside Buckingham House or St. James's Palace.

De la Rochefoucauld saw soldiers "plastering their hair, or, if they had none, their heads, with a thick white mortar, which they laid on with a brush, and afterwards raked, like a garden bed, with an iron comb; and then fastening on their heads a piece of wood, as large as the palm of the hand, and shaped like the bottom of an artichoke, to make a cadogan [a knot of hair worn on the nape of the neck], which they filled with the same white mortar and raked in the same manner as the rest of their headdress."

Desertion into the lonely North where a man with an axe, a knife, a musket, and a sack of salt could survive for years by hunting, was common. Many troops deserted over the border and were lost in the well-populated towns of New England. Desertion was so common it threatened the military security of both Lower and Upper Canada, and was controlled only by the deterrent of severe punishment.

The Government paid a reward of eight dollars, and the officers of the regiment concerned offered an additional eight dollars, for the apprehension of a deserter. Indians were often used to track them down. Court martials sentenced deserters to 999 lashes, and even to death. The full number of lashes, however, was rarely inflicted. Death sentences were nearly always commuted to transportation for life. Only in one case was the extreme penalty paid. In Upper Canada, "from the absolute necessity of a public example", Governor Simcoe consented to the execution of a Private Charles Grisler, who had deserted while standing as night sentry over Government ships on Lake Erie. It was customary to make Army executions as macabre as possible in order to impress the troops. Grisler, for example, was shot while kneeling on his own coffin.

The number of desertions from the Fusiliers also compelled Edward to make an example of someone. He chose a French-Canadian soldier named La Rose, a man of whom he was particularly fond. Because Edward had frequently complimented La Rose on parade for his soldierly bearing, the man's desertion caused him especial pain. Determined to bring him back, Edward headed the pursuit party, which caught up with the deserter as he was eating supper in a peasant house at Pointe au Tremble, nearly two hundred miles to the west. When the royal giant strode into the little cabin, La Rose got up from his seat and smiled grimly. "Sire," he said, in front of Edward's accompanying officers, "you are fortunate I am without arms. If I had a pistol, by God, I'd shoot you where you stand."

Back in Quebec, La Rose was sentenced to 999 lashes. It has been said that Edward stood by without intervening as the full punishment was administered. But there are good reasons for doubting this. According to several accounts in French, La Rose, when he was untied from the stake, strode up to Edward, snapped his fingers, and said defiantly: "Sire, it is only the bullet that punishes. Never has the lash crumpled a French soldier!"

Who can believe that a man suffering from 999 lashes would be able to speak, let alone to snap his fingers or walk? And was Edward's reaction that of a tyrant? He simply turned to one of his officers and said: "This is a brave man."

The most frequently quoted instance of Edward's supposed

62

cruelty is the case of Private Joseph Draper. This soldier was one of a group of conspirators who planned to assassinate Edward in Quebec City. The plotters were betrayed and arrested. At the court martial Draper was sentenced to death. One conspirator, named Timothy Kennedy, was sentenced to seven hundred lashes, and another, William Rose, to five hundred lashes. The proceedings appear to have been scrupulously fair. A private named James Lanegan was acquitted for lack of sufficient evidence, and a sergeant named Thomas Dryton was released before trial for the same reason. Curiously enough, Dryton insisted on facing trial. He was allowed to do so. Evidently he incriminated himself, for he was found guilty and sentenced to four hundred lashes and reduction to the ranks.

The trial was held *in camera,* and in consequence the motive for the plot against Edward's life must remain a matter for conjecture. One theory is that the proposed assassination was to be a reprisal for suffering under Edward's regimental discipline. This surmise is weakened, however, by the fact that men from several different units were parties to the plot. There are stronger grounds for supposing that the conspirators, by assassination, hoped to draw public attention to the general oppressiveness of service in Canada, and that they decided their ends would best be served if they chose for their victim the most exalted individual available.

Colour is lent to this theory by the anxiety of Dryton to face trial. From this it may be deduced that the plotters wished to use the court martial as a public platform on which to air the grievances of the garrison as a whole, and that Dryton was regarded as spokesman for the group. Unfortunately, what he said at the trial has never been made public. There is no direct evidence, therefore, to suggest that the plot was motivated by hatred of Edward. As there *is* indirect evidence to suggest that Edward was to be a purely political victim, chosen for his rank to suffer for the sins of the régime as a whole, it is unfair to ascribe the plot to the Prince's harshness. Nor does the remainder of the story justify the extent to which it has been used for blackening Edward's character.

It is true that on the day scheduled for the execution Draper was marched through the streets in a shroud; that Draper was forced to march in the middle of the Fusiliers' band, which played funeral dirges, and saw his own coffin born on a gun-carriage; that Edward himself rode at the head of this grisly procession; and that in front of two thousand spectators the terrified Draper was tied to a stake while the firing-squad formed up opposite him. But what happened next?

Edward, the man who might have died so violently by Draper's hand, approached the man and said: "You have now reached the awful moment when a few more seconds could carry you into the presence of the Supreme Being. You must be aware of your guilt and that you have no right to pity. But I, your commanding officer, may show pity. As the son of your sovereign, whose greatest prerogative is the dispensation of mercy, I feel myself able to do that which as your colonel the indispensable laws of military discipline rendered it impossible for me even to think of. The Lieutenant-Governor, Major-General Sir Alured Clarke, has listened to my pleas on your behalf. As your plot was directed against my person he has agreed that I should be the first to obtain from His Majesty your pardon. Let us hope that this terrible scene will be a warning to you and that for the rest of your life you will repent what you have done. Joseph Draper, you are free."

It was unnecessary to expose Draper to such suspense, even as a deterrent to other disaffected troops who might be contemplating murder in high places. But in days when a boy could be hung for stealing a sheep, when executions were popular public spectacles, and when life generally was held in contempt, the incident hardly qualified Edward as a sadist.

A sadist would have enjoyed the march to the gallows, but he would not have deprived himself of the pleasure of the execution. Sadism and mercy are incompatibles. Draper's dreadful experience was not so much Edward's fault as it was a phenomenon of the callous times in which both lived. The repeal of his sentence revealed at least a touch of compassion in the disciplinarian's heart.

In 1793 a combination of two events provided Edward with an opportunity to demonstrate his real worth as a soldier on active service. The first of these happenings, which took place early in the year, was the birth to Edward and Julie of a son. Though both parents were pleased and proud, the new arrival was an embarrassment. Instead of flaunting the child, as most parents do, they felt compelled to keep its existence a secret from all but their closest friends.

Edward was influenced to adopt this attitude, firstly by the certainty that wide-spread knowledge of the son in Quebec would tend to increase public curiosity about the precise nature of his relationship with Julie. This he wished to keep as vague as possible. Secondly, he was well aware that news of an addition to the collection of royal bastards already sired by his brothers in England would intensify the hostility toward him of the King. This he was naturally anxious to avoid.

So Edward decided on a curious expedient. Instead of rearing under his own roof his first-born by the woman he loved, he put the child out to foster-parents. His choice of them was most odd.

He selected for the foster-father a man named Robert Wood, who had served in the Royal Navy as a chief petty officer. At some time during his service Wood had found himself in the same ship as Prince William, Edward's older brother; and eventually he had become the Prince's personal servant. When Prince William arrived in Quebec City in 1789, Robert Wood went ashore one day and fell in love with a French-Canadian girl whose parents kept a gift store in the Rue Sous le Fort, and specialized in the sale of souvenirs to the garrison.

Wood was so fond of the girl that he asked Prince William to release him from the Navy, and permit him to marry and settle in Quebec City. William consented. Later Edward secured for Wood the job of door-keeper at the Legislative Assembly. Wood was fulfilling this modest function when Edward and Julie asked him to care for their child. Thus, while Prince William's ten illegitimate children by Mrs. Jordan were raised openly in England and married off into the nobility, the first son of Edward and Julie was brought up in a lower-middle-class colonial home.

Edward was clearly over-optimistic in expecting that a former royal servant of Wood's humble rank could remain silent about so remarkable an arrangement. The news got back to George III in the winter of 1793, and once more that old curmudgeon tried to break up Edward's liaison with Julie by sending him far away from her. The King seized as his opportunity the fact that England was once again at war with France and that officers were needed to fight under General Sir Charles Grey, who was preparing to attack Martinique, Santa Lucia, and Guadeloupe, in the French West Indies. Shortly before Christmas in 1793, Edward received orders to proceed forth-with to General Grey's headquarters in Barbados.

One can imagine Julie's feelings on hearing she was to be de-prived of her lover at such a time, especially in view of the fact that she was already pregnant again. One may just as easily imagine her taking consolation in the fact that Edward would soon be in a position to give her first-hand accounts of conditions in and about her old home at Martinique. There is documentary evidence to suggest that Robert Wood, the foster-parent of her child, ac-companied Edward to the West Indies for the specific purpose of carrying such news back to Julie in the event of Martinique's fall to the British.

When news of Edward's impending departure spread through Quebec, scores of addresses to him arrived at the Chateau St. Louis. One, from a group of *Québecois,* said: "The amiable qualities of benevolence and attention manifested by Your Royal Highness to-ward the relief and protection of our fellow citizens in the hour of distress, as well as your condecension and urbanity to all who have occasionally had the honour to approach Your Royal High-ness, have invariably claimed our admiration and gratitude."

Another read: "The Roman Catholic Clergy of Quebec, protected by the best of kings, comes to bring Your Royal Highness a testi-monial of their affliction at the approaching departure which will deprive the Province of so kind a Prince. The social virtues which make you the object of general love, the activity and military vigilance by which you have strengthened the confidence of the subjects, assure you of the general gratitude of all and sundry. We are assured by your goodness that you will deign to receive our best wishes for your health and the success of your arms."

Lord Dorchester, who had now returned from England, ex-plained in a public proclamation that Edward was going to the West Indies by way of the United States, a risky journey in those days for a prince of the blood. "In order to lose as little time as possible," said the proclamation, "he has taken the shortest and most expeditious route to join his command."

Edward left behind him a reply to the warm expressions of fare-well he had received. "Nothing can flatter me more," he wrote, "than to learn from you that my conduct during my residence in this Province has gained your friendship. Be assured that though I go

66

with cheerfulness to the post assigned to me by the King, my father, I shall not leave Quebec without real regret, nor without carrying with me a remembrance of the marks of friendship and consideration I have experienced here."

Early in January, 1794, Edward drove west with his retinue in a convoy of sleds up the grey and frigid St. Lawrence. Then he turned south down Lake Champlain, which runs out of Canada into the United States. Shortly before they came to the frontier, two sleds, carrying the whole of Edward's equipment, his maps, tents, camp beds, saddles, weapons, uniforms, books and wines, broke through the ice and sank to the bottom of the lake. The loss cost Edward more than two thousand pounds sterling. His Gibraltar debts, despite the repeated promises of his father to honour them, remained unpaid, and the disaster added a heavy strain to his slender finances.

When he reached the little town of Burlington, in Vermont, Edward possessed nothing but the clothes in which he stood. The republicans of Burlington were sympathetic, and being aware of Edward's popularity in Quebec, were curious to meet him.

At the Burlington Inn, where he stayed one night, the following note was delivered to Edward:

Sir: Dictated by the principles of common civility and politeness, and possibly urged by an unwarrantable anxiety to have an interview with Your Royal Highness, in behalf of the most respectable gentlemen of this place, we have to request you to appoint an hour (commencing after 6 p.m. on account of the business of the court) which will be most agreeable to you to receive that respectful attention due to your rank, and you may be assured, although in a strange country, that protection is equally at your command, with the greatest subject in the United States.
We are with the greatest respect
Your Most Obedient Servants,
Elnathan Keyes
John Bishop
William Prentice

The petitioners received the following reply from one of Edward's aides:

Gentlemen:

I am commanded by His Royal Highness Prince Edward to return you his best thanks for your polite attention and at the same time to say that if half-past-six o'clock this evening will be a convenient hour to you, he shall esteem himself much flattered by having the pleasure of seeing you.

I have the honour to remain

With great respect,

Your most obedient humble servant

Fred. Augt. Wetherall

Frederick Augustus Wetherall, a veteran of the American Revolutionary War, was by now one of Edward's most intimate confidants. Though thirteen years older than the Prince, he was remarkably similar in temperament, and a devoted subordinate and friend. He had been first attracted to Edward in Gibraltar, where he had approved of the Prince's attempted reforms. There Edward had taken Wetherall on his staff. Though Wetherall's progress in Edward's train is shadowy, it is continuous. He remained in Edward's service until the end of the Prince's days, rising from ADC to equerry and eventually to comptroller. Finally he was the executor of Edward's estate. So in the West Indies Edward was to have the benefit of the advice and companionship of a man who had fought at Boston and Brandywine, and with the marines under Rodney at the Battle of Cape St. Vincent.

On February 13, 1794, Edward reached Boston, where he heard that Sir Charles Grey had already established several beach-heads on Martinique. He embarked for Martinique direct in what he described later as "a wretched little packet boat of six guns". Off the Massachusetts coast a squadron of French frigates was cruising hungrily in search of British prizes. On several occasions, as it ran the gauntlet, Edward's little packet replied to enemy fire with its puny batteries. The packet, however, was fleet and managed to outrun the French. "Providence has extended to me remarkable favour," wrote Edward.

Though Edward was doubtless glad of the chance to show his prowess in battle and to satisfy Julie's curiosity about Martinique, he was saddened by a suspicion that his father cared little for his fate on the field. Some months later he wrote to a friend: "The West Indies! The wish entertained about me in certain quarters when serving there was that I might fall."

Chapter VI

BY MARCH, 1794, the headless body of Louis XVI had been in its grave for fifteen months. The National Convention, the longest-lived of France's Revolutionary Assemblies, was in the middle of its three-year span. Out of the dark intrigue of rival contenders for office, Robespierre had emerged as victor. He was drunk on the blood of his enemies. Under his Reign of Terror France cringed. Dissenters were fed to the guillotine at the rate of sixty a month. Robespierre sought to have himself appointed "the Supreme Being". He had already prohibited, by public proclamation, the worship of God.

Europe, stunned by the barbarism that prevailed in the name of liberty, fraternity and equality, ringed France with guns. But France, having conscripted nearly a million men, was advancing on several fronts. One British expeditionary force, through the bungling of its commander, the Duke of York, had failed to capture Dunkirk and now was in full retreat to Holland. Another which for several months had invested Toulon—with the help of French royalists—had been driven out by a rising young colonel named Napoleon Bonaparte.

Meanwhile the Revolution had spread to the French colonies in the West Indies, where thousands of Negro slaves saw in it an opportunity of winning their freedom. French West Indian royalists, defeated largely by Negroes under white revolutionary command, had invited forces from the British West Indies to help them stage a counter-revolution. The invitation had been accepted. A small-scale British attempt to seize Martinique in 1793 had failed. The French West Indies were now defended for Revolutionary France by Marshall Jean Baptiste Donatien de Vimeure, Comte de Rochambeau.

Rochambeau was one of those high-born soldiers who sacrificed the interests of their class to their careers in the army. He had fought against the British during the American Revolution, and like Lafayette had fallen to some extent under the influence of republican ideals. For a time, in France, he had been disgusted by the excesses of the revolutionary leaders, and had even been imprisoned briefly by Robespierre for making his feelings known. But his value as a soldier had resulted in his release and his posting to Martinique.

During the winter 1793-94 Rochambeau studded the island of Martinique with strong redoubts against the threat of a combined operation from Barbados under General Sir Charles Grey and Admiral Sir John Jervis. Rochambeau, however, failed to establish good communications between his many scattered fortresses. His defenses were static and his troops were incapable of massing for strong, decisive counter-attack at any one point. In consequence Grey and Jervis, by a series of brilliantly co-ordinated landings from the sea, managed, during February, 1794, to reduce the fortresses one by one.

On March 4, 1794, Grey was established on the heights around Fort Royal, the capital of Martinique, and was ready to launch the final assault. It was on this day that Edward reported for duty.

Rain fell heavily through the blanketing tropical heat, and the British troops were racked by yellow fever. But with final victory in sight, morale was high. Edward was given command of two battalions, one of light infantry, the other of grenadiers. Having lost his equipment in Lake Champlain, he was fitted out with borrowed uniforms and weapons.

The city of Fort Royal was defended by two redoubts, Fort Bourbon and Fort Louis. Both were strongly armed with heavy guns. Day and night the British troops ashore, and the nineteen Royal Navy warships standing in the bay to the south of the capital, were harassed by savage and continuous French fire. On March 6, however, Grey was ready to attack. His field guns opened up on the two French fortresses from eight hundred yards. The artillery fire was augmented by the guns of Jervis's fleet in the bay. For ten days the barrage fell on the French while the British infantry advanced yard by yard. As the infantrymen moved forward they cleared paths through the jungle, and by degrees the guns were brought along these, closer and closer to the French fortifications.

It is interesting to note that this dour and bloody manoeuvre evoked Edward's sense of humour. On March 17, urging his troops onward in face of withering fire, the Prince raised his sword and shouted: "This is St. Patrick's Day! The English will do their duty in compliment to the Irish! And the Irish in compliment to the Saint! Grenadiers! Forward!"

On March 19 the British field guns were within two hundred yards of Forts Louis and Bourbon. On March 20 a flotilla of small boats laden with troops put out from the battleships *Asia* and *Zebra* and landed on a beach under one of the walls of Fort Louis. While these troops were being engaged by the French, Captain Robert Faulkner of the *Zebra* ran his ship ashore under another wall of the same fort. Deep water enabled him to put *Zebra*'s bow within a few feet of the masonry. Bluejackets then threw ladders against the wall and fought their way over the top into the redoubt. A murderous struggle within the fort continued for some hours, and Rochambeau eventually yielded to the temptation to summon reinforcements from Fort Bourbon.

As this movement was being carried out, Edward, with his light infantry and grenadiers, led a land-based attack against the city of Fort Royal, which stood between the two bastions. He strode forward at the head of his troops, facing severe musket fire from outlying pickets. One by one the pickets were overwhelmed. Finally Edward and his men surged into the city and disorganized the movement of troops between Fort Bourbon and Fort Louis. After a sharp fight Edward seized a number of strong-points. A second wave of infantry followed and occupied warehouses containing the city's supplies and ammunition.

Seeing the city invested, Fort Bourbon reduced in strength, Fort Louis on the point of falling, and the whole battle area littered with wounded and dying French, Rochambeau hung out the white flag. Firing ceased and for three days both sides negotiated a surrender. On March 23 Rochambeau's garrison marched out with full military honours and laid down their arms. Grey gave Rochambeau a passage to the United States on the condition that he would not serve in the French armies again. (Although he eventually returned to France, Rochambeau kept his promise.) Thus Martinique fell to the British.

Edward was rebuked by Grey for taking too many personal risks in the battle. In tribute to the Prince's courage, Grey renamed Fort Royal, Fort Edward.

The carnage among the French was great. The British spent three days helping them to bury their dead. Among the dead was a French artillery colonel whose head had been blown off by a British cannon-ball. The discovery of this body must have filled Edward with mixed emotions, for it was that of the Baron de Fortisson, Julie's husband. This extraordinary coincidence is vouched for by a direct descendant of Edward and Julie. The gentleman told this writer: "My father heared the story at first hand from my great-grandmother, Julie de St. Laurent."

On parting from Edward and Julie at Gibraltar, three years before, the Baron de Fortisson had taken advantage of an amnesty which the French Government had extended to *émigré* officers who would agree to serve in the Republican army. He had been posted to the West Indies, only to lose his life in battle with the man to whom he had lost his wife.

Edward at once dispatched Robert Wood—his courier, and the foster-parent of his first child—with a note to Quebec City. This informed Julie of her husband's death and reminded her that they were now free to contract a morganatic marriage. Edward also asked Julie to prepare to meet him soon in Halifax, Nova Scotia. He was already planning to bring Julie to her old home in Martinique as soon as the campaign ended. Although the note has not survived, there is documentary evidence of its transmission in the hands of Wood. In a letter to Mr. Hector Bolitho, the late Colonel William Wood, of Quebec City, one of Canada's foremost historians, wrote: "I have the pass given to Robert Wood at Martinique in 1794 authorizing the said Robert Wood to pass any and all of His Majesty's posts by land and sea." The pass was signed by Edward.

There can be little doubt that Edward would have liked to linger in Martinique for the purpose of investigating conditions at Julie's family's estate at Trois Ilets. But the need to pursue the campaign left him no time.

On March 30, seven days after the fall of Martinique, Edward was ordered to embark with his troops in Jervis's fleet, which was now readying itself for an attack on the adjacent French West Indian isle of Santa Lucia.

Despite windless weather, the voyage was made in two days, and on April 1 Grey began to repeat the tactics he had employed so successfully at Martinique. His objective was the capital city, the port of Castries, which stands in the north-west region of Santa Lucia. He landed four parties, two to the north of Castries at Pointe de Cap and Choc Bay, and two to the south at Anse Latoc and Marigot. The northern and southern groups were to march toward each other along the coast, taking the seaward batteries from the rear. At the head of one column Edward stormed several batteries during the night of April 1. By April 2 all four columns had converged on Morne Fortune, the major fortress protecting Castries. Two batteries adjoining the main fortress were taken by surprise at the bayonet point, one by Edward, the other by a Colonel Coote. Thirty of the enemy were killed, but the British did not lose a man.

The Santa Lucia commandant, General Ricard, was caught off balance by the pace of the British attack. On the evening of April 2 he capitulated. He was shipped to Franch with the one hundred and twenty regular white troops who had stiffened the Negro garrison. Edward was invited by Grey to rename the fort of Morne Fortune. He chose his mother's name, and to this day it is called Fort Charlotte.

On April 4 Grey wrote to the War Office: "The exemplary good conduct of the brigade of Grenadiers under the immediate command of His Royal Highness Prince Edward . . . affords me the highest satisfaction." After selecting a small garrison force for Santa Lucia, Grey re-embarked his troops the same day, returned to Martinique, and took on supplies and ammunition. But again Edward had no time to visit Trois Ilets. On April 8 Grey set sail for the twin islands of Guadeloupe, fifty miles to the north. He landed his troops at Gozier Bay, near Pointe à Pitre, on Grande-Terre, the eastern of the two islands of Guadeloupe. The landing was achieved with little loss after Lord Garlies, captain of the Battleship *Winchelsea,* laid his vessel close under the French shore batteries and pounded them into silence with broadsides.

The most formidable defenses of Grande-Terre—Morne Mascotte and Fort Fleur d'Epée—lay a few miles to the east. Here most of the French garrison was concentrated. At midnight on April 11 Grey divided his force into three groups. He gave orders that the advance eastward was to be carried out in complete silence. All outposts were to be taken by the bayonet alone. To ensure compliance with this order, flintlocks were removed from the men's muskets. For these tactics the commander earned the nickname "No-flint Grey".

One column under General Thomas Dundas took the coast trail; another under a Colonel Symes took an inland trail; Edward's force

73

advanced along a road between them. During the night Edward's column stumbled on an outpost, which immediately opened fire. Though he was unable to return the fire, Edward urged his men on, making good use of tropical foliage as cover. Casualties were heavy, but eventually the outpost was rushed and taken with cold steel.

By five in the morning the three columns were reunited below Morne Mascotte and Fleur d'Epée. Flintlocks were returned to the muskets. Edward's objective now was Morne Mascotte, that of the other two columns Fort Fleur d'Epée. On a signal from a gun in Jervis's flagship *Boyne* the double assault began, under a ferocious fire of French grape and musketry. Once more Edward led his troops forward in a series of rushes. Each rush was cleverly timed and covered by musket fire.

At a critical moment, when the Light Infantry reached the base of the walls, and Grenadiers kept the French heads down with covering fire, bluejackets raced up with scaling-ladders. These were not quite high enough to reach the embrasures, but a number of plucky seamen clung to the top of the ladders and hoisted their messmates in over their shoulders. Many dead and wounded fell from the ladders, but the walls were finally carried. Soon the fighting was in the confines of the fort. This was hand-to-hand combat, and Edward was noticed by one naval officer to be "in the thick of it".

At Fort Fleur d'Epée the struggle was equally bitter. When French communications between the two forts were finally cut, the surviving French panicked and fled. The eastern island of Grande-Terre was thus captured before midday on April 11. After twenty-four hours of rest, Grey advanced across the causeway that spanned the gulf between Grande-Terre and the western island of Basse-Terre. Once again the operation consisted of storming isolated posts at the bayonet point by night. By the morning of April 21 both Basse-Terre and Grande-Terre were in British hands.

Six thousand French had defended Guadeloupe and the number of British against them had never exceeded three thousand. Grey's dead numbered eighty-six. J. W. Fortescue, in his *History of the British Army*, wrote: "The whole campaign was an extraordinary example of the power of a small and efficient army working in perfect harmony with a small and efficient squadron upon a fortified coast."

Edward's gallantry was again mentioned by Sir Charles Grey in dispatches. Both Houses of the British Parliament and the Irish House of Commons passed a special vote of thanks to the Prince. This was the only time a member of George III's family was publicly commended for service in the field. The Duke of York, smarting under the press and parliamentary criticism he had incurred for his fumbling of the Dunkirk campaign, became jealous of Edward. In later years Edward was to suffer much from this unbrotherly attitude.

For his valour in the West Indies Edward was rewarded with the post of C-in-C British troops in Nova Scotia. But he felt free to pursue his private interests before taking up these duties. He planned to marry Julie morganatically with all possible speed. On April 23, two days after the final victory at Guadeloupe, he embarked in the frigate *Blanche,* evidently hoping for an early meeting in Halifax with his mistress. The *Blanche* was commanded by Captain Robert Faulkner, the naval hero of Martinique, whose former ship *Zebra* was still stuck on the beach below Fort Louis. Captain Faulkner, in a letter to his mother, said he found Edward "a pleasant, kind companion".

The *Blanche,* said Captain Faulkner, took only eleven days on the voyage from Guadeloupe; and therefore it must have landed Edward in Halifax on May 3. About this time Robert Wood would have completed the longer voyage to Quebec City with Edward's letter to Julie.

While waiting for Julie to arrive in Halifax, Edward spent several weeks touring Nova Scotia and New Brunswick. By July 14 he was back in Halifax and disappointed by Julie's failure to appear. In a letter of that date to de Salaberry he described his experiences in the West Indies, thanked God for his survival, and added: "My good fortune would have been completed if on my arrival here I had found my friend Madame de St. Laurent." Clearly, however, he must have received news of Julie's imminent departure from Quebec City. He added a postscript for Madame de Salaberry, saying he expected Julie to reach Halifax "in three weeks or a month at most".

Julie's delayed departure from Quebec City was probably due to her pregnancy and to the difficulty of finding a ship that carried a surgeon. Eventually she was given a passage in a British man-of-war. Aboard it on the way to Halifax, she gave birth to a son, her second by Edward. He was christened Jean. He grew up under the surname de Mestre, one of the de Fortisson family names.

There is no record of the date of Julie's arrival in Halifax, but one of her descendants says that soon after she joined Edward in that city they sailed together for Martinique, taking their second son with them. In Martinique Julie was delighted to find her mother the Comtesse de Montgenet in good health. During the visit the Comtesse agreed to bring up the baby Jean. A descendant says that Edward and Julie were married in Martinique by a Roman Catholic priest in the summer of 1794, Edward using the name "Captain Armstrong".

Unfortunately the writer has been unable to trace any record of the marriage. Monsieur A. Michaud, secretary to the Bishop of Martinique, told the writer in 1956: "In so far as religious ceremonies are concerned there is nothing to be found older than 1902, when St. Pierre's volcano destroyed all our records."

In 1939 the Reverend Charles E. Rivers, of Oriel College, Oxford, wrote a note to Mr. Hector Bolitho in which he said:

A member of my own family married some years ago a direct descendant of Madame de St. Laurent and the Duke of Kent. This lady was in Canada on a visit and met the Archbishop of Quebec and the Vicar General of his diocese. They told her that the Duke was privately married to Madame exactly in the same way as Mrs. Fitzherbert to George IV and that there was documentary evidence to this effect in their possession.

In many enquiries about this document in Quebec City the writer has met only with equivocal replies. Luis Carrier, a member of the Montreal Historical Society and an authority on Quebec of the eighteenth and nineteenth centuries, told the writer in 1954: "It has always been believed that proof of the morganatic marriage of the Duke of Kent and Julie de St. Laurent lies in the archives of the Catholic Church in Quebec. But nobody, not even one of the Duke's descendants, has been able to uncover it."

The story of Edward's and Julie's voyage to Martinique in 1794 is strongly supported by the memoirs of Sir Brenton Haliburton. Sir Brenton says he was in the guard of honour which met Edward in Halifax in October 1794 on the Prince's return from a voyage to the

West Indies. The date of this arrival is five months later than the date in May, 1794, when Edward disembarked there from the frigate *Blanche*.

So it is probable that Edward, upon taking up his duties in Halifax in October 1794 as Commanding Officer, British Troops in Nova Scotia, was married, not only in the eyes of God, but also in the eyes of the church Julie revered.

Chapter VII

DURING the winter of 1794-95 the Twenty Years War, which was to last until the defeat of Napoleon at Waterloo, increased in sweep and violence. Europe thundered to the tramp of marching feet. At sea warships and merchantmen burned and sank. In the West Indies reinforcements from France recaptured the islands of Guadeloupe. An invasion of Canada was expected any day. The War Office in London feared that the French might try to seize Halifax, inflame Quebec to revolt, seek another alliance with the United States, and, in a northward thrust, attempt to make an end of British rule in North America. To de Salaberry, Edward wrote: "We are ever on the alert."

In fortifying Halifax, Edward was handicapped by an impoverished and disordered population that was dominated by a decadent local oligarchy, and by the lethargy of troops whose officers had slipped through idleness into dissipated habits.

Ever since the loss of the American colonies, Halifax had been decaying. Funds from England had been sufficient to sustain the port only as a naval base. Cut off from natural commerce with the United States, trade had stagnated. American Revolutionary War defences had crumbled or disappeared under a growth of weed and thicket. The tumble-down wooden houses overlooking the harbour were riddled with brothels and the streets were plied by a motley collection of beggars and peddlers.

Halifax's moral tone had been set largely by Edward's naval brother, Prince William. Between 1783 and 1791 William sailed into Halifax on many occasions. In view of his pointed red-thatched cranium the Haligonians had nicknamed him "Coconut". Once his vessel arrived under the command of a fourteen-year-old midshipman because William and his senior officers were too drunk to walk the quarter-deck. Ashore in Halifax, with a party of six companions, William once drank twenty-eight bumper toasts of champagne and claret followed by fourteen bottles of Burton ale. A young buck of a subaltern named Dyott, who recorded the incident in his diary, said William "sang two or three songs and for three hours laughed incessantly". At a dinner some nights later, William and Dyott joined a party of twenty who shared sixty-three bottles of wine.

The carousing was usually followed by a tour of the town's stews, wherein William whetted his carnal appetite by watching the women engage in Lesbian exhibitions. On several occasions his goatish caprice drove him straight from the arms of a prostitute to the embraces of Frances Wentworth, an unfastidious matron of forty-two who was delighted to share her bed with any man in a position to further her social ambitions.

Beautiful, intelligent, and wanton, Frances was married to John Wentworth, a plodding, cunning civil servant who held the rank of Keeper of the King's Woods. He tolerated his wife's promiscuity partly because she had cowed him into the habit of indulging all her whims, and partly because she often influenced his personal promotion.

In 1791 Wentworth's moment came. During a visit to England Frances strayed from her husband and hunted William down again. Although the Prince was then living with Mrs. Jordan, Frances enticed him into a resumption of past pleasures. William bought her a sofa, and, according to a letter written home by a Haligonian in London, "they tried the length of it on the Queen's birthday".

As usual, Frances mixed business with pleasure; and a few weeks later, when John Wentworth took her back to Halifax, he boasted the rank of Lieutenant-Governor of Nova Scotia. A knighthood soon followed.

When Edward settled in Halifax, Frances Wentworth was making her husband's office the excuse for a life of perpetual Saturnalia, in which the leading clique participated with relish. "It was no unusual thing," wrote the well-restrained Haliburton, "for the gentlemen to join the ladies in a state of intoxication." This was "merely laughed at by the ladies".

The officers of the garrison found relief from the routine of gambling, tippling and wenching in fighting duels, breeding game-cocks, coursing hares, and hunting. The troops filled the taverns and a row of filthy bawdy-houses along Barracks Street. An exotic streak was added to some of these stews by freed Negro slaves, many of whom lived by pimping and prostitution.

In addition to the older established Negroes was a tribe of six hundred new-comers from Jamaica. Known as Maroons, they were descended from absconded slaves who had taken to the hills of the British West Indian colony and had lived by raiding outlying plantations for food and money. It had been feared that they might become infected with the spirit of the French Revolution, serve as a fifth column in Jamaica for the rebel slaves in the French West Indies, and so sharpen the very real threat of a new Negro empire in the Caribbean. In a resolute military operation in Jamaica, the Maroons—men, women and children—were rounded up and shipped to Halifax. The British Government sent £25,000 to Halifax to defray the cost of settling them on the land, and added a grant of £240 a year for a school in which they were to be educated.

Wentworth got his hands on the money, and though he talked about "disseminating piety, morality and loyalty among them", he consoled himself during his wife's absences by taking the most beautiful young virgin in the tribe to his bed. He took another fifty Maroons to work as low-paid retainers on his estate at nearby Preston. The rest of them were housed in a collection of shanties around the estate, where, discouraged by the cold winters and damp summers, they made a poor show of farming and study, and lived largely by their wits. The Maroon nights were often given up to African rites that had somehow survived many generations of exile; and it was no secret that some white men paid handsomely for the privilege of sharing in the orgiastic climaxes.

The economy of Halifax was disrupted by the growing number of French prisoners who were shipped in from land battles in the West Indies and naval engagements in the Atlantic. To save himself from the worry of maintaining the French prisoners, Wentworth permitted them to wander about the town doing odd jobs and selling handicrafts. Out of beef bones some made snuff-boxes, knives, forks, dominoes, and model ships. Others bought textiles and leather to make stockings, gloves, and purses. Among them were painters, goldsmiths, shoemakers, music teachers, and dancing-masters, who followed their trades at cut rates in order to buy a few provisions. Such chaotic conditions offered many opportunities to the corrupt, and Wentworth was quick to take advantage of them. His wife's demands on his purse were endless. He even bought her a galley rowed by many pairs of oars; and aboard this, as she sailed about the harbour on her amorous quests, she reclined like a celebrated Egyptian queen.

We may be sure that Frances toyed with the idea of embroiling Edward in a profitable liaison. We may be equally sure that after taking one look at the ravishing Julie, more than twenty years her junior, the Haligonian Messalina was discouraged. Edward's arrival in Halifax put an end to the more flagrant venery of Frances Wentworth and saw her beginnings as a drawing-room rather than a boudoir hostess.

On the northern slopes of Citadel Hill Edward bought a wooden mansion with a Corinthian portico, well-kept gardens running down to Cogswell Street, and lodge gates lit by two handsome copper lanterns. Here he began to entertain in the stately style of Quebec. At levees, dinner-parties and balls, officers, colonial officials, gentlemen farmers, richer merchants, and local politicians were expected to hold their liquor and restrain their flirtations. Whist was permitted for nominal stakes because Julie liked the game. But Haliburton says that Edward "never touched a card".

It would not have been surprising if, in his determination to bring about rapid and radical reforms, Edward had antagonized the Wentworths. But of course they were snobs and the last couple on earth to quarrel with a prince. After summing up Edward's character, they were just as anxious to earn his esteem by putting on a show of rectitude as they had been ready to ingratiate themselves into his brother's favour by lifting the lids off the flesh-pots.

It was not Edward alone who inspired an elevation in Haligonian morals. Back in England, a revulsion from the atheism of revolutionary France had prepared the ground for the seeds of that evangelism, piety, and strict personal conduct which later characterized the majority of Victoria's subjects. The puritanical convolvulus germinated first among the poorer nonconformist industrial classes of the North, but the tendrils sprang upward quickly and spread into the Established Church. Thence they entwined themselves through the houses of the new rich and the old nobility. The humble folk of England became accustomed to seeing the carriages of the gentry choking the roads to the churches every Sunday. It is remarkable that Edward, who had been out of England for ten years, and who belonged to the pinnacle of a leisured, self-indulgent society, should have been so sensitive to this changing morality and so quick to adjust his own code to it. In Halifax he surprised the local citizens by limiting his entertainment on the Sabbath to quiet conversation and an occasional solo on the harpsichord from Julie.

Frances Wentworth must have been bored by these bleak Sundays, but she put up with them for the sake of royal patronage. Knowing of Edward's energy as a place-seeker for his friends, she insinuated herself deftly into his good graces. Wouldn't it be pleasant, she suggested, if he could have a country place too? She knew just the place. She and John owned a little cottage at Bedford Basin, six miles out of town on the Windsor Road. It rejoiced in the lyrical name of Friar Lawrence's Cell. There was land enough about it for a bigger home. The estate was Edward's for the asking.

Julie was already weary of the town and the importunity of socially ambitious visitors. The street outside her sitting-room rang at dawn with the bugles and drill commands of Edward's first parade. Throughout the morning and afternoon it resounded to the shrill of fifes and tattoo of drums. At sunset the sad notes of taps floated in through the windows. The endless martial music made Julie's head ache. The flogging of army delinquents on Citadel Hill distressed her. And then one day there was a public hanging outside her window. This was the last straw. On Julie's urging, Edward accepted the Wentworth's offer and soon was engaged in his first house-building experiment at Bedford Basin.

He soon revealed those same exotic architectural tatses that had prompted his brother the Prince of Wales to build a Byzantine palace at Brighton. The white wooden frame building was in imitation of the rococco Italian style. It had a flat roof surrounded by an ornate railing, long narrow windows, and a double-decked portico with lattice-work up which many coloured creepers climbed. Inside were a big ballroom and a large central hall, used for levees. Behind the house was another building in the Gothic style. This contained the guardroom, the kitchens, and Edward's private office. Opposite was a circular bandstand consisting of a gilded Moorish cupola mounted on Greek columns.

Hidden in the woods of the grounds was a Chinese temple with strings of copper bells ringing as they were swung by the wind. A gravel path twisted tortuously through the natural woodlands. A balloonist drifting over the estate would have noticed that the path spelled "Julie". At points where it commanded a view of the Basin, there were seats under tiny shelters that looked as if they had been cut out with a cookie-cutter. Among the rafters of these shelters little strips of hanging glass tinkled musically in the breeze. The *pièce de résistance* was an artificial brook, led into the grounds from a nearby stream, which tumbled over a series of pretty waterfalls into a lake. Edward had had the lake's natural shape altered to that of a heart as a mark of his love for Julie. It was surrounded by Julie's private garden.

The lake and the bandstand still survive. On visiting them, generations of Haligonians have pictured Edward, the six-foot red-head in his high black boots with gold tassels, his tight white breeches, and his blue coat heavy with gold braid, strolling tenderly with the slight, black-haired Julie, in her white muslin dress and high-heeled shoes, while through the trees drifted the sentimental concert music of the Fusiliers' band. If Julie felt the love-nest was a trifle vulgar, she took consolation in the knowledge that it was the expression of Edward's simple and truly romantic ardour.

There were receptions every week, conducted with such decorum that the Haligonians began to consider their former excesses out of style. One ball honoured the arrival in the city of Julie's old friend the Duc d'Orléans, who, accompanied by his aides the Duc de Monpensier and the Comte de Beaujolais, had escaped from France and was seeking asylum in America. The trio arrived destitute. Edward lent Orléans two hundred pounds. With this the Duc left for Philadelphia, where for several years he made his living as a school-teacher. Half a century later, when he was Louis Philippe, King of France, he repaid the sum to Edward's daughter Queen Victoria.

(During a state visit to France, Victoria rode through cheering crowds with Louis Philippe, and recalled in her diary how "The King repeated again and again to me how attached he was to my father.")

Every Sunday afternoon Edward paraded his regiment in full-dress uniform and rode at their head through the streets. He organized among his officers another dramatic society, which presented plays—free now from the disapproval of Colonel Simcoe—at the Grand Theatre on Argyle Street. During the winter Edward and Julie rode at the head of jolly processions of sleighs down to the heart-shaped lake, where they skated with their guests under Chinese lanterns to the music of the band.

But Edward limited his dalliance in order to fulfil his military duties with more vigour than ever before. First he cleared the streets of the mendicant French prisoners and locked them up in a proper compound. Next he dragged the Maroons out of their dissipation and idleness and paid them for work on his new fortifications. Old American Revolutionary War trenches on Citadel Hill were filled in. Edward got the earth for this by removing fifteen feet from the top of the hill. On the plateau thus levelled he built a square fort with a bastion at each corner. The approaches to the battlements were obstructed by a ten-foot-deep moat with up-pointing spikes in the bottom.

In the centre of the redoubt was a parade ground, surrounded by a barracks for 650 men. On the flat roof, which was reinforced by huge timbers, the snouts of heavy cannon pointed towards the harbour. The defences were stocked with enough ammunition and supplies to withstand a twelve-month seige. This was to be the keep in case of a successful French landing.

In the harbour Edward prepared a hot reception for any enemy. At Sandwich Point, overlooking the entrance to the harbour, he sited heavy guns. Across the North-west Arm he hung a chain boom, and covered it with four cannon on traversing platforms. At Fort Ogilvie, Fort Sackville, and Imperoyal old defences against the Americans were strengthened and equipped with the latest type of armaments. On St. George's Island Edward built a star-shaped fort from which three hundred riflemen and thirty cannon crews could fire in any direction. The fort had two furnaces for making shot red hot and so adding an incendiary effect to its impact on wooden ships.

It was only two years since a British force attacking Cape Mortello in Corsica had encountered a small enemy fort consisting of a slender tower with immensely thick walls. Hard to hit with the inaccurate cannon of the day, it had proved a potent obstacle. Its only door was located twenty feet above the ground. During battle the ladder giving access was pulled inside, making seizure by infantry a difficult and costly operation. Now, along the southern coast of England, Mortello Towers were going up against the threat of French invasion. In Halifax Edward revealed himself abreast of the times by erecting Mortello Towers at Point Pleasant, Eastern Battery, and York Redoubt.

Edward was far from blind to the fast-growing importance of

military communications. His telegraph in Halifax was not only the first in North America, but was an improvement on all known types in Europe. In fact it was the Prince's greatest single contribution to military science. The French were first in the field of long-range signalling in 1793, with lines of intervisible semaphore towers built on hill-tops. With a telescope their signals could be observed from great distances and relayed onward. From Paris the French command could communicate rapidly to army points on all the country's frontiers.

In England the War Office and the Admiralty were using a telegraph of Swedish design. This consisted of shutters, similar to Venetian blinds, which, when raised or lowered in various combinations, represented letters of the alphabet and a number of key words. Messages could be sent from London to Channel ports in less than an hour. Edward's telegraph was even more speedy. Its code depended in daytime upon arrangements of flags and large black wickerwork balls, and at night on a combination of lanterns and drums.

Within the Halifax area signals could be exchanged between strong-points in two or three minutes. Edward's home at Bedford Basin was within the network. His original idea was to extend the telegraph around the Bay of Fundy to Saint John, New Brunswick, onward to Fredericton, and thence to Quebec City, a total distance of six hundred miles. The line was completed as far as Fredericton, 250 miles to the north-west of Halifax; but Bay of Fundy fogs interfered so seriously with vision and audibility that it proved impractical outside the limits of Nova Scotia. Annapolis Royal, Windsor, Truro, Yarmouth, and other settlements in Nova Scotia were all linked by the telegraph. Brief messages were sent to a point fifty miles distant in twenty minutes.

Once, in Halifax, a Captain Daniel Lyman was surprised to note preparations at the barracks for a flogging of army defaulters. He knew that Edward insisted on endorsing every court-martial sentence of corporal punishment, and wondered if the royal order was being ignored, since, at the time, the Prince was in Annapolis Royal, 140 miles away. Lyman made enquiries. In a letter to Edward Winslow, published in *The Winslow Papers,* Lyman explained that the endorsement of the flogging came by signal. "I was told," he wrote, "that the men were to be flogged, by telegraph! A hundred miles off the Prince was still acquainted with what was going on, and giving orders the same as usual. You will have this mode of communication all the way to Fredericton very soon. I suppose our friend Leonard will have one atop his windmill!"

In May of 1795 Dorchester was preparing to retire to England. Edward hoped to succeed the gallant old man as Governor of Lower Canada. Failing this, he hoped that the Governor's military and civil responsibilities would be divorced, and that he, Edward, would receive at least the command of British troops in North America. Now he was writing to England, beseeching his father to give him an audience and listen to his plea for promotion. George III chose to keep his son on tenterhooks.

On May 11th, 1795, Lyman wrote to Winslow:

It does not seem to be clear yet, from what the Prince mentioned to me yesterday, that it is determined whether he stays here or not. He said "if I should remain here and have the command," why then he would have the posts go so and so; that he would endeavour to have them go quicker; and he proposed to alter their route in the province. The officers of his regiment say that the Prince wishes to go home but that the King will not allow it.

Early in 1796 Edward's dreams of reward for his diligence were shattered. He heard that the governorship and the command of British troops in North America were to go to an octogenarian named Major-General Robert Prescott.

Edward's failure to secure the bigger command in Canada did not discourage his administration of the lesser. His pride and interest in, and extensive knowledge of, each man in his Fusiliers, is shown in a letter he wrote on June 10, 1796, to Thomas Carleton, a relative of Dorchester, who was Lieutenant-Governor of New Brunswick. After saying that he had complied with Carleton's wishes that one thousand stand of arms should be sent to the militia in New Brunswick, Edward turned to smaller, but, in his eyes, equally important matters. He wrote:

I am infinitely obliged for the permission you have granted to MacMullen and Granger of your Provincial Corps to join the Fusiliers in lieu of two other men to be sent from here. If you will direct your men to be sent to St. John's I will embrace the first opportunity that offers of sending a sergeant round with the two men I mean to transfer in their stead, by which means the sergeant will be enabled to take charge of the others on his return.

In another letter to Thomas Carleton, Edward asked that a Mr. Goldsmith, an elderly and recently discharged lieutenant, should be appointed agent for the settling of a boundary argument with the United States. Carleton declined to meet Edward's wishes, on the ground that Goldsmith was too weak. Edward wrote to Carleton:

Your Excellency is extremely polite in explaining so fully your reasons for not appointing Mister Goldsmith as agent in the business of settling the boundary. Having therefore nothing more to say on that subject I shall only observe that I flatter myself should an opportunity offer of befriending that worthy old officer you will not suffer it to pass.

Edward was forever travelling about Nova Scotia and New Brunswick on inspection tours, covering up to seventy-five miles a day. In the rugged month of November, 1797, Lyman wrote to Winslow from Windsor, describing how Edward fitted in innumerable calls on friends. At John Ruggles' home in Windsor they stopped for an hour, then drove thirty miles to Aylesford, where they were entertained at "a magnificent dinner" by Bishop Charles Inglis. From here they drove onward several more miles, to sleep at the Horton home of Edward de Wolfe. The following morning they were back in Windsor.

All this followed an exhausting trip to Annapolis, where Edward had checked the repairs to a barracks. Now he was proposing to return to Halifax by driving overnight. Lyman wrote wearily: "But as I have not so great an object in view I shall probably stay here to-night and see how my friends are. I do not exactly understand what the Prince's object has been in this violent journey." He added, however, that the Prince had "been very pleasing and in great spirits and good humour during the jaunt".

There were not hours enough in any day for Edward's unflagging program of painstaking work and ceremonial play. Planning, punctuality, and procedure were so important to his peace of mind, both on the barrack square and in the drawing-room, that he became obsessed with the instruments of time. He collected watches and clocks so avidly that they cluttered every room in the house. Elaborations of the dials were evidence of his preoccupation with mechanics and ceremony. A clock that would play a tune every quarter of an hour meant more to Edward than one that merely chimed; and if he could find another which also released a jack-in-the-box, or set an endless circle of statuettes chasing each other around the face, or started a pair of silver horses to prance, then he would buy it, no matter what the cost.

In the late eighteenth century the power of the uncoiling spring was being applied to an ever widening range of knick-knacks, often fashioned out of precious metals and stones. Edward was fascinated by this marriage of the jeweller's and the watchmaker's art. He bought music boxes by the dozen, clockwork singing birds and toy organs, and all sorts of figurines that hopped, skipped, or jumped, or in any way simulated life.

The keys he kept, carefully numbered, on large rings, and employed a man to give his collection a daily winding. His ear was so well attuned to the quarter-hourly chimes, booms, clatterings and bird calls all over the house, that if one clock out of scores failed to add its sound to the cacophony Edward missed it, sent for his winder, and directed him unerringly to the defaulting instrument.

This harmless foible has been ridiculed by some writers, who argue that Edward was more occupied with the fact of time than with its application. It has been suggested in many biographical works that he was also excessively interested in the administrative side of army life. Why, ask the critics of his command in Halifax, did he concern himself so deeply with the postings of individual privates, with the most trifling details of his telegraph or fortifications, with the cut of uniforms, the size of buckles, the design of badges, and all the other minutiae of army life? Why, in other words, wasn't he more concerned with fighting?

The answer is, of course, that in Halifax he never had a chance to fight. The French failed to challenge him. In the absence of an enemy, an army, theoretically, has nothing to do. In practice a lengthy period of inactivity represents an army's sternest test. Edward was one of the first British officers to grasp the fact that waiting to fight imposes a more severe stress on soldiers' morale than fighting itself.

Ever since Edward's day it has been axiomatic in the British Army that if uncommitted troops are to remain in fighting trim, they must be subjected to a rigorous daily routine of spit and polish, drill, fatigues, and form-filling, just as children must be given chores to keep them out of mischief in the holidays. No satisfactory alternative to this tedious and much maligned ritual has ever been found. Drop it, and leave troops to amuse themselves, and at once you get the kind of deterioration that Edward encountered on his arrival in Gibraltar, Quebec, and Halifax, but did not encounter, significantly enough, in the West Indies, where the shot was flying. Nobody knew better than Edward that troops, like boxers, run quickly to fat if they are allowed to relax their muscles or their minds for too long.

For his soldiering in the West Indies, where he saw action for the first and last time, Edward incurred nothing but praise. For his soldiering in other parts, where he saw only garrison duty, he was condemned. And he was condemned for the very policies by which he saved his troops from dissolution. In Halifax Edward had the misfortune to perpetuate his reputation as a fusspot and a martinet. Yet his misfortune was England's good fortune. Had the French been able to stage an invasion of Nova Scotia and New Brunswick before Edward's arrival, Canada might have been lost by the British Commonwealth and Empire. Until his arrival the regional defences were puerile.

Between 1794 and 1797, the years of Edward's first command on the Atlantic Coast of Canada, he transformed a legion of sloppy drunks into an agressive fighting force, and a scattering of mouldering forts into a bristling bastion. The fact that the French never tested his Nova Scotia defences is testimony to his preparedness. All Canada was crawling at the time with French spies, and there can be no doubt that the intelligence they sent to Paris, describing the kind of reception Edward had in store for invaders, discouraged a landing.

A letter Edward wrote in 1796 to Louis de Salaberry reveals the calm confidence with which he waited for a chance to show his mettle:

Undoubtedly you must have heard of the arrival of the French fleet on our coast. It escaped from Brest and made a descent on Newfoundland. According to our latest information it was preparing to attack the port of St. John's which is defended on land by a force of four thousand five hundred men, including Provincials, and at sea by a ship of fifty guns, two frigates and four corvettes. From this force I flatter myself St. John's cannot be taken, but the fisheries will certainly suffer this year from the devastations which these *Carmagnoles* [a French term for soldiers of the Revolution] commit wherever they go. As for us we keep ourselves constantly on the alert, lest they should honour us with a visit, which is not impossible, though it may be improbable. But I flatter myself that in the event of a visit we should so conduct ourselves that they would be glad to retire as quickly as possible.

At home Edward enjoyed agreeable respite from his arduous routine. He was ideally happy with Julie. She made a brilliant hostess, and her French cuisine enraptured local epicures. Her clothes were gorgeously feminine, and as a leader of fashion she encouraged Halifax to resist the more severe modes that were creeping in from across the Atlantic. Under Julie's influence the wig and the beauty patch remained *obligatoire* for Haligonian women long after they had been abandoned in England. In manners as well as attire, she maintained her own distinctive style. She detested, for example, the English custom of men lingering for hours over the port after dinner, while the women repaired to the drawing-room. Fifteen minutes was all she allowed Edward and his friends for those extra stimulants and masculine discussions. Then it was necessary for them to "join the ladies". (Curiously enough, this was one of Queen Victoria's social disciplines.)

Junior officers doted on Julie. Instead of having to remain listening respectfully to their seniors on matters military, and laughing at old men's jokes, they were released at the peak of their postprandial glow to unfold their peacocks' tails among the women.

Solemnity would surely have engulfed Edward's parties had he been left to conduct them alone; but as Julie tossed a barrage of light banter across the room, and clever subalterns delivered a counter-battery fire of gallantries, the gatherings were invariably atwinkle with roguish eyes and atinkle with affectionate laughter. One can see Edward standing back, aloof, as became his rank, a little flabbergasted by the rapid exchanges of wit, a tiny bit envious of the high spirits which Julie evoked in lighter-hearted persons than he, but always beaming with controlled pleasure and pride.

At the end of most of his letters to Louis de Salaberry, Edward added a postscript mentioning Julie with, for a royal personage, unusual tenderness. She had cut her finger. She had slipped and bumped her head. She had had a chill. She was packing to accompany him on a journey. She was writing to Madame to Salaberry by the next mail. Always Edward referred to Julie as Madame de St. Laurent. In these postscripts, upon which we are so dependent for an image of Julie, we can sometimes see her standing over him as he finishes the letter and encouraging him to add such gushing lines as: "Both of us charge you with a thousand compliments to Madame de Salaberry and the children."

Louis de Salaberry's oldest son Charles had joined the British Army in 1794 at the age of sixteen, and was one of Edward's many protégés. In that year Charles de Salaberry went to the West Indies to serve under Sir Edward Grey, and he proved a lad of spirit. He fought through the same West Indian campaigns as Edward. Once, in a duel, he killed a German mercenary officer who slighted the French-Canadian race. On account of his youth, and his connections with Edward, he escaped a court martial, and progressed through a military career which, in the War of 1812, brought him fame as the victor over an American force at Chateauguay on the Quebec-New York State border.

Edward's affection for Charles de Salaberry, and later for several younger de Salaberry sons, was deep and abiding. In a letter to Louis de Salaberry, dated July 2, 1796, Edward mentions the boy's unexpected arrival in Halifax in command of a contingent of troops which had been posted from the West Indies to Nova Scotia.

There was excessive humility in the words Edward chose to tell the father that he was serving as the son's host. "He is now staying with us," wrote Edward, "for want of better quarters." But in the remainder there is sincere admiration for the young lieutenant. "He is now in perfect health," Edward continued, "though he says he suffered much from the fever in Dominica. He is tall, being, I think, nearly five feet eight inches. He is well formed and his manners are very good. He speaks English thoroughly, and writes, I believe, as well. Everybody gives him the best possible character in every respect, and your old friend Governor Hamilton, of Dominica, in particular, has written me a letter very much to his credit, which, I believe, you will be very much pleased to read. Consequently I enclose it but beg of you to return it by the next mail."

As will be seen later, Edward and Julie became surprisingly emotional in their letters to de Salaberry on the subject of their friend's sons. This may well have been an outlet for sentiments about their own two sons which for reasons of discretion they felt bound to bottle up. Their first son, born in Quebec City, took the name of his foster-father, Robert Wood, and made his home in Canada. Their second son, Jean de Mestre, born during Julie's 1794 voyage from Quebec City to Halifax, was reared by Julie's mother in Martinique until he was seven. Then he was sent to a Jesuit school in Philadelphia. Eventually he joined the French consular service in Australia. Mélanie, Julie's daughter by de Fortisson, lived with her mother in Halifax until 1798.

In October of that year Edward was riding home from manoeuvres when his horse put a hoof through a rotting plank of a wooden bridge. The Prince took a bad toss, wrenching muscles in his back. He was carried to Bedford Basin on a stretcher. From wrenched muscles the average man of thirty-two makes a quick recovery; but Edward, hitherto resilient in health, now appeared to be curiously frail. He stayed in bed for several weeks, with Julie ever at his side, fetching and carrying trays, patting his pillows, straightening his covers, and seeming extremely worried.

A Dr. North soon realized that Edward, with Julie's connivance, was pretending to be worse than he was, and was intent on making his injuries a means of realizing some unadmitted wish. When the doctor, after giving much thought to the problem, suggested that the waters of Bath in England might prove remedial, Edward immediately brightened up. This time his desire to visit England was unopposed by George III. Cool though he still remained toward his son, the King had the grace to acknowledge that Edward—especially an apparently ailing Edward—deserved some small reward for creating Halifax's formidable defences. As soon as the King's permission to visit England was received, Julie went into a flurry of packing, and was so busy she hadn't time to suggest a postscript to yet another letter to de Salaberry.

In the home of Frances Wentworth, news of Edward's impending departure precipitated similar activity. Edward at last was going to

92

see his father, and possibly to glean some small favours for himself and his friends. If there was anything to be had out of this visit, Frances was going to have her share. On the excuse of taking one of her younger sons to school in England, she booked passage in a ship that left several weeks before that in which Edward and Julie were due to sail. Lieutenant-Governor Sir John Wentworth was invited by Edward and Julie to assuage his supposed loneliness by leaving the drafty old Government House in central Halifax, and enjoy during their absence the clockwork wonders of Bedford Basin. (Rumour has it that on more than one occasion Wentworth's lissom young Negro paramour was permitted to take a peep at those wonders between her services in bed.)

In great excitement Edward and Julie embarked late in November, 1798, accompanied by Mélanie, who was now ten. Seas were high but the wind was favourable, and they reached England a few days before Christmas, 1798.

Frances Wentworth was on the dock to meet them, already in possession of an honour which permitted her to adopt a slightly less deferential approach to Julie than had been necessary during their Halifax association. At nearly fifty she had made, in less than three weeks, an opportunity to burn brightly once more in the arms of her old lover Prince William, now Duke of Clarence, and through his influence to gain an audience with Queen Charlotte. The Queen's susceptibility to blandishments, particularly those of the middle class, had resulted in the appointment of Frances as a "lady-in-waiting with permission to reside abroad", a position that carried with it five hundred pounds a year and relatively easy access to the royal presence.

Though there had been little genuine warmth in the relationship of Frances and Julie, their interlocking social interests now brought them closer and a mild affection sprang up between them. Frances wished to keep in Julie's good books for the sake of favours she expected from Edward. Julie, a stranger in London, and highly apprehensive about her reception, found in Frances a social sponsor.

The two women were much together after Edward had established himself officially in one of the royal bachelor suites at Kensington Palace and had found for Julie a small house in Knightsbridge. Frances introduced Julie to Maria Fitzherbert, the Prince of

Wales's morganatic wife. The meeting provided Julie with another sponsor.

Both Julie and Maria were Roman Catholics, able to converse with equal ease in French or English; both were vivacious, beautiful, intelligent, and worldly. They were so much alike, in fact, that they might easily have tangled talons. Women are usually as affronted by a replica of their own natures as they are by another model of their own dress. Perhaps the odd absence of rivalry between them arose from the fact that their domestic circumstances were similar and that each divined in the other's face an omen of her own unhappy destiny.

Accompanied by Frances and Maria, Julie gained an audience with Queen Charlotte and made a favourable impression. Soon the Queen was speaking in kindly tones of Julie as "Edward's French lady". George III consented to see the woman from whom he had been trying to separate Edward for more than ten years. He too must have been captivated by Julie's charm, for never again did he try to disrupt the association. Without qualms Julie was able to visit Edward in his Kensington Palace apartment, and on occasion to share with him the room in which, years later, Queen Victoria was born.

From Maria Fitzherbert, Edward and Julie bought a house at Ealing—Castle Hill Lodge—which later became their favourite home. In society they appeared openly together. Julie's public demeanour was so prudent, discreet and inconspicuous that her association with Edward never provoked in the press the bitter ribaldry that other unofficial royal liaisons aroused. To discourage awkward questions, she placed her daughter Mélanie with some of her own French relatives who were living in London as refugees from the Revolution.

In April, 1799, four months after reaching England, Edward was given the titles and estates of Duke of Kent and Strathearn, and Earl of Dublin. This brought him a parliamentary grant of twelve thousand pounds a year. In June he realized another wish. He was appointed Commander-in-Chief of British Forces in North America, to lighten the responsibilities of the aged Governor Prescott.

Meanwhile the Wentworths were helping Edward to recover still more of his father's approval. In Halifax, John Wentworth raised a subscription of five hundred guineas for the purchase of a diamond star to be presented to Edward as a token of thanks for his services to Nova Scotia. In London, Frances made sure the star was presented to Edward in a formal ceremony at Kensington Palace by her older son Charles, a graduate of Oxford. Highly impressed, George III immediately gave young Charles Wentworth an appointment to His Majesty's Council in Nova Scotia.

This shower of good fortune on the Wentworths and his own *ménage* caused Edward to forget the pretext on which he had visited England. Julie wisely reminded him of it, and for a few weeks he perfunctorily took the waters of Bath. Then with Julie, and Lady and Charles Wentworth, he embarked eagerly in the Frigate *Arethusa* to resume duty in Nova Scotia. Off Chebucto Head, in September, 1799, the *Arethusa* was sighted by Nova Scotia lookouts, and Edward had the satisfaction of learning later that news of his impending arrival had been signalled by telegraph to Windsor, fifty miles distant, in less than twenty minutes.

Ever since his first arrival in Canada eight years earlier, Edward's debts had been mounting. A twenty-thousand-pound debt in Gibraltar still remained unpaid. The five thousand a year general's pay he had received in Canada had been hopelessly insufficient for his needs. He assigned a portion of his new twelve thousand a year parliamentary grant toward liquidation of his debts, but it would take many years to pay them off.

Recklessly he ordered a new equipment from England to befit his dignity as C-in-C British troops in North America. It included a library of five thousand volumes and cost him eleven thousand pounds. It was lost when the transport *Recovery* was captured in the Atlantic. Two earlier outfits he had bought to replace the one lost in Lake Champlain had been sunk in the vessels *Antelope* and *Tankerville*, at a cost to Edward of ten thousand pounds.

Edward felt that these losses by enemy action should be made good by the British Government, but his pleas for compensation were ignored. He bought still another outfit, again for eleven thousand pounds. This was shipped to Halifax in the transport *Amelia*, which was wrecked on Sable Island, a sand-bar off Nova Scotia. The fantastic run of bad luck in connection with outfits plunged Edward into greater financial difficulties than ever before.

While desperately short of personal funds, he handled with scrupulous honesty huge sums allocated to him for the development of Nova Scotia. He built a new barracks on George's Island and a hospital for infectious diseases on Navy Island. In Halifax he built a mansion for the senior general under his command, and a new Government House for the Wentworths. Joyfully Sir John Wentworth wrote: "The Duke of Kent has entered on his command with infinite activity and ideas extremely enlarged since his departure. The arrangement in contemplation promises a plenteous circulation of money and improvement to this province."

As public funds got into circulation through wages, the prosperity of Halifax began to increase. Merchants built fine homes. Even the poorer people had enough money to improve their wooden hovels. Edward laid the foundation of a new St. George's Church on Brunswick Street and a new Freemasons' Hall.

His responsibilities frequently kept him at his desk from dawn until midnight, and his continuing concern for the smallest details of military economy was evident in a letter he wrote in November, 1799, to Lieutenant-Governor Major-General Thomas Carleton of New Brunswick. It concerned the uniforms of the New Brunswick Corps.

I have recommended that the old jackets be turned and cut up so as to make into round jackets, which will answer both for the purpose of wearing under the greatcoat in the winter and for drilling in summer. I have always adopted this custom for my own regiment and find it answers remarkably well. The clothing, after being worn the first year in the proper form, with white waistcoat, breeches and gaiters, for all duties with arms, such as Review, Parade, Etc., and the second year when altered into neat jacket with trousers for exercise, is still able to answer the third year for all purposes of fatigue, and when men are employed on King's work.

Edward then turned to the matter of haircuts, which he made standard throughout his command:

I have directed my adjutant and quartermaster to give every possible information to your Captain Clopper, in order that during the winter he may be enabled to instruct the regiment in many points in which they may differ from the present method. As there is none in which they are so out of the way as the hair I request you will give the strictest orders that both officers and men conform most accurately to the pattern established here, of which Captain Clopper has been made perfectly acquainted.

General Carleton was so irritated at being asked to interest himself in such trivia that he resigned. His attitude was out of date.

As a result of Edward's pioneering, it became standard practice in the British Army for commanders-in-chief to save their country's money by turning and recutting worn uniforms to serve as fatigue dress; and ever since Edward's day inspection of British soldiers' haircuts on parade has been regarded as essential to the maintenance of smart appearance, and therefore inseparable from good discipline.

During his service in Halifax, Edward constantly advocated reforms in army dress, and some of his suggestions were incorporated in the new uniforms that made their appearance in 1805. In that year cocked hats, pigtails, breeches and gaiters disappeared, and in their place troops wore shakos, short haircuts, red tunics, and trousers.

Despite the heavy volume of work he undertook, Edward never closeted himself behind locked doors. He gave an audience to almost any man who sought one. Among the visitors Edward received in Halifax was Alexander MacKenzie, the great fur trader and discoverer of the MacKenzie River. On Edward's recommendation, MacKenzie was given a knighthood.

Another of Edward's visitors was William Cobbett, the old soldier and journalistic reformer. Ten years before, during service in Nova Scotia, Sergeant-Major Cobbett had come in contact with a royal commission sent out from England to enquire into the economic condition of the colony. Because the commissioners were too drunk to write their report themselves, Cobbett wrote it for them. The matter was supposed to be a secret. Cobbett was surprised to learn, however, that Edward knew all about it. In his autobiography Cobbett said that Edward "asked me how much the commissioners gave me. When I told him not a farthing he exclaimed most bitterly and said that thousands of pounds had been paid by the country for what I had done."

Administrative reforms occupied so much of Edward's time that in February 1800 he wrote to de Salaberry: "My business has accumulated to such a degree that neither myself nor my secretary nor five under-secretaries can overtake it." Having been accustomed in the past to riding every day on parade or in manoeuvres, he found the desk work required of the C-in-C, and consequent lack of exercise, detrimental to his health. He began to complain of biliousness. Furthermore he was disappointed at not being given the governorship of Canada. De Salaberry, whom he had promoted to the rank of reserve major, raised the point in correspondence. Edward replied:

> As to the idea, my dear Major, that the time has arrived when it would be advantageous to place me at the head of the Civil as well as the Military Government believe me your wish cannot be realized, for under the rule which the present Ministers have established as to Princes of the Blood the thing is impossible.

In June, 1800, at Vinegar Hill, the insurrection of the United Irishmen, an organization dedicated to the overthrow of British colonial rule in Ireland, was crushed. By means of extensive patronage, Prime Minister William Pitt the Younger prepared the ground for the Legislative Union of Great Britain and Ireland which was to become law on January 1, 1801. Henceforth, Edward knew, the position of Commander-in-Chief in Ireland would be one of great importance. It would call for a skilled soldier, a diplomat, and a man whose sympathy for the Roman Catholic Church was sincere and well known. Edward believed, not without justification, that he was just the man for the job. From England he received hints that he might be given the appointment if he returned.

At the same time momentous events in Europe were beginning to diminish the strategic importance of Halifax. Napoleon was rising fast toward absolute power, and the greatest military threat was against England herself. Edward wrote to his father for permission to return to England once more, so that he might be ready to take up a new and more responsible post. Permission was received.

On May 11, 1800, Edward wrote to de Salaberry:

> You already know from my last letter that Madame de St. Laurent has wholly recovered from her fall. She has passed the winter without any sickness, a thing which we feared as the climate of North America is by no means favourable to her. You

know that the Union of Ireland is said to be so far completed that I have reason to believe that the command of the troops there is destined for me.

In early July, Edward wrote again to his friend:

Though I find myself today in the midst of preparations for my departure for England, His Majesty having approved my return for the present . . . I do not wish to leave without giving you the news and offering you my thanks for your letter of the 9th July which arrived at the same time as the pretty present from yourself and the children. . . . One of his Majesty's ships, *Assistance,* of fifty guns, has been prepared for me. As I wish to avoid the possibility of encountering the equinoctial gales, and as everything will be ready in two days, I propose to embark on Saturday 3rd, August. Consequently I will almost immediately be in England. But you may be persuaded of this: that the distance will not ever change my sentiments towards yourself and family. At all times you may be firmly persuaded of the continuation of my esteem and friendship.

Before his departure Edward reprieved eight of eleven men who had been sentenced to death for mutiny and desertion. He took away with him the following testimony from Lieutenant-Governor Sir John Wentworth and the Legislative Council of Nova Scotia: "To your benevolence the indigent have owed their support; the tradesmen and mechanics employment; and the industrious of every description the means of reaping the recompense of their skill and diligence." Edward never returned to Canada; yet he did not forget Halifax. Two years later the city received from him a souvenir that is still its most familiar landmark: the chiming clock that keeps perfect time in the Tower of Citadel Hill.

Chapter VIII

WHEN EDWARD and Julie disembarked from H.M.S. *Assistance* at Plymouth toward the end of August, 1800, they found England in a state of apprehension. The anxiety was especially distressing because it followed precipitately on a period of exultation. From December, 1798, to October, 1799, the alliance of England, Russia, Austria, Naples, Portugal, and the Ottoman Empire had shown promise of an early victory over France. Serious defeats had been inflicted on the French in Italy, Switzerland, Germany, and even in Egypt, where Napoleon was in command.

Having lost the French Mediterranean Fleet to Nelson, in the Battle of the Nile, Napoleon recklessly marched eastward, with Britain's Indian colonies as his goal. He was turned back at Acre, Syria, by British marines serving under Admiral Sir Sidney Smith. Domestic troubles deepened his despair. While brooding over the plight of his thirty-five thousand men, stranded without ships to take them home, and facing years of exile in the desert sand, Napoleon received news of Josephine's flagrant infidelities in Paris. In his bitterness he retaliated by taking to his tent the young wife of an ensign who, dressed as a man, had smuggled herself into the ranks of his expeditionary force. In the arms of this black-eyed, nubile beauty, a former pastry-cook, Napoleon recovered his resolution, and laid plans that were to turn the tide of his own and France's fortune. He divined precisely what the French were saying two thousand miles to the west: that France needed a strong young man to restore her losses.

Despite his failure in Egypt, and despite the public shame of his cuckolding by Josephine, Napoleon decided that if he returned to France and presented himself as the man of the hour he would be accepted. And he was right. He deserted his army, embarked in one of the few small ships that were left to him, and in the Mediterranean evaded the pursuit of Nelson's corvettes. When he landed in

France on October 8, 1799, he was hailed as the "Conqueror of Egypt".

Napoleon's impact on French morale was magical. Immediately news of his arrival spread, the French Army in the Netherlands, hard pressed by an attacking force of British and Russians, began to show a new spirit of resistance. The commander of the attacking force was Edward's brother, the Duke of York, who, astonished at the enemy's sudden change of heart, wrung his hands and halted his advance. On October 18, 1799, only ten days after Napoleon set foot on French soil, the Duke of York, at the Convention of Alkmar, entered into a disgraceful agreement with his opponents. In return for the surrender of his French prisoners, he received a guarantee under which he was permitted to evacuate British troops from the Netherlands without obstruction. In disgust Russia quit the Alliance, and France's waning star began to wax again. At once the Duke of York was vilified by the British press for kneeling to the French.

On November 9, 1799, twenty-two days after the Duke of York's humiliation in the Netherlands, Napoleon brought off the *coup d'état* which made him First Consul of France and gave him almost absolute authority. The following summer he redeemed French losses in Germany, Switzerland, and Italy. Thus Edward and Julie came to England to find that while George III still ruled the waves, Napoleon was the overlord on land.

The King was in no condition to worry unduly about Napoleon. His mind was fully occupied with the preservation of its own balance. In a desperate effort to save his reason, George III was indulging in a new social custom. He was resting by the sea at Weymouth. Thither went Edward to pay his respects, leaving Julie in her little Knightsbridge home. He wrote to de Salaberry: "I remained three weeks with the King during which I took advantage of hot sea baths which certainly did good to my rheumatism."

Edward also pressed his claims to the military command of Ireland. For a time he obviously had high hopes that the King would consent to this appointment, for he wrote to de Salaberry: "I flatter myself that it may yet be arranged." But he was out of luck. Early in 1801, before he had made up his mind to grant his son's wish, the King had another mental breakdown. Edward's future was deposited in the lap of his brothers, the Prince of Wales and the Duke of York.

If Edward had entertained any hopes of preferment in reward for his defense works at Halifax, these were soon dashed by the attitude of the Duke of York, who despite his military incompetence was now Commander-in-Chief of the British Army. Flinching under continuous press criticism, and fearful of unfavourable comparisons being drawn in Parliament between his own martial prowess and that of Edward, the Duke of York became his younger brother's sharpest detractor. It was his custom to belittle Edward in the family circle by ridiculing his solemnity.

His dislike of Edward even transcended the bounds of professional jealousy. York was an idler, a voluptuary, a sophisticate, and a knave. Edward remained temperate, industrious, regular in his habits, and doctrinaire in matters of honour. As such, he was to York a living reproach. It was Edward's greatest misfortune to score a success in the military field at a time when York was a failure. Ever afterward York stood between Edward and any post that promised the younger brother glory or advancement.

All through 1801 Edward remained unemployed, a situation that rasped his temper. News that de Salaberry had been tossed out of a job in the Indian Affairs Department at Quebec deepened his resentment. In a bitter written protest to the Duke of Portland, Secretary for the Colonies, Edward classed his friend's dismissal as "one of the many mortifications I have experienced".

While Nelson was putting his blind eye to his telescope at the Battle of Copenhagen, and British forces were rebuilding national pride by capturing the Cape of Good Hope, Edward fretted for action. Because nobody appeared to be interested in finding him a command, he began seeking something to occupy his mind. This has been described as "meddling" in the affairs of his brothers.

From the youngest up, Edward's brothers were by now a footling lot, living in a mire of fatuity, gluttony, and concupiscence.

The Duke of Cambridge was an officer in the Hanoverian Army, an enthusiastic but excruciating singer, an off-pitch violinist, a student of Jewish culture, and an incessant prattler. In church, where he always occupied a front pew, he almost unhinged the clergymen by keeping up a running commentary on the sermon, often so vigorously that his face flushed, and his elaborate blond wig fell askew. The Princess of Wales, far from fastidious herself, once wrote of Cambridge: "He looked exactly a sergeant, so vulgar with his ears full of powder."

The Duke of Sussex had been living since 1793 with a Lady Augusta Murray, even though George III had annulled their marriage. Lady Augusta was eleven years older than Sussex. He called her Goosy and spent much of his time writing childish poetry about her. When he wasn't scribbling he was taking singing lessons or staggering about in dramatic exaggeration of the pain he suffered from asthma.

The Duke of Cumberland, who was shockingly scarred about the face from battle against the French, was a man of great physical courage in war. But he was universally detested. His nickname was The Ogre. He spent hundreds of pounds hanging the walls of his bachelor quarters in St. James's Palace with mirrors for the stimulation of his bizarre sexual pursuits. Later Cumberland was to be suspected of deflowering his sister, of violating his valet's wife, and of murdering the outraged valet during a scuffle with a razor.

The Duke of Clarence had been living with that coarse and adipose actress, Mrs. Jordan, for ten years, and was in process of begetting from her a family of ten illegitimate children. They all lived at Bushy Park, where Clarence had enjoyed, since the end of his navy days, the sinecure of Ranger. Wholly unabashed by his own flagrant liaison with Mrs. Jordan, he had had the gall to speak in the House of Lords on the Adultery Bill, which was designed to prevent marriage between the guilty parties to a divorce. "Let us not assemble here," he thundered, "to forge the galling chains of prostitution and degrade the English fair sex. But let us adopt the Christian charity of a right reverend prelate towards a female sinner." He then bored the House to the point of groans by reading a long sermon of the Bishop of Rochester on the theme of Mary Magdalen.

The Duke of York, who had already been described by Lord Brougham as "that Prince of blackguards," had set up house with a Mrs. Mary Anne Clarke, whose good looks, ready wit, audacity, and perfidy had made her the nation's most prosperous courtesan. His legal wife the Duchess, formerly Princess Frederica, a dim, pock-marked, childish niece of Frederick the Great, had lived alone at Weybridge, since her unsuccessful marriage in 1791, with a houseful of dogs, cats, parrots, and monkeys.

The Prince of Wales, after a period of estrangement and heavy over-indulgence in women, wine and food, was living once more with Mrs. Fitzherbert, his morganatic wife of sixteen years. His legal wife, Caroline of Brunswick, Princess of Wales, with whom he had cohabited for only a few weeks, was living at Montagu House, Blackheath, with their daughter Charlotte.

The Princess of Wales's social habits were comparable to those of a raffish circus artist. She was addicted to pornography and off-colour jokes, and if she did not engage in homosexuality she was preoccupied by its varying forms. But she had a certain engaging frankness, and she enlisted the sympathy of a wide circle of friends who excused her frailties because she had been exiled for so long from the marriage bed.

Oddly enough, Mrs. Fitzherbert, who might well have been the Princess of Wales's greatest enemy, was tenderly disposed toward her. It was she who enlisted Edward's aid in a matter concerning the Princess from which he would have been wiser to abstain.

At Montagu House the Princess was careless about money matters. She was generous, and easily imposed upon by spongers. Her servants and tradesmen robbed her. Her books became so confused that the Prince of Wales made the matter an excuse for appointing a Colonel Thomas to look after them. The Princess of Wales loathed Thomas, looking upon him as a spy sent by her husband to catch her out in a profligate act and so make possible a divorce. Furthermore, in her opinion, Thomas was even more hopeless than she in financial matters. She complained to Mrs. Fitzherbert about his ineptitude, and Mrs. Fitzherbert suggested to the Prince of Wales that Edward should be called in to investigate the situation. Reluctantly Wales agreed to this proposal.

The painstaking and conscientious Edward found that the Princess of Wales's complaints against Thomas were justified, and recommended the bumbling Colonel's dismissal. This was strongly resented by the Prince of Wales, who probably did appoint Thomas as a spy, and who, in any event, never would accept the idea that his unwanted wife could be right about anything.

Wales was so angry about the Thomas affair that he refused to see Edward. In distress the latter wrote to Mrs. Fitzherbert on November 21, 1801, asking her to intercede in his behalf:

I really felt it a duty to point out that the Colonel was in every respect unfit for the business, and that the plan could not go on without a more capable person to direct it. I trust it will need no great exertion to convince the Prince of my zeal in his service. I have been compelled from a sense of what in honour I owed him to speak a little against what I know to be his sentiments. I am apprehensive that at the first outset it may put him in a little ill-humour with me. Permit me therefore to hope you will asist me in convincing the Prince that I have acted only from the sense of duty.

Mrs. Fitzherbert intervened and took the edge off the Prince of Wales's wrath. Thomas was relieved of his post. Once again Edward was left to twiddle his thumbs. He soon found something else to pass the time.

As Earl of Dublin, he found himself president of the St. Patrick's Charitable Society. Normally it was sufficient for a prince to lend his name to such an agency. But at the London Tavern, on St. Patrick's Day, 1802, he consented to occupy the chair at the society's dinner. Children who were being educated by the society were paraded before him, and he was so impressed by their appearance that he contributed a hundred guineas toward the good work. He also made a neat speech and, according to one newspaper, joined in "the excellent songs" and "the utmost conviviality and harmony" that marked the occasion.

We can imagine the bulging balefulness such middle-class altruism would light in the eyes of Edward's self-centred and haughty brothers. Against the background of this monstrous fraternity, Edward, in spite of his many weaknesses, appeared to the British people as a tower of wisdom, rectitude, and democracy. But he was not alert enough to detect a cunning undermining of his foundations by the green-eyed Duke of York.

To his astonishment Edward was invited, early in 1802, to proceed to Gibraltar as Governor, in succession to his old enemy Major-General Sir Charles O'Hara, who had died. He accepted because the Rock was in the forefront of the battle against the French and their Spanish allies. In July, 1801, Admiral Sir James de Saumarez had scored in Gibraltar Bay a brilliant naval victory over Franco-Spanish forces twice his strength. Nelson said of it, "A greater action was never fought." But the Gibraltar garrison, under O'Hara, had not been committed to direct action for years, and in consequence was in a low state.

The troops had had to endure a prolonged state of seige. No communication with the enemy Spanish mainland was possible, and they were confined to an area two and a half miles long and a quarter to three-quarters of a mile wide. All food had to be brought by sea, and there were frequent outbreaks of plague resulting from the consumption of rotten salt meat. The shortage of water was chronic. Mail from England was rare and erratic. The unmarried men could find solace only in the arms of a handful of worn-out hags. The only provision for the troops' recreation was a single small room full of tattered magazines and old newspapers. Boredom induced lethargy in troops and officers alike, and drill parades and exercises were perfunctory. But the worst elements in Gibraltar life were the ninety wine shops, from whose license fees O'Hara, as a Governor's perquisite, had derived seven thousand pounds a year, over and above his pay. Drunkenness and insubordination were rife.

It was Prime Minister Henry Addington, later Lord Sidmouth, who offered Edward the onerous appointment of Governor of Gibraltar. Describing to Edward the conditions there, he said: "This state of things cannot be permitted to endure. It has lasted already too long. It must be put down, and Your Royal Highness is the man to do it." He added a glib promise: "You may reckon on the support of the Cabinet at home." Edward did not accept without caution. He asked Addington: "Now as to the second-in-command, Barnett, can I depend on him?" "True as steel, rely on him," was the reply. It was an empty assurance.

Though Addington offered Edward the job, the man behind the proposal was the Duke of York, who anticipated correctly that Edward would be enraged by the condition of the garrison, and would initiate severe disciplinary remedies. He hoped that Edward would eventually provoke a mutiny, and so wreck his career and cease to exist as a military rival.

In a letter to Edward, the guileful motives of York were clear. "I consider it my duty," he wrote, "to make Your Royal Highness aware that much exertion will be necessary to establish a due degree of discipline among the troops." Then he added a phrase that would place him in a position from which he would later be able to say "I told you so." He urged Edward to accomplish reforms "gradually" and by a "moderate exercise" of the powers invested in him. To ask moderation of Edward in coping with the situation on Gibraltar was like urging forebearance upon the angels at Sodom. York knew this well, and his sole purpose in securing the command for Edward was to create a noose in which he hoped the younger Prince would hang himself.

The tone of the King's words on Edward's departure for the Rock reflected the extent to which Edward's record had already been minimized by York's mischievous tongue. "Now sir," said the dim-witted King, "when you go to Gibraltar do not make *such a trade* of it as when you went to Halifax."

Edward and Julie reached Gibraltar on May 10, 1802, eleven years to the day after his earlier transfer from the Rock for supposedly undue severity. The moment Edward stepped ashore he showed anger at the slovenliness of the guard of honour, and so began to play into the waiting hands of York. Of the guard, an officer in Edward's retinue wrote to a friend:

> The inaccuracy of their movements even in the most common manoeuvres, and their unsteadiness, as well as that of their officers, was beyond the power of language. Nor was their discipline less worthy of the severest censure, for the grossest irregularities were evident in the conduct of the men off duty, even in the public streets, where they were to be seen in groups wallowing in a state of the most shameful intoxication. No unprotected female could walk the streets even during the day without being subjected to the grossest insults and in several cases to brutal violence.

Reasonably enough, the writer ascribed this state of affairs "to the carelessness of the officers and their inattention to duty".

Edward installed himself in the Convent, a Franciscan monastery dating back to 1480. This had been used as the official residence of British governors ever since the seizure of Gibraltar by England in 1704 during the War of the Spanish Succession. Most of the time Julie lived discreetly in the Convent, but for the sake of propriety she occasionally occupied a small house on the fringe of Cork Woods, which is still known as the Duke of Kent's Farm.

As was to be expected, Edward set about restoring Gibraltar's morale by a relentless drill-and-training plan. He ordered reveille for three-thirty in summer, four-thirty in spring and autumn, and five-thirty in winter. He made sure the men got enough to eat by calling the roll at each meal. Insobriety at mealtimes became a punishable offence. In the evening there was another roll-call of men confined to barracks for misdemeanours. Men out on pass at night had to report to the guardroom on their return.

The unsoldierly custom of carrying umbrellas in wet weather had spread among the officers in Gibraltar. So Edward banned umbrellas, much to the chagrin of the army's dandies. Many stubbly faces caught his eye, so he laid down regulations which enforced shaving every day of the chin, and of the cheeks up to the level of the corner of the eye.

Edward also insisted on uniformity of the appearance of sentries. All sentries were ordered to don or remove greatcoats at the command of the orderly officer, and not merely when they felt too cold or too hot. At daylight every day each member of a guard or picket had to wash, untie his hair, comb it, tie it afresh, and brush his clothes to the satisfaction of the orderly officer.

Some women of Gibraltar who had combined in a monopoly to overcharge the men for laundry were put out of business. Edward made laundry work the perquisite of NCO's wives, and laid down regulation charges.

He tried to encourage the profitable use of free time. To the Garrison Library for Officers and Government Civilians—founded at his suggestion during his earlier tour of duty on the Rock—he gave a hundred pounds.

He abolished the custom of naming battalions after their commanding colonel, and from this beginning all units of infantry were given a number.

Modifications of many more of Edward's innovations are still standard practice in the British Army. These are to be seen closest to their original form in canteen regulations. Edward forbade sergeants to drink with corporals and corporals to drink with privates, thus inaugurating the sergeants' mess and the corporals' room.

The reform that brought about Edward's downfall in Gibraltar was his reduction of the ninety wine shops to forty. Even the surviving wine shops were placed out of bounds to troops. These changes were made at great personal cost to him, for he lost four thousand pounds a year of the Governor's emoluments from licence fees.

To replace the services of the wine shops, Edward built a brewery at Europa and gave a franchise to brew "wholesome beer" to a civilian named Ninian Douglas. He then licensed and named three big taverns, to be run on the same lines as English inns. These were The Three Light Infantrymen, in Cooperage Lane; The Three Grenadiers, between Southport and South Bar Rocks; and The Three Guns, in Cannon Lane.

G. T. Garrett, in his *Gibraltar and the Mediterranean,* says:

If Edward had been wise he would have waited until he had collected more support among officers before he started any drastic reforms. Instead of this he appears to have quarrelled with the senior officials. In closing half the wine shops and putting the rest out of bounds he . . . united against him the wine-sellers, the soldiers, and the deputy governor, Sir Thomas Trigge. The wine-sellers promptly retaliated by supplying liquor gratis to the garrison. The result was a kind of mutiny. It was a lamentable affair. *The officers seemed to have connived at the riot.*

The troops under Edward's command on Gibraltar were the 2nd Foot (now the Queen's Royal West Surrey Regiment), the 8th Foot (now the King's Liverpool Regiment), the 23rd Foot (now the Royal Welsh Fusiliers), the 25th Foot (now the King's Own Scottish Borderers), the 54th Foot (now the 2nd Battalion of the Dorset Regiment), and supporting units of Royal Artillery and Royal Engineers. On Christmas Eve, 1802, during his customary daily inspection tour of mess-halls, armouries, kitchens, guardrooms, canteens, and billets, Edward warned the troops that Christmas Day was not to be spent in drunkenness.

For reasons best known to themselves, and probably well known to the second in command of the garrison, General Barnett, the adjutants of the 8th Foot, the 25th Foot, and the 54th Foot made Edward's warning an excuse for confining their men to barracks on Christmas Eve. The adjutant of the 25th went even further; he held back the pay due to his men that day.

There is no evidence that Edward endorsed these extreme and absurd precautions. But there is abundant evidence to suggest that they were taken deliberately in the hope and expectation of trouble.

Two years after the trouble was over, Private Henry Salisbury, late of the 25th Regiment, signed an affidavit to the effect that *officers had been the real power behind the Gibraltar mutiny,* and that it was plotted in one of Edward's new taverns, The Three Guns.

The mutiny began on Christmas Eve, when some of the disaffected wine-sellers managed—evidently with great ease—to smuggle cheap brandy into the 8th's billets. There they harangued the men about the supposed iniquity of closing the wine shops. The men got drunk and broke out of barracks. They marched on the barracks of the 25th and the 54th, and tried to persuade these comrades to join them in a riot. But the latter regiments were at that time sober, and they resisted the overtures of the 8th. Indeed the 54th, taunted for timidity, opened fire from the barracks windows on the catcalling 8th, and wounded five. Thereupon the 8th withdrew to their own barracks. On Christmas Day Edward visited the 8th and delivered to them what modern troops call "a rocket". But he forgave them and ordered no further punishment.

On Boxing Day the 25th received their pay, began drinking cheap wine and brandy smuggled in by the wine-sellers, and started listening to a group of hotheads who reminded them of the insults they had taken from the 8th on Christmas Eve. When they were thoroughly inebriated, the 25th marched on the 8th's barracks and provoked a fight. It lasted three hours. Two of the 25th and one of the 8th were killed in the drunken tumult. Artillery was used to subdue the combatants.

This was too much for Edward. Ten of the ringleaders were brought to trial and all were sentenced to death. Three of them, two Dutchmen and an Irishman, were shot. In the other seven cases Edward commuted the sentence to transportation to Australia. Order was restored.

In the strict sense of the word it was not a mutiny; it was more of an inter-regimental fracas. It was provoked by the adjutants who confined the troops to barracks on Christmas Eve, yet none of the violence was directed against the person of any officer. The incident was made much of, however, by some officers who resented being dragged from their cards, billiards and mistresses by Edward's intensified training programs, and by others who stood to profit from his dismissal. General Barnett, the second in command of the garrison, was overheard to say when the riot was over: "It is the best thing that could have happened. Now we shall get rid of him." He meant, of course, Edward.

Barnett's sentiments were shared, naturally, by the Duke of York, who looked on the riot as a fruition of his deep-laid schemes. The incident enabled York to discredit Edward at the War Office. His misrepresentations, and constant allusions to earlier charges of undue severity against Edward, were effective. To his astonishment, Edward was invited by the War Office to explain his actions.

To Thomas Coutts, his banker, he wrote on February 7, 1803: "I cannot boast of being either in good spirits or finding my situation comfortable, for my feelings have been very severely wounded." He added that he was sending Captain Thomas Dodd, his aide-de-camp, to England "for the express purpose that the real truth may be known and that the facts as well as their causes might be fully stated without addition or diminution". As Edward's advocate before the War Office court of enquiry, Dodd appears to have been unsuccessful, for on April 3, 1803, Edward was writing to Coutts to express his fear that "reports dictated by calumny and malevolence might have reached you and injured me in your good opinion".

The findings of the War Office court of inquiry were reviewed by Lord Pelham, the Home Secretary, and by the Duke of York. As a result Captain Dodd—an officer who later allowed his devotion to Edward to overcome his discretion—returned to Gibraltar with humbling orders. Dated March 5, 1803, they were addressed to Edward and signed by Lord Pelham. They contained the King's command that His Royal Highness should "return to England immediately".

Edward was ordered to hand over his military authority to his disloyal second in command General Barnett, and his civil authority to his hostile deputy governor Sir Thomas Trigge. To his anger and shame, Barnett and Trigge immediately rescinded some three hundred orders the Prince had laid down for the improvement of military and civil discipline. But the Rock never slipped back to the loose moral standards that had prevailed before Edward's arrival.

Before he left Gibraltar Edward lost one of his favourite privates, a man who preferred to spend his free time fishing instead of drinking. When his boat capsized during a squall the man was drowned. He had been one of those who were allowed to bring their families to the Rock. Edward waited three days for the widow to get over the first shock; then he called upon her. For several hours he sat in the humble army billet dandling one of the children on his knee and trying to comfort the woman. He gave her twelve gold dollars. The next day he returned with more gifts for her and the children. She was pregnant at the time, and Edward arranged for a good doctor to atttend her later lying-in. For years afterwards he continued to send her money.

One of the most curious things that happened to Edward on Gibraltar also took place just before he left. He was accosted by a gipsy fortune-teller in the street. Instead of pushing her aside, in the manner of most officers, he listened to her politely. "Your Royal Highness will have losses and crosses," she said. "But you will die in happiness. You will have a daughter and she will become a great queen."

Edward and Julie left Gibraltar on May 1, 1803, and reached London on the 26th. Immediately Edward wrote four letters to Lord Pelham, demanding for himself a court martial before which he would be able to justify his measures on the Rock. Pelham failed to answer the first three letters, and in reply to the fourth he stated briefly and coldly that the matter had been laid before the King.

The King made no move. Whereupon, in June of 1803, Edward wrote five letters to the Duke of York, demanding an opportunity to clear himself. The letters were verbose, and even in parts maledictory, but they evoked no reply from canny York. Early in 1804, frustrated to the point of fury, Edward called the Duke of York "a rascal" in the King's hearing. The King still had a very large soft spot for the Duke of York, and as a result of this abuse of his brother Edward lost all the ground he recently had gained in his father's favour.

Yet Edward was not without warm partisans. Civilians in Gibraltar sent him a thousand guineas as an expression of their gratitude for his reforms. Edward spent this on a diamond garter to match the star he had received from the equally thankful citizens of Nova Scotia.

A Methodist preacher, a representative of a sect with little love for royalty in those days, rose at a meeting of the British and Foreign

Bible Society to pay tribute to "the upright courageous conduct of the Prince and the beneficial regulations for the soldiery and inhabitants which he so wisely devised and so perseveringly maintained" at Gibraltar.

General Sir William Fawcett, a man who had risen from the ranks to become Adjutant-General to the Duke of York, risked his chief's displeasure by describing Edward's action on the Rock as "the model that had long been needed". Even the Prince of Wales, who had been suspicious and resentful of Edward ever since the Colonel Thomas affair, turned one day in 1804 to Henry Addington, who had been succeeded as Prime Minister by the younger Pitt, and said: "You send a man out to control a garrison all but in open mutiny. You tell him to terminate such a disgraceful state and assure him of the Government's unqualified support. He goes out and finds things infinitely worse than stated. The impending outbreak occurs. He quells it thoroughly. By way of reward you disgrace him. If you want to deter an officer from his duty or encourage a mutinous soldier your tactics are admirable. Edward may well complain. He were neither an officer nor a man if he were silent."

The championship of the Prince of Wales was, however, worse than useless to Edward. The King detested the Prince of Wales for his persistent attempts to get himself established as Regent, and for his continued association with the hated Whig, Charles James Fox.

On his return from Gibraltar, Edward was denied any official position of importance. Yet the last sixteen years of his life were not entirely wasted.

Chapter IX

O N THEIR return to London in the spring of 1803, Edward and Julie found England clinging to the last cultural strands of the eighteenth century. At their stately homes the belted and booted squires lived as their sires and grandsires had lived before them for a hundred years. They studied Latin, Greek and English poetry, consumed rich foods and fine wines, and sat long after dinner discussing politics without emotion. Sometimes they bedded their hosts' wives or servant girls, and arose next morning to shoot grouse, partridge, and rabbit for their larders. Already they were demonstrating a type of democracy peculiar to Englishmen: they played games with the lower classes. Most of them were on cricket teams that were under the captaincy of a local footman, blacksmith, innkeeper, or groom.

Once in a while they took a fast coach up to London to see Sarah Siddons in *Macbeth* or to watch Mendoza meet Humphreys with bare fists. They fought duels on Hampstead Heath, roistered in the clubs of St. James's Street, and bought and sold stocks in the Cheapside taverns. Sometimes they dressed up in middle-class attire and visited the Vauxhall Gardens amusement park to pick up a tart. And often they went down to the Fleet Prison to bail a spendthrift cousin out of the debtors' compound.

To these engaging and imperturable bucks Napoleon was an infernal nuisance, a froggish upstart who played the game of war with a shocking disregard for the sporting rules, a low-born mercenary who, sooner or later, would be put in his place by the gentlemen amateurs of England. But Napoleon never upset their equanimity. In the House of Commons the members, still largely drawn from the upper classes, wore silk hats, heavy greatcoats, and strap-bottom trousers over the top of their riding-boots; and they lay about on benches, cracking nuts, eating oranges, and yawning as news of Britain's victories and reverses reached them by messenger from the War Office. If Napoleon caused them fits of occasional nervousness, they rarely showed it, and there was never any element of defeatism in their thinking, for it seemed to them that the playing-fields of Eton were turning out enough gallant youngsters each year to guarantee a perpetuation of the golden *status quo.*

A cartoon of the early nineteenth century depicted a shrimpish Napoleon wearing a sword and a cocked hat that were too big for him. He was weeping and pointing to the window of a toy shop that was full of models of the Bank, St. James's, Carlton House, the Tower, and other famous institutions. To John Bull, who stood on guard outside the toy shop in the uniform of a British sentry, Napoleon was pleading: "Please, Mr. Bull, let me have some of those toys." And Bull was replying: "I tell you, you shan't touch one of them. So blubber away and be damned."

Another cartoon showed Napoleon greedily cutting a slice off the globe, a thin slice labelled Europe. From the other side of the globe a nonchalant Pitt was cutting a huge slice, a slice including Canada, India, Africa, and the Antipodes.

One of the most prominent external signs of noble phlegm in England was George Brummell, that friend of the Prince of Wales who reached the peak of his fame as a coxcomb, wit and iconoclast at a time when Napoleon's guns were barking fiercely.

The aristocracy formed a protective and not too disagreeable crust over the English social pie. It would be long before that crust would crack, though the meat and vegetables underneath were now beginning to bubble in the heat of economic and scientific changes. The waxing middle class was the most mechanically-minded class in the world. Profiting from the demand for improved weapons and supplies of war, they stippled the country north of Nottingham with engineering shops and mills, powered sometimes by the fast-flowing streams of the Pennine Range but more and more by coal and steam. On the proceeds of the machines a new plutocracy was rising, with money to invest in all manner of industrial enterprises. Phillippe Lebon, for example, a refugee Frenchman, was already trying to float the company that four years later lit Pall Mall with gas lamps.

The Rothschilds had been in London for six years and were busily founding those practices of high finance that brought wealthy land-owners and wealthy industrialists closer and closer together. In the ardent common pursuits of dividends, caste was forgotten. The blue-chip families began to marry into the blue-blood families, and money ran in an ever increasing torrent from the silent earth toward the roaring mills.

With the flow of capital, peasants, dispossessed of land by the enclosure practices, and impoverished by the war-time rise of the price of imported corn, flocked into urban manufacturing or emigrated to the colonies. Their sufferings, in the mean streets that were jerry-built around the factories, and in the boundless wildernesses of Canada and Australia, were appalling; but within a decade they changed the structure of the Empire. Before the Napoleonic War was over, Britain had taken on a new role. She was a floating factory off the coast of Europe, and her people were dependent for their victuals largely on the nation's overseas possessions.

Edward was better acquainted with this change than any other member of the royal family. Eventually he was in the van of the humanitarian forces that sought to alleviate the misery which low wages and periodic unemployment inflicted on the industrial poor. But now, in 1803, he was heavily preoccupied with his own affairs.

Having failed to recover his military position, he could not help brooding over his grievances. In an attempt to forget these, he devoted himself to the establishment of a *ménage* that was little short of fantastic. His official home, where most of his correspondence was written and received, was a bachelor apartment in Kensington Palace. Julie's home, which Edward also used occasionally as a town house, was a pretty little dwelling in Knightsbridge. The couple shared a third home, The Pavilion, in Hampton Court, which Edward acquired when he was appointed, as a sop, to the undignified sinecure of Ranger of the Park. But it was at Castle Hill Lodge in Ealing, the house he had bought from Maria Fitzherbert, that Edward spent most of his time with Julie. Here he let rip his florid ideas on interior decoration and imparted a martial touch to his domestic arrangements.

Mr. Justice George Hardinge, who visited Castle Hill Lodge one week-end, left an amusing description of its character. He wrote in part:

> I followed my servant, in undress and in boots, to the lodges of the Duke's palace. Between these wings I was received in due form by a porter in livery, full trimmed and powdered. He opened his iron gates for me, bowed as if he had been a king, and rang the

alarm bell as if I had been a hostile invader. I looked as tall, as intrepid and as affable as I could, but I am afraid I was not born for state.

The approach to the palace door is magnificent, graceful and picturesque. The line of the road, flanked by a row of lamps, the most brilliant I ever saw, is a gentle serpentine. It commands to the right, through young but thriving plantations, Harrow-on-the-Hill. The lodges are quite new, and in Mr. Wyatt's best manner.

A second gate flew open to me. It separates the home garden from the lawn of entrance. The head gardener made his appearance, in his best clothes, rang his bell to the house and withdrew.

When I arrived at the palace door, my heart went pit-apat. An aspen leaf in a high wind stood better upon its legs than I stood on mine. Indeed, I am not sure it was not upon my head instead of my legs. I invoked all the saints of impudence to befriend me! Think of little me attended by six footmen! Three of a side! And received at the head of this guard by the house steward, a venerable Frenchman of the old court, who had very much the appearance of a Cabinet Minister. He conducted me with more solemnity than I wished up stairs into my toilet room. At the door of it stood the Duke's valet who took charge of me into the room, bowed and retired. In this apartment I found my own servant.

The exterior of the house has an elegant and chaste as well as princely air. But the interior struck me infinitely more. There was not one speck to be seen. Everything was quite exquisite in outlines and proportions. My dressing-room in which there was an excellent fire, attached its-self to my bedroom, and was laid open to it by a folding door.

My toilet was *à peindre* and there was not anything omitted which could make a youthful Adonis out of an old hermit. A gentle tap at the door alarmed us. We opened upon a messenger who told me in French that His Royal Highness was dressing and would soon do himself the honour of taking me by the hand.

On opening one of the doors of the bedchamber I discovered in an adjoining closet a running stream and a fountain. I began to think I was in the fields of Elysium.

117

The bed was only to be ascended by a ladder dressed in flowered velvet. There was a cold bath and at night hot water. Pen, ink and paper of all descriptions made love to me. Books of amusement were dispersed upon the tables like natural flowers.

I was in my shirt when His Royal Highness knocked at the door. Not waiting for an answer, he opened the door himself and gave me a shake of the hand with his royal fist. I hurried into my coat and waistcoat and then he walked before me into the library. All the passages and staircases were illuminated with lamps of different colours. This library fitted up in perfection of taste is the first room of a magnificent range commanding at least a hundred feet. All the contiguous apartments in that suite were lighted up and thrown open to this apartment. By a contrivance in the management of the light, it seemed as if the distance had no end.

The Duke, among other peculiarities of habit bordering upon a whim, always recommended *the very chair on which you are to sit*. I suppose it is a regal usage. He opened a most agreeable and friendly chat which continued for half an hour. It embraced a variety of topics and was unremitted. He improved at close quarters even upon his pen—and you know what a pen it is. The manly character of his good sense, and the eloquence of his expression was striking. But even they were not so enchanting as that grace of manner which distinguishes him. Compared with it, in my honest opinion, Lord Chesterfield was a dancing master.

I found next morning that he has infinite humour. At breakfast the Duke himself poured out the tea. Then, suddenly rising from operations with his ample platter, he opened a door and gave an order in German. Immediately a band of thirty wind instruments burst into a march.

I was all ears and entranced. Then, upon a sudden they performed the dirge upon our naval hero. It threw me into a burst of tears. [The dirge honoured Hardinge's son, who had been killed in battle at sea.] He took me by the hand and said, "Those are tears which do none of us any harm." He then made the band play all varieties for an hour. He walked me round his place and parted

118

in these words: "You see we are not formidable—do come to us again. Come soon and come very often."

May I not—must I not—love this man?

Mr. Justice Hardinge diplomatically referred to Julie as "a third person".

Edward controlled his servants at Castle Hill Lodge in military style. He employed a resident hairdresser who every day tended their locks, and a resident tailor who kept their uniforms immaculate. Each morning the menservants were paraded and Edward inspected them for neatness and cleanliness. The six footmen could be called, individually or as a group, by bell-pulls hanging side by side in every room. There was an endless dusting by the women servants of the enormous collection of clockwork music boxes, animated toys, and timepieces that Edward had bought on his travels, and of the hundreds of coloured lamps that burned fragrant oils all night in the long corridors. As always, one servant sat up by night in Edward's room to keep the fire going and to call his master at five o'clock with a cup of chocolate or coffee.

After breakfast a housekeeper presented Edward with an account of the previous day's expenditures. This he studied carefully, reproaching the woman for extravagance, or if it was warranted, congratulating her on her thrift. Edward kept a particularly close eye on the price of tea, which by this time was beginning to replace coffee as the national beverage. A subaltern who came to breakfast one morning was astonished when one of the servants handed Edward a big tea-caddy. Taking a key from his pocket, Edward unlocked the caddy, spooned the tea into the pot, and then relocked the caddy and handed it back to the servant. "Take a lesson from me," said Edward to the subaltern. "You are just starting in life. Never be above attending to particulars. Aye, and minute particulars. What is a trifle? Nothing that has reference to our comfort, our independence or our peace."

While Edward was stingy about small items like tea, he was prodigal in his spending on the decorations of Castle Hill Lodge and on its staff. James Denew, a surveyor, estimated that Edward spent £100,000 on renovating the lodge, but predicted that it would not fetch more than £50,000 if it were put on the market.

The Court Register of 1803 published the following details of Edward's household:

Comptroller	Maj.-Gen. William Anne Villette
Grooms	Lt.-Col. John A. Vesey
	George Strachey-Smith
	Willoughby J. Gordon
Equerries	Lt.-Col. Frederick A. Wetherall
	George Anson, Esq.
	Capt. F. Hardyman
Treasurer	William Dalrymple, Esq.
Sub-Treasurer	John Barton, Esq.
Secretary	Capt. Thomas Dodd (Artillery)
Chaplains	(13 in all)
Physicians	Dr. Mervin Nooth,
	Dr. Hayworth
Physician to the Household	Dr. G. Hazelton
Surgeons	Messrs. Robert Keate and P. Travers
Surgeons to the Household	Mr. Tuson, Mr. Thomson
Surgeon Extraordinary	Mr. J. Nooth
Surgeon Dentist	Mr. Clement Brotherton
Apothecaries	Messrs. Atkinson & Tegart
Apothecaries to the Household	Mr. Thomson, Mr. Merryman, Mr. Mildmay
Seal Engraver	R. Brook, Esq.

About a year after settling in England, Edward became embroiled once more in the affairs of Caroline, the Princess of Wales, who was now a pitiable figure. Plump, dark and florid, Caroline suggested in appearance a Latin rather than a Teutonic descent. But she was German to the core. Her personality was marred by a taste for vulgarity, which she associated with candour and honesty. Her experiences at various courts had led her to connect punctiliousness and fine manners with deceit and hypocrisy. As a result she exuded belligerent coarseness.

When he was first introduced to her, the Prince of Wales had turned to a footman and said: "Fetch me a glass of brandy." Caroline was so repellent to the Prince that at their wedding he was tipsy. He lived with her only long enough to beget their ill-fated daughter Charlotte. Afterwards, when he was compelled by reasons of state to appear at the same social functions, the Prince of Wales acknowledged Caroline with only a slight nod and from the greatest possible distance.

At Montagu House, Blackheath, her separate home, Caroline tried to assuage the humiliation of her rejection by leading an intensely gregarious life. She gave endless balls, dinners and intimate parties and drove frequently to the theatre and opera, often embarrassing Wales as he sat in an adjacent box. Edward and Julie visited Caroline occasionally because they felt sorry for her. The Dukes of Sussex and Gloucester, and even Maria Fitzherbert, were among a few other notables who accepted and returned Caroline's hospitality because they too felt that she had been wronged and was in need of moral support. But she also had a flock of free-living acquaintances who associated with her simply for the social prestige reflected on them by her rank, or because they openly enjoyed the smutty gossip, salacious stories, and sexy antics that were characteristic of her smaller parties.

Caroline spoke English with a gutteral German accent and mixed in a dash of French; she even wrote like this. Her favourite topic was *"amour"*. Describing one of her receptions, she referred to a man named Lewis "who did play de part of Cupidon, which amuse us, as you will suppose. He tink himself charming and look so happy when he make *les yeux doux* to de pretty ladies dat it is cruel to tell him 'you are in de paradise of de fools.' "

In the same letter she spoke of the Misses Butler and Ponsonby, who shocked society in the early nineteenth century by quitting London and setting up a home together in Wales. "They must be mad," wrote Caroline, *"mais chacun à son gout.* My dear, I do dread being married to a lady friend. Men are tyrants *mais* de women, heaven help us! Dey are *vrais* Neros over dose dey rule."

Caroline's attitude toward some of her women guests indicated, however, that she was susceptible herself, on occasions, to the cult of Lesbos. For a certain Lady Douglas, she displayed one of those violent affections which in her youth had been noted with dismay by Lord Malmesbury. Lady Douglas was married to Sir John Douglas, a colonel of marines, who had fought under Admiral Sir Sidney

Smith in that battle at Acre, Syria, which had confounded Napoleon's designs on India. The Douglases were introduced to Caroline by Sir Sidney Smith, who at this time was at the height of his fame. Caroline invited the Douglases to become house guests, and this they accepted, living at Blackheath for several months.

Lady Douglas appears first to have encouraged and later to have rejected Caroline's advances. In a statement made during the "Delicate Investigation", the sensational inquiry that resulted from the two women's relationship, Lady Douglas recalled Caroline's attitude thus: "She would exclaim: 'Oh believe me you are quite beautiful; different from any other Englishwoman. Your arms are fine beyond imagination, your bust is very good and your eyes, oh I never saw such eyes. All other women who have dark eyes look fierce. But yours are nothing but softness and sweetness, and yet quite dark, my dear Lady Douglas.' In this manner she went on perpetually before strangers."

Caroline's infatuation for Lady Douglas was once demonstrated at uncomfortably close quarters before Edward. He was sitting in the presence of the two women and a Mrs. Harcourt at Montagu House one day when Caroline said, indicating Lady Douglas: "Your Royal Highness must look at her eyes. But she has disguised herself in a large hat, you cannot see how handsome she is." Edward politely pretended not to hear and went on talking to Mrs. Harcourt, an act for which Lady Douglas felt "very much obliged". But Caroline was determined that Edward should inspect Lady Douglas's eyes, and said to her: "Take off your hat." When Lady Douglas demurred, Caroline removed the hat herself. Lady Douglas recalled that Edward "conceiving it could not be very pleasant for me took little notice and talked of something else".

When Lady Douglas began to discourage Caroline's ardour, the Princess, probably in an attempt to recover her dignity by pretending that the advances had not been serious, began to boast of affairs with men. Her most dangerous boast was that she was with child by one of her lovers, and that she was going to pass off the infant as an adopted orphan.

Lady Douglas realized that if this kind of boasting reached the ears of the Prince of Wales, he would have grounds for divorce from Caroline. And Lady Douglas feared that she might be involved in the court scandal as a witness. Consequently she and her husband left Montagu House and began, as tactfully as possible, to withdraw their friendship from Caroline.

Caroline's reaction was full of jealousy and malice. She developed the conviction that her rival for Lady Douglas's favours was not Sir John Douglas, but Sir Sidney Smith. In the mail one day in 1804, Sir John and Lady Douglas received a lifelike pornographic drawing. It showed Sir Sidney Smith and Lady Douglas in the act of coitus. The drawing was embellished with obscene remarks in the handwriting of Caroline.

Instead of burning the drawing and keeping quiet about it, Sir John Douglas flew into a rage. Perhaps he believed its insinuation. He summoned Sir Sidney Smith, who, in chorus with Lady Douglas, heatedly protested his honour. Whereupon Sir John Douglas communicated with Caroline, demanding an audience and an apology. The apprehensive Caroline refused to see him. Sir John Douglas remained undaunted. He pestered Caroline so persistently for an audience, and threatened so strongly to expose her indiscretion, that the Princess got into a panic. For help she turned to Edward, one of the few members of the royal family who had ever shown her any genuine sympathy.

At first Edward believed Caroline when she said she was not responsible for the drawing. When he visited Sir Sidney Smith, who was now in possession of the drawing, Edward asked to see it. He took one look at it, recognized the handwriting of the comments, and knew that Caroline was guilty. He tried, however, to hush the matter up. Studying the drawing, he said: "Abominable. If this matter makes a noise it may distress the King and injure his health. So I wish that Sir John and Lady Douglas would, at least for the present, forget it. I will speak fully to the Princess of Wales and point out the danger of such things."

On speaking to Caroline, as he had promised, Edward did not seek any admission of guilt. He merely suggested to her that it would be better for everyone concerned if the matter were allowed to drop. Caroline, however, was too emotionally wound up to heed Edward's advice. Lady Douglas was her obsession and a continuing target for the barbs of her jealous tongue. At her social gatherings she persisted in hinting that Lady Douglas and Sir Sidney Smith were lovers, and it was patent to her listeners that the thought distressed her.

Lady Douglas, her husband, and Sir Sidney Smith became enraged at Caroline's continued insinuations and could bear them no longer. In 1805, Sir John Douglas went to the garrulous Duke of Sussex, told him the whole story, and asked him to intervene. Sussex relayed the story of the drawing to the Prince of Wales. In addition, he repeated the boast that Caroline was now making at her indelicate parties—the boast that Willie Austin, a small boy she had recently adopted, was in fact her own son by a lover. In the course of this conversation with the Prince of Wales, Sussex implicated Edward. "The Duke of Kent," said Sussex, "has known it for a year."

Wrathfully the Prince of Wales summoned Edward and asked him why he had for so long kept to himself matters affecting so deeply the good name of the royal family. Edward explained that he had wished to avoid a scandal, having kept in mind the effect such disclosures might have on the health of the King.

The Prince of Wales would have waded through scandal up to his neck, completely indifferent to the King's health, if this would have helped him to rid himself of Caroline, free him to marry again, and permit him to face with pleasure, instead of insurmountable disgust, the duty of begetting a male heir to the throne. He regarded Edward's discretion not as an act of filial concern for the welfare of the royal family, but as a deliberate attempt to rob him, the Prince of Wales, of a golden opportunity to cast off an intolerable burden through the indictment of Caroline with ruinous charges.

In his response to Edward's explanation, the Prince of Wales made a sarcastic reference to the "well-known uprightness" of his brother's "character and principles". The Prince of Wales also called Edward "Simon Pure", after the humbuggish Philadelphia Quaker in Mrs. Centlivre's popular stage comedy *A Bold Stroke for a Wife.* The jibe was repeated in society and compared laughingly with the earlier nickname "Joseph Surface", that had been hung upon Edward by his sisters. The effect was to perpetuate and exaggerate Edward's reputation for hypocrisy, a reputation that really arose from a misunderstanding of his unsophisticated nature.

In the highly publicized "Delicate Investigation" that followed, Edward repeated his statement that Caroline had asked him to intervene on her behalf in the distasteful matter of the drawing. Gallantly Edward refrained from stating whether or not he believed

Caroline to be guilty. Gratefully, while still protesting innocence, Caroline attempted to vindicate Edward. In a statement to the King she said that Edward saw Sir Sidney Smith on her behalf. She added: "Being impressed by him [Smith] with the belief of Lady Douglas's story that I was the author of the drawing and anonymous letter he did that which naturally became him under such belief: he endeavoured for the peace of your Majesty, and the honour of the Royal Family, to keep from the knowledge of the world what, if it had been true, would have justly reflected such infinite disgrace upon me."

The "Delicate Investigation" petered out. While the evidence left her reputation in shreds, it was insufficient to prove Caroline guilty of adultery. Although it must have been obvious to Caroline that she had escaped by a hair's breadth from a public shaming, she failed to profit from the lesson. Instead her foolhardiness increased. In society she went on to relate her troubles with embarrassing frankness and lewdness, and she maligned with her pen many real or imagined oppressors. To her relatives and friends in Germany she wrote scores of letters containing reflections on almost every member of the British royal family. By chance, or deliberate subterfuge, a package of these letters fell into the wrong hands.

Caroline had entrusted the letters to a Reverend Doctor Randolph as he was about to depart on a trip to the Continent. At the last minute Randolph was prevented by other business from going. He said later that he mailed the letters back to Caroline immediately. Unfortunately they never reached her; somebody got hold of them. Within a few days the Queen had read them and, in her shock and anger, had passed them around to other members of the royal family. Now the House of Hanover was sulphurous with hatred of Caroline.

In the family heat that Caroline had generated, Edward alone was moved to take a stand dictated by coolness and probity. He flatly refused to read the letters, although they were offered to him many times. He could not, however, prevent his relatives from telling him what was in them; nor, despite the hearsay nature of the evidence, could he quell his indignation when he heard.

In a note on the matter which Edward circulated to his relatives, he wrote: "They were unjustifiable letters which it was hardly possible to reconcile with the rank of the writer." But, in the same note, Edward drew the attention of his family to a question of principle which, in his opinion, was even more important than the question of Caroline's malice. "I have not seen the letters," he wrote, "for various reasons, among them being a conviction that their being in existence at all, and certainly in the hands of the parties who held them, was a breach of that honourable confidence which ought to actuate all persons in matters where private correspondence is concerned."

For reminding the royal family that their pain was the result of their own prying, Edward was rated as Caroline's defender. In this unwanted capacity he had to contend with the increasing enmity of his three most important brothers, the Prince of Wales, the Duke of York, and that Duke of Clarence who later was to become William IV.

Steadily the shadows darkened over Edward. To some extent he had brought them upon himself, through stumbling into affairs more subtle men would have avoided, but he was motivated by kindness rather than caprice.

The gentle side of Edward's nature is manifest in the help and hospitality he extended to the four sons of his old Quebec City friend Louis de Salaberry. All were commissioned into the British Army under Edward's patronage. They were Charles, now a captain, and a veteran of the wars in the West Indies; Maurice and Chevalier, now cadets; and Edward's namesake and godson Edward, who was expecting to leave Quebec City soon to enter Woolwich, the artillery academy. Whenever the boys passed through London on their way to join their regiments, or *en route* from one colonial outpost to another, they were entertained by Edward and Julie. It is in Julie's few surviving letters, most of them to de Salaberry on the subject of his sons, that we get further glimpses of her blithe and affectionate spirit. For this reason the letters are quoted almost in full.

Kensington Palace, 5th April, 1805

The departure of Captain Vesey, my dear de Salaberry, has been so suddenly announced, that being today very busy I see with regret that I must deprive myself of the pleasure of writing you a long letter, but I promise that I will make amends for it at the first opportunity.

Nothing could be more delightful than your letter but its

author. I have read it with extreme pleasure. What you say of Maurice enchants without surprising me. During his infancy I was always struck with something chivalrous about him, and you will recollect my passing my fingers through his fair sunny hair, and comparing him to the famous Maurice, Count Saxe. I do not think less of my *little Chevalier,* now that he is at least as tall as you are.

I hope that you are satisfied with the way our Duke has disposed of both. His Royal Highness has certainly shown great zeal. I would likewise inform you that Colonel Vesey, who is a very great friend of yours, has contributed everything in his power with the Secretary of the Duke of York, and has eulogized in the most flattering manner the brilliant talents of both young gentlemen. He assures me that they are really charming, and noted over the whole country for their politeness and elegant manners.

I hope that this letter will find Captain de Salaberry [Charles] in better health. His tender mother's care, and your own, cannot fail to re-establish it speedily. On thinking how fatal those islands [the West Indies] are to the health and lives of so many brave men, one cannot but regret their possession. Pray assure the invalid of my most tender regard.

I am very happy to learn that Madame de Salaberry—alias *Ma Souris*—enjoys such good health. It will not fail to give me great satisfaction when I hear of the marriage of my three young friends, to whom I send a thousand loves.

Adieu, dear and ever dear de Salaberry. I have only a minute left to dress and go out. It is go and come from morning to night. Ah! London, I will not call you a *hole*—the greatest and most beautiful city in the world—but every place has its drawbacks.

Your sincere friend, J. de St. Laurent

Kensington Palace, 3rd September, 1805

My Dear de Salaberry:

Our young men have arrived fresh, vigorous and in good health. I will not attempt to express to you the pleasure I had in receiving them. Captain de Salaberry is as usual very well, but the two Cadets, both of whom I last saw when so small, are to me *perfect wonders*. The Duke being at Weymouth with the Royal Family, I myself had the pleasure of doing the honours of Kensington Palace and I hope that they are quite satisfied with the friendly and cordial manner in which I acquitted myself.

Captain de Salaberry, in whom I am happy to recognize *the true son of his father,* has had the gallantry to say to me that he found no change in me. I have not failed to let him know I was much pleased with the good intention which led him to pay a compliment so agreeable to a lady after an absence of ten years. The tall Maurice and the amiable Chevalier (your living picture) also said they would have recognized me. My dear de Salaberry, you see they are made for the world, and they will be successful without doubt.

Our dear Duke did not fail to see them immediately upon his return, and partook of my enthusiasm in regard to them. He has arranged with them their journey to Scotland, where they will repair immediately by sea. Captain de Salaberry will remain with us during the three months he proposes to remain in England, but till such time as we have a vacant room at Kensington the Duke has asked him in the meantime (which will not be long) to *mess* every day with us.

It is a very fortunate thing for Maurice and Chevalier that your old friend Colonel Hardyman is at the head of their regiment [the Royal Scotch] for he is ever grateful for the politeness he received from Madame de Salaberry, and will not fail to be very friendly. And as he is just married he will have greater opportunities of shewing them many attentions. I have also recommended them myself to Mrs. Hardyman, an amiable person who will be very useful to them, *so everything is safe and perfectly well*.

You may believe that I put question on question to these three amiable *sons of yours,* and I have learnt with pleasure that my dear *Souris,* my little friends, and my godson, are enjoying brilliant health. Master Edward will, I flatter myself, be lucky enough, for he has made a fortunate entrance into the world, His Royal Highness having already nominated him as a Cadet at Woolwich, and you must send him to us next year, when he will have completed his fourteenth anniversary.

The letters of your sons for you, my dear de Salaberry, being already here, I am again prevented for want of time, to write you at leisure, but this I again promise to do on the first opportunity. Believe me in the meantime, dear de Salaberry,

Your sincere friend, J. de St. Laurent

Castle Hill Lodge, September 16th, 1806

As the Duke has told me, my dear de Salaberry, that from the delay of the departure of the packet there is time for me to write, with great pleasure I take up my pen to announce the arrival of your Edward. The boy, who came to spend some days with us here, and who conducted himself with all possible grace, has really charmed us and nearly turned our heads. Nobody could be better bred, more polished or gentle, and his countenance is so intelligent and open and he smiles so sweetly. You had good reason to say in one of your former letters, that his pleasing mien would charm me. I am absolutely carried away, for never did a boy of his age inspire me with so much interest. He will tell you, I am sure, how much I have caressed him—more than he desired—but he endured it all with the best grace and the most perfect good temper. He permitted himself to be kissed and questioned without ceasing with great good nature and without any fear, for it is not possible to spoil him.

Today at length we decided to let him go to school, accompanied by General Wetherall, where we hope he will do well. It is the first and best school in the country, and there he will remain till such time as it is judged that he is sufficiently advanced to go to Marlow and from thence to Woolwich.

Before placing him under the roof of his master, we could not refuse to show him in the meantime the sights of London. He went with us to Drury Lane, and he had our box *for himself and company* at Covent Garden. His company was Dr. Wetherall, the General, Mrs. Wetherall, etc. We intend to go and see him in the course of next week, to recommend him favourably to his Academy. I repeat there is not such another amiable boy. During his stay here he played draughts, dominoes and backgammon, and I am happy to say he won our money at all these games. It is impossible, with the intelligence he showed on every occasion, that he will fail to carve himself a brilliant career. He certainly will not fail for want of application, and I hope still further from the great desire he shows to please his illustrious godfather and his tender godmother. He will come to spend the Christmas holidays with us and you may be sure that from now to then we will not lose sight of him, and the curricle will be employed to see how he gets on.

I would write a great deal longer on this interesting subject but I have not time at present, having a large dinner party today. I hope that this rapidly traced letter will suffice to set you at rest in regard to the success of our charming little *man in miniature,* who has entirely, absolutely and decidedly made a conquest of us.

I am delighted that my dear *Souris* has decided to try the wig (for my little finger tells me that she has done so). I hope that she will wear it for my sake. It is a head-dress which she will find very comfortable, when she has become accustomed to it. Everybody wears it. I hope that it arrived safely with the letter which accompanied it. I am delighted that my dear *Souris* is quite well. Kiss her tenderly for me. I embrace with my whole heart the amiable and tender mother of my little godson, and not less tenderly my dear Adelaide. And thank her a thousand times for her interesting letter, which I read with great pleasure.

Adieu, my dear de Salaberry, believe me ever to be your most sincere friend.

J. de St. Laurent

P.S. Your eldest remains well. He has enlisted not less than one hundred and fifty recruits for the Royals within two months and you can be sure he has delighted the Duke. I hope his majority is not far off. As for the two Cadets their conduct is perfectly good. The room paper is for Beauport, that home dear to my heart, and which I delight to call to mind as the home of that amiable family that I so much love.

Castle Hill Lodge, 28th July, 1807
I have received all your letters, my dear de Salaberry. Each day I wished to reply and each day something prevented me, but you know well that the silence of my pen by no means

130

indicates that you are absent from my thoughts. Edward who writes you, can also tell you if I have forgotten you, and if I always love you. I shall leave to that amiable boy the care of writing you on this head, and truly I could not have a better mouthpiece or a truer interpreter of my sentiments, so sincere and so true, for you and all pertaining to you.

The beautiful embroidery, and the other charming work accompanying, from my young friends, are now on my table, as also the pretty flag, which I must thank them for very much, as a mark of attention both kind and ingenious.

Our two young voyagers must by this time have arrived at the Cape of Good Hope, and if they have called there, they will undoubtedly have written us. I hope we will learn the good news of their having had a pleasant passage. I hope they will find the country healthy, and have rapid promotion in their profession.

The Duke, who saw them at Portsmouth, assures me that they embarked in excellent spirits, and I believe him, for nothing could be more natural, for if one is convinced that the country is good for *speculators,* it must be advantageous to others, and all officers on that account strive to get the preference to accompany troops to India.

I am delighted, my dear de Salaberry, to find by your letter that you look upon the thing in its true light.

J. de St. Laurent

Castle Hill Lodge, 15th November, 1807
I have received, my dear de Salaberry, all your letters from the 4th August inclusive to this date, in which you announce to me the recovery of our dear *Souris* from a severe illness. You have put me under a real obligation by not announcing it to me before her recovery, otherwise I would have been most uneasy. Long may she enjoy health. Long, for the happiness of her family and friends, who knowing her amiability, her winning disposition and strong mind, are able to appreciate her virtues at their true value. Kiss her tenderly for me, in assurance that I love her with my whole heart.

I have seen, with sincere regret, that nothing has yet been done for you, but the Duke, in accordance with your wish, has again written to General Craig, and we shall see what success will attend this next step. I see that there is something wrong, and that too many have been recommended at the same time. The Governor has fulfilled one part of his promise to his illustrious friend, but unfortunately has not yet performed that regarding you. But you may rest sure the Duke is determined and this he will tell you himself in a letter which he proposes to accompany this. I hope then this affair will end well, and that in a short time I shall be able to congratulate you on the attainment of what you have so long waited for.

I have received all the pretty things which have been sent me by my young friends. Edward and your eldest, who were present at the opening of the box, will tell you much better than I can how much pleasure this kind of attention has given me, and how much the charming work of Adelaide, Hermine and Amelia was admired. Be assured then of my gratitude and friendship, and of the pleasure I will have in sending them in the spring, in return for their kind presents, some pretty trifles of the fashion.

I have not yet received the snowshoes, and Edward has not yet written on the subject, but as he is coming before long to pass the vacation with us he will be able to let us know all about them. He continues to make great progress in his mathematical studies, drawings, etc. He is now taller than his mother and godmother, of which he is very proud, not wishing to be a single line less tall than Maurice. He has a fine appearance, is ambitious, but not vain.

I shall now relate a little anecdote which has caused us a good deal of anxiety. It is true I have not the permission of him who is the hero of it but I cannot deprive myself of the satisfaction and I hope he will pardon this little indiscretion, as the story only does him honour.

During the sojourn of Capt. de Salaberry in Ireland, his first care was to inform himself of the residence of his aunt, Mrs. Fortescue, where he presented himself with that eagerness to enjoy the society of relatives which is always felt in a strange land. The lady of the house received him with open arms, as did her husband and daughter, a young and pretty girl of twenty or twenty-two years. A connection so attractive could not but be dangerous for a young soldier, and a young soldier was naturally a formidable cousin to a young girl. The familiarity which resulted under the pretext of relationship was changed very speedily into a more tender sentiment, and you see from this our young people thought of nothing less than love and marriage, when Capt. de Salaberry was obliged to return suddenly to England. Thus being under the necessity of separating from his fair cousin, sad were the adieus, there is no reason to doubt. But in this kind of trouble, the sorrow of those who are left is the more painful, while those who go away, distracted by the cares of the journey and a thousand different objects, bear it more easily.

De Salaberry when he arrived here was as calm as usual, and some time afterwards, having lost his enthusiasm for Miss Fortescue, I began to doubt if there was anything, as he always replied to my joking with a good grace, and I believed I was mistaken, and thought no more about it. Judge then my astonishment when after he had rejoined his regiment some fifty miles from this, I received a letter requesting my advice on his intention of marrying his cousin. I was astonished, not believing that there was any way of changing his resolution, but I hastened to secure a powerful auxiliary, and at once communicated to the Duke the untoward news, which I regarded as certain to ruin your son, Miss Fortescue having no fortune. [Despite the irregularity of her relationship with Edward, Julie conformed to the social mores of her time.]

Our illustrious friend taking the same view as myself, saw that no time was to be lost to get him out of the scrape, if possible, promised me to write him and did it immediately in terms the most strong though kind, pointing out how he would embarrass himself if he proceeded in a step so calculated to affect his future well-being, and I added a few lines to that long letter, though we had little hope of the success of our effort.

Well, my dear de Salaberry, would you believe it, the dear generous young man heroically thanked the Duke in the most grateful terms for his good advice so full of wisdom, solemnly promised to think no more of marriage, and to write at once to Ireland, excusing himself to Miss Fortescue, on the grounds of the advice given by his illustrious protector, and sending at the same time to the young lady's brother-in-law a copy of the letter which had induced him to change his resolution.

Rejoice then, my dear friend, that you have given being to one so noble, and let the pleasure of having such a child console you, at least in a great degree, for other causes of disquiet. Embrace him with redoubled tenderness when he returns to you in spring, as Major of Brigade to General de Rottenburg, for there is without any doubt this prospect of advancement.

I believe I have done right, but if I am wrong, you must pardon me on account of my good intentions. Adieu, my dear de Salaberry, I have been very lazy in not writing you oftener, but this long letter will ensure my pardon. I shall now lay down my pen, hoping that this rhapsody will find in good health all the amiable family at Beauport, whom I embrace most sincerely with my whole heart.

J. de St. Laurent

Whenever we get letters from India, you may depend they will be sent to you without loss of time.

Young Edward de Salaberry added a brief but illuminating letter to this valuable correspondence. Writing to his father on New Year's Eve, 1807, he said:

I am at present staying with H.R.H. the Duke of Kent at Kensington Palace, where I have fine apartments. H.R.H. and Madame de St. Laurent are at present at Knightsbridge which is some distance from here. It is a superb mansion, beautifully furnished. I have dined there several times. I dined there on Christmas Day with the Duke of Orléans and his brothers. I have been at the opera with H.R. Highness and Madame, when I saw the Duke of Cambridge to whom I was presented as godson of H.R.Highness and Madame. I have also seen the Swedish Ambassador the same evening. I have been at the play with H.R.Highness. H.R.H. has given orders that we shall always have music at dinner. The dinner is at seven o'clock, which is supper for me. The Duke and Madame have been very kind to me and their kindness, if possible, is greater every day. I hope, my dear Papa, you will write me by every mail: the letters cost me nothing: they all come first to H.R.H. and then to me: the postage is paid at the Palace where I am now. . . . Adieu my dear Papa. I believe I shall see you before long, and I am with the most lively affection,

Your devoted and obedient son,

Edward Alphonse de S.

P.S. Madame de St. Laurent has given me six guineas since I came to England, a jolly sum for me.

The devotion which Edward and Julie were lavishing on the de Salaberry boys in the year 1807 arouses curiosity about the progress of their own children. Little is known of these offspring, for the very good reason that in later years they were an embarrassment to Queen Victoria. Throughout Victoria's reign it was always politely pretended that Julie de St. Laurent had never existed, and it would have been a brash writer indeed who dared to make reference to the Queen's half-brothers by Julie.

By 1807 the half-brothers of the yet unborn Queen were in their teens. Robert Wood, the elder, was still in Quebec City, living with his foster-father and namesake, and enjoying the discreet and watchful protection of the de Salaberry family. His presence in Quebec City probably stimulated the verbose nature of the correspondence between Edward and Julie and the de Salaberrys. His parents would naturally be concerned about his welfare.

It is believed, however, that Robert was kept in ignorance of his true parentage until he reached manhood. Letters containing references to him in the de Salaberry correspondence were probably destroyed. He visited England several times, escorted by his foster-father, and it is likely that Edward and Julie saw him. But he settled permanently in Canada and, as will be seen, founded one of Quebec City's most distinguished families.

Jean also visited England several times—each time, curiously enough, in the company of his brother's foster-parent, Robert Wood, who called for him at the Jesuit College in Philadelphia before departure for England. Jean's permanent home was still the Montgenet estate in Martinique. In the West Indies, the United States, and England, he moved in *émigré* French circles close to

Louis Philippe, Duke of Orléans, who later became King of France. As a man, Jean settled in Australia.

Mélanie, Julie's daughter by de Fortisson, was twenty in 1807. She had by this time sailed across the Atlantic to marry in New Orleans a former official of the old French colony of Louisiana. This official, whose name was Levison or Lewison, had become an American citizen after the United States purchased Louisiana in 1803. By profession he was a hydraulics engineer and was responsible for many of the early dams and water-power plants in North America. Later Mélanie and her husband settled in Philadelphia, where many of their descendants still live.

Being far more sensitive to convention than his brother the Duke of Clarence—who openly married off his large illegitimate brood into the British nobility—Edward preferred to deny himself the company of his own sons. It was a harsh restriction that he imposed upon himself, and upon Julie too, for the sake of outward propriety. But appearances meant a lot to him, as they do to most born soldiers.

By 1807 a house empty of children was not Edward's only worry. The final eclipse of his career was imminent. Young Captain Charles de Salaberry, writing home to Quebec, said of Edward: "The Duke has not now that influence which, as a Prince of the Blood, he might be supposed to have, and yet he is undoubtedly far more correct in his conduct than his royal brothers." The observant young officer was quick to put his finger on the source of Edward's distress. "The Duke of Kent," he said, "made me wait on the Duke of York. He appeared to be a very different man."

Chapter X

BY the year 1808, Napoleon had been Emperor of France for four years. All Europe, save the United Kingdom and Russia, lay at his feet. He had conquered the Prussians at Jena and grouped the German states into the submissive Confederation of the Rhine. He had brought to an end the Holy Roman Empire.

Though once he had sneered at hereditary rulers, Napoleon no longer hid his true esteem for the functions and fruits of a throne. His bourgeois Corsican kin, rising in the trail of the Napoleonic rocket, were already peopling the royal palaces of subject countries with a new crop of young pretenders. His brothers Joseph, Louis, and Jérome were respectively the Kings of Spain, Holland, and Westphalia. His brother-in-law, Joachim Murat, was King of Naples. Another brother-in-law, the great French general Jean Bernadotte, was soon to be declared Crown Prince of Sweden. In distributing honours to his tribe, with the object of founding a Bonaparte continental dynasty, Napoleon did not forget even his step-son, Eugène de Beauharnais. This youngster, the Empress Josephine's child by her first husband, was now Viceroy of Naples.

Only one monarchy in Europe was safely belted against the Corsican rape, and this was the United Kingdom's House of Hanover. George III and all his sons still spoke of Napoleon's aspirations as "insolent". Their defiance was fortified, of course, by the Royal Navy, which, at Trafalgar three years before, had so decimated the French fleet that Napoleon could not hope to mount a cross-Channel offensive for years to come. But another offensive, almost equally arrogant and frightful in British eyes, was rumoured. King Joseph Bonaparte of Spain, according to intelligence agents, was planning to recapture Gibraltar.

This report pricked the most tender spot in Edward's pride. He still retained the rank and pay of Governor of Gibraltar. Now, as the Rock stood in danger once more, he was overcome by the intolerable indignity of his absence from its battlements. His appeal to the King for permission to return to Gibraltar was like a shout of pain. "I beg leave," he said, "to impress upon Your Majesty's attention everything most dear to me in life. My character, my professional credit as a soldier, are at stake."

George III did not reply. Instead he handed the letter over to the Duke of York, who, on February 6, 1808, wrote to Edward from the Horse Guards with his customary prolixity:

It is at all times a matter of great regret to me to recall to your recollection the unfortunate events which led to your return from that fortress, and which have already and must ever preclude the confidential servants of the King from advising His Majesty to permit you to resume your station there. I had hoped from the number of ineffectual applications which you have at different times made upon this unlucky subject that you would have been prevented from renewing them; and I can only repeat how much I have lamented that no arrangement could be made to relieve you from the embarrassment which you must undoubtedly always labour under so long as you retain the government of Gibraltar.

The letter might have driven other men to resign, but it only stiffened Edward's stubborn clutch on his empty office. He began to write querulous notes to Lord Castlereagh, Secretary of State for War, demanding an explanation of his continued exile from Gibraltar. Castlereagh replied in polite but equivocal terms, and Edward's frustration soon became a matter of public knowledge. Some passages from the letters were slipped before the eyes of the radical press, which was growing fond of Edward for his unprecedented royal interest in the poor. By this time he was a patron of such institutions as the Westminster Infirmary, the London Orphan Asylum, the Irish Charitable Society, the Smallpox Hospital, and the Lying-in Charity for the Delivering of Poor Women at Their Own Habitations.

Stirred by Edward's benevolence, many radical newspapers assumed the role of his defender and began to present him to their readers as the victim of a palace plot. Editorial writers directed their sharpest barbs at Edward's brothers, who, they said, were denying the soldier Prince the right to resume his command in Gibraltar because they were jealous of his martial record. So profuse were their representations on Edward's behalf that they weakened rather than strengthened his hopes of re-engagement.

A scathing pamphlet entitled *Observations on His Royal Highness the Duke of Kent's Shameful Persecution Since His Recall from Gibraltar* did particular damage to Edward's prospects. It was circulated in 1808 by a journalist named Pierre Franc MacCallum, who enlarged, somewhat inaccurately, upon "the affection in which the Duke of Kent is held by every member of his family—one only excepted, our virtuous, wise and conscientious Commander-in-Chief". The sarcasm of the last sentence was underscored when MacCallum followed up with the opinion that the Duke of York would be better employed as "a Prussian drill sergeant or a master tailor". If Edward replaced his brother as Commander-in-Chief, said MacCallum, the British Army in Portugal would "attain speedy victory".

The pamphlet almost fired the Duke of York with apoplexy. He accused Edward of secretly providing MacCallum with intimate truths about private royal affairs, and with thus inciting MacCallum to write the pamphlet. Edward heatedly denied the allegation. He admitted, however, that he had circulated among friends, for the protection of his own reputation, copies of his official correspondence over the Gibraltar dispute. In this admission Edward implied that one of his friends had passed the information to MacCallum.

Some of Edward's intimates, however, were more inclined to the opinion that Captain Thomas Dodd, Edward's military secretary, was the man responsible for the disclosures. After all, they said, Dodd would have strong motives for such an act. His devotion to Edward, and his personal ambitions, were well known. If by propaganda Dodd could bring about the dismissal of the Duke of York and the investment of Edward with the rank of Commander-in-Chief, he would, at one stroke, ease his beloved master's anguish and render brilliant his own hopes of promotion.

While Dodd's motives were widely discussed during the din of the controversy, Edward refused to believe that the captain could be guilty of leaking information from confidential correspondence. He remained in Edward's service. The loyalty that Edward always displayed toward his personal staff was particularly touching in the case of Dodd. This earnest young officer was undoubtedly much to blame for the next cloud of scandal that darkened Edward's life. It was a scandal that impelled the Duke of York to resign from his post and imposed on naive Edward the incongruous reputation of a Machiavelli.

In the autumn of 1808, the handsome, saucy and highly mercenary Mrs. Mary Anne Clarke, the one-time wife of a stonemason in Fetter Lane, had to face the world as the discarded mistress of the pot-bellied, heron-shanked Duke of York.

This middle-aged, slightly tottery, but still avid rake was now coupling, down in Fulham, with a more demure woman named Mrs. Cary. Mrs. Clarke's position was far from enviable, but it hardly justified the degree of revenge that she was plotting against York.

During six or seven years as the Duke of York's mistress, Mrs. Clarke had amassed enough money to acquire an elegant home in Gloucester Place, two carriages, and eight horses. She also employed a butler, a coachman, a postilion, a groom, a chef, two gardeners, two footmen, and several maids. Where she found the funds for such high life was something of a mystery, for the Duke of York was notorious among London's courtesans for his parsimony.

The source of Mrs. Clarke's wealth was particularly interesting to a certain Colonel Wardle, a Whig Member of Parliament who, like the rest of his party, was looking for some mud to sling at Tory conduct of the war. How he made Mrs. Clarke's acquaintance is not known, but in Brighton one day he was seen driving with her. They were accompanied by Captain Dodd. During the jaunt Mrs. Clarke chattered with gratifying abandon about the Duke of York. Although she spoke fondly of her former lover's romantic predilections—"He called me Darling," she giggled, "and I called him Doctor"—she was at pains to point out that during their days and nights together he had been astonishingly stingy. Mrs. Clarke said she had been driven, in order to keep up the appearances expected of a royal mistress, to arranging with the Duke, in return for cash bribes, the promotion of many ambitious army officers.

She disclosed a fixed scale of charges for her services. For using her influence with the Duke of York to obtain an officer a majority she had charged £2,600; for a captaincy, £1,500; for a lieutenancy, £550; and for an ensigncy, £400. She also revealed that she had obtained for one of her footmen a commission in the army, and had taken money from an army chaplain for securing him an opportunity to preach before the King.

140

Wardle must have thrilled at the volume of political ammunition that fell into his lap that afternoon; and Dodd, no doubt, began to dream of what would happen to him if his master Edward were to replace as Commander-in-Chief the now incriminated Duke of York.

Wardle rose in the House of Commons on January 27, 1809, and employed Mrs. Clarke's indiscretions as the grounds for moving that "a committee be appointed to investigate the conduct of His Royal Highness the Duke of York in his capacity of Commander-in-Chief, with regard to appointments, promotions, exchanges, the raising of new levies and the general state of the army".

The motion caused such a public stir that the Government decided that the charges against the Duke of York should be heard, not privately before a committee, but openly, before the press, at the bar of the House of Commons. The proceedings lasted seven weeks, and Mrs. Clarke convinced the Commons over and over again that she had received money from numerous aspiring officers.

The Government defended the Duke well. It produced War Office documents to prove that all the promotions mentioned had taken place in the ordinary course of events, and that the officers' bribes had thus been a waste of money. Although it was suggested in the course of the proceedings that the Duke might have taken money himself for bringing about the promotions, no evidence was offered to prove it. Nor was there any evidence to suggest that the Duke knew that Mrs. Clarke stood to profit from the promotion of the officers she praised in his company. In other words, the Duke of York was revealed by the inquiry to have been childishly indiscreet in discussing promotions with Mrs. Clarke, but hardly corrupt.

During the evidence Dodd's name cropped up several times, and this reflected suspicion on Edward. Toward the end of the hearing, Edward, though suffering from influenza, went down to the House of Lords to refute the wide-spread gossip that he was the power behind Wardle in the attack on his brother. He told the Lords that while there were many professional differences between him and his brother, he believed that the Duke of York was wholly incapable of the conduct imputed to him by Mrs. Clarke. He added, untruthfully, "No animosity subsists between the Duke of York and myself and all reports to the contrary are unfounded.'

Edward's words were not without impact on opinion in the Commons. By 278 to 196, the Members expressed their confidence in the Duke of York as Commander-in-Chief. But the majority of 82 votes was not big enough, in York's opinion, to vindicate his honour. Nearly two hundred gentlemen of England regarded him as guilty of "personal corruption and connivance at the infamous practices disclosed by Mrs. Clarke". York resigned and his post was left open.

Thus the inquiry produced little but a lot of smutty verses in the British press on the subject of Mrs. Clarke, a wave of snickering before the drawn bed-curtains of the Duke of York, and many significant winks at the crafty part Edward was supposed to have played in the revelations.

Across the Channel, news of the proceedings filled Napoleon with bewilderment. His armies had just driven the British into the sea at Corunna. What kind of people were those English, he asked, who at a time of such national crisis could think of nothing else but the public unbosoming of a wanton woman?

Many spurned women would have rested content with the ignominy suffered by the Dukes of York and Kent, but not Mrs. Clarke. Now she revelled in twisting the dagger in the wounds of her victims. Early in 1810 she published two volumes of circumlocution and ambiguity entitled *The Rival Princes*. Basing this maundering twaddle on society gossip, the tittle-tattle of high-class harlots, and the eavesdropping of servants, she prattled away at the theory that the Duke of York had been cut down from office by the hidden hand of his brother Edward. She claimed that Dodd, who was still in Edward's service, and now a major, had been the liaison agent between Colonel Wardle and Edward in the planned destruction of the Duke of York's character. She alleged that Dodd, in Edward's name, had offered her five thousand pounds cash and four hundred pounds a year if her evidence at the Commons inquiry resulted in the deposing of the Duke of York and the appointment to his command of Edward.

Mrs. Clarke also sharpened the salacious appeal of her "best seller" by making two allusions to Julie de St. Laurent. Outside the royal circle Julie's background was a mystery and the subject of considerable speculation. Mrs. Clarke whetted the curiosity of her readers by writing: "As I am in possession of all the circumstances attending the Duke of Kent's conduct while Governor of Gibraltar it is not improbable I shall publish a curious history of his courage,

142

his military and political actions, together with an interesting account of the discovery of the St. Lawrence." In another passage she paid a dubious compliment to Edward and Julie by quoting an authority she described as Mister Glennie. "Mister Glennie observed," she said, "that the Duke's affection for his old French lady, whom he lamented he could not marry, was proof of his steady disposition and domestic good qualities, added to which he regularly went to church and was never seen inebriated."

This mischievous literature, despite its rambling and vapid charater, was lapped up by the reading public of both high estate and low, and it amplified the drawing-room babble that was reducing Edward and Julie to a state of nervous prostration. In desperation Edward countered in 1810 with a publication of a questionnaire he had put to his secretary Dodd a year before. It consisted of questions dictated by Edward in the presence of Dodd, and Dodd's written and signed replies. Its authenticity was vouched for by the signatures of two witnesses, the Earl of Harrington and Colonel J. A. Vesey, one of Edward's grooms. It ran as follows:

Question: Have I either directly or indirectly sanctioned, advised or encouraged any attack upon the Duke of York to your knowledge?

Answer: Never.

Question: Have I had to your knowledge, any acquaintance or communication with Colonel Wardle or any of the persons concerned in bringing forward the investigation respecting the Duke of York's conduct, which took place in Parliament last winter, either direct or indirect?

Answer: I feel confident that your Royal Highness has had no such knowledge or acquaintance.

Question: Have I, to your knowledge, ever had any acquaintance with, or knowledge of, Mrs. Clarke, or any communication with her, direct or indirect, upon the subject above named or any other?

Answer: I am confident that your Royal Highness never had.

Question: Have I ever expressed to you any sentiment which could induce you to believe that I approved of what was brought in Parliament against the Duke of York, or to any proceeding that would tend to his obloquy or disgrace?

Answer: Never. I have heard your Royal Highness lament the business *viva voce,* and you made the same communication to me in writing.

Question: Have you ever, to your recollection, expressed yourself either by word or in writing either to Colonel Wardle or to Mrs. Clarke, or to any other person connected with the investigation of the Duke of York's conduct, in any way that could give them reason to suppose that I approve of the measures or would countenance those concerned in trying to bring it forward?

Answer: Never. But I have, in the contrary, expressed myself that your Royal Highness would have a very different feeling.

Question: What were my expressions on the subject of the pamphlet which appeared passing censure on the conduct of the Duke of York and others of my family—and holding up my character to praise; and what have been the sentiments which I have uniformly expressed on similar publications, whether in the newspapers or otherwise?

Answer: I have invariably heard your Royal Highness regret that any person should attempt to do justice to your own character at the expense of that of the Duke of York, or of any other member of your family.

Question: During the ten years you have been my private secretary, when in the most confidential moments I have given vent to my wounded feelings upon professional subjects, did you ever hear me express myself inimical to the Duke of York, or that I entertained expectations of raising myself by his fall?

Answer: Never. On the contrary, I have frequently heard Your Royal Highness express yourself very differently.

Dodd's statement that he had never represented himself as Edward's agent to Colonel Wardle and Mrs. Clarke is difficult to believe. If Dodd had not been a party to the plot, neither Wardle nor Mrs. Clarke would have tolerated his presence in the carriage at Brighton during the fateful conversation. It seems fair to assume that Dodd, without Edward's knowledge, pledged Edward's support to Wardle and Mrs. Clarke. Edward himself must have detected Dodd's frailty. We are indebted to Roger Fulford's *Royal Dukes* for a translation of a letter on this matter which Edward wrote in French, in April, 1810, to the Duke of Orléans. Edward said that

Dodd was "more to be pitied than blamed in many things, and the imprudent things which he has unfortunately done have come from too great an enthusiasm for my service and too lively a sense of all the injustices we have suffered." Edward added that Dodd had resigned voluntarily from his service as "a necessary sacrifice to public opinion". It was typical of Edward's fidelity to his subordinates when he concluded with the remark that he had not lost any "esteem" for Dodd.

Early in 1810, Colonel Wardle was revealed as the man most directly responsible for initiating the scandal. He was sued by an upholsterer for the cost of refurnishing Mrs. Clarke's home, an expense he had undertaken as the price of her evidence before the Commons inquiry. The public was beginning to tire of the whole affair, and after this last flicker of sensation was glad to forget it.

From the opprobrium of the Commons inquiry the Duke of York recovered quickly. In 1811 it was apparent that the Duke of Wellington owed much of his success in the Peninsular War to the planning that had been carried out during the Duke of York's tenure as Commander-in-Chief. York, therefore, was reappointed to his old post and cheered by the House of Commons. This put him into a conciliatory mood, and he made an uneasy truce with Edward. At the funeral of their sister Princess Amelia, who had died of consumption, York lifted his glass and said with condescending magnaminity: "Though this is a sad occasion I must drink the health of poor Edward."

In another letter to the Duke of Orléans, poor Edward said he did not think the reconciliation would bring him any advantage. To his pessimism he now added caution. He avoided with elaborate and nervous care any act that might be construed as intervention in the affairs of his brothers. A good example of his wariness at this time was provided by his reaction to the troubles of Mrs. Fitzherbert, who was now separated once more from the Prince of Wales.

The Prince of Wales, who had a passion for women old enough to be his mother, had taken to the venerable but volatile embraces of Lady Hertford. For some probably degenerate reason, he insisted on Mrs. Fitzherbert being present in the Pavilion at Brighton when he flaunted this new paramour before his guests. Mrs. Fitzherbert revolted against such an indignity and refused to obey the summons. At this thwarting of his caprice, Wales was livid.

Generally speaking, the royal family regarded Mrs. Fitzherbert as a good influence on the Prince of Wales, and various members tried to patch up a peace between the heir to the throne and his morganatic wife. The Dukes of York and Clarence were among those who made these attempts, only to flee the room before Wales's wrath. Then, indirectly, Edward was entangled in the trouble. During a quarrel with the Prince of Wales Mrs. Fitzherbert let slip the remark that Edward, an old friend of hers, agreed with her policy of remaining away from the Pavilion when Lady Hertford was present. The Prince of Wales began to prance about the room cursing his brother.

Apprehensively, Edward took up his pen and reproached Mrs. Fitzherbert for dropping the unfortunate remark. "What has passed on this occasion," he wrote, "renders it absolutely necessary for me to implore you, whenever I have the happiness of seeing you again . . . that we never should touch upon that most delicate subject— the state of things between the Prince and yourself."

Edward needed to handle the Prince of Wales with care, because in 1811 the older brother's authority became the highest in the land. The King's mind collapsed completely and the Prince of Wales, in face of strong parliamentary opposition, was appointed Regent. By now the Regent was as bloated as a water-melon, and his arrogance was in proportion to his tumescence.

Edward, at forty-three, was also bulky, but hard and agile through much walking and riding. Determined to keep his virile appearance, he dyed his now greying red hair a dark brown. If there was vanity in this act there was also strategy, for he wished to impress the Regent as a man outstandingly fit for active service. Much as he disliked the Regent, Edward did everything possible to earn his brother's esteem, in the hope of getting back into the army. For example, he strongly opposed, in two speeches to the House of Lords, an act designed to restrict the Regent's power, and he organized a petition signed by thirty-two peers protesting against these limitations. But the Regent was unmoved by Edward's contriving. Sulking still over old grievances, he refrained from suggesting to the Duke of York that Edward should be given another command.

Through the great events which began in 1812 Edward fidgeted bitterly in a gilded pigeon-hole. "Just occasionally," writes Roger

Fulford in his *Royal Dukes,* "his field marshall's baton was drawn out of its case to attend a review, and he would sit his horse grimly watching defects in the troops he was powerless to correct."

Napoleon suddenly squandered four hundred thousand men in the snows of Russia. Returning to Paris almost alone, he was unable with the remnants of his once invincible legions to save the capital from invasion by vengeful Russians, Prussians and Austrians. Nor could he halt the advance onto French soil from Spain of the Duke of Wellington's British divisions. During the same period, on the other side of the Atlantic, British troops, freed from commitments in Europe by Napoleon's advance on Moscow, supported by Canadian militia, repelled triumphantly the ill-organized United States Army which attempted to conquer Canada.

In April, 1814, Napoleon abdicated and was exiled to Elba.

After twenty years of privation and bloodshed, England drained the cup of victory. Edward and Julie took part in the brilliant celebrations, though they were now an obscure and almost forgotten couple.

Edward glimmered briefly in the festivities that attended the restoration of the Bourbon dynasty to France. Louis XVIII, brother of the guillotined Louis XVI, was brought out of his long retirement in Hartwell, Buckinghamshire. The Regent made Louis' departure for France a state occasion, to be marked by balls, carnivals, ox-roasting, and processions.

On April 20, 1814, the Regent in Field Marshall's uniform set out from London to meet at Stanmore, Middlesex, Louis' royal procession, which was driving toward the capital. The Regent's postilions wore the Bourbon colours—golden fleur-de-lis on a white background. Eight white horses in gilded harness drew his carriage. When the Regent reached Stanmore he saw that the villagers had removed the horses from Louis' carriage and were hauling it themselves up a high street aflutter with Bourbon flags and brassy with the music of local bands. The enormous Louis, puffed up with years of idleness and epicurean dishes, smiled good-naturedly.

The two processions formed into one and headed for London. Crowds lined the entire route, waving flags and cheering. Louis and his niece, the Duchess of Angoulême, rode in the Regent's carriage beneath the royal standard. The Regent sat opposite them, with his back to the horses. Alongside clattered a sovereign's escort of Life

Guards and one hundred mounted gentlemen, including the burly
Edward. The occasion was so cordial that Peter Pindar wrote:

> And France's hope and Britain's heir
> Were, truth, a most congenial pair;
> Two round, tun-bellied thriving rakes
> Like oxen fed on linseed cakes.

Later the Regent gave a reception for Louis at Carlton House,
which was hung with banners inscribed: RUSSIA: AUSTRIA:
VIVENT LES BOURBONS: PRUSSIA: ENGLAND. Edward was among the
first to be presented to the French King. Far back in the order of
precedence was Julie, now in her middle forties, but still petite,
sparkling, and graceful; a little out of date, perhaps, in the modesty
of her neckline and in the wig to which she still clung, but far removed from that image of lace, lavender, and knotted veins that was
conjured up when Mrs. Clarke described her as an "old French
lady". One can imagine Julie, when the formalities were over, com-
forting poor Mrs. Fitzherbert, who felt lonely, neglected, and guilty.

Although she had been passed by when the invitations were
issued, Mrs. Fitzherbert could not bear to miss so great an event. So
she suffered the malignant glances of Lady Hertford and the em-
purpled rage of the Regent, as she tiptoed about the background,
seeking out good friends like Julie who would understand her and
forgive her gate-crashing.

On April 23, 1814, Louis XVIII and his *entourage* left London
for Dover, where he was to embark for France. Edward, in his field
marshall's uniform, and the Duke of Sussex, in Highland dress, rode
at the windows of his carriage. From Dover, Louis set sail amid the
cheers of ten thousand English spectators. At the end of the pier the
Regent, with Edward and the Duke of Sussex, stood bowing.

In June the Regent received, with more bands and bunting, Tsar
Alexander of Russia and the King of Prussia, who was accompanied
by his military hero, Marshal Blücher. The Regent led a state procession to the Guildhall, where the sovereigns dined with the Lord
Mayor of London. Each of the Regent's brothers, including Edward,
rode alone in his own carriage.

There followed in July the glittering reception to Wellington, in
honour of his victories in Spain and Portugal. Carlton House was

not big enough to accommodate the hundreds of guests, so the Regent ordered it surrounded with huge tents hung with silken drapes and interconnected with covered walks. The climax of the evening was the grand entrance of all the members of the royal family save the poor demented King. The Regent and the Queen came first, then Edward with the Princess Augusta. Other princes and princesses followed, and the Duke of York, making one of his rare appearances with his wife, strode in last, to the new music of "The Prince Regent's March". Supper was served and then, to the tune of "Voulez-vous Dancer, Mademoiselle", the thirty-eight-year-old Princess Mary, partnered by the stripling Duke of Devonshire, opened the ball. Dancing continued until six o'clock in the morning.

During the festivities a pretty young Diana who was hunting for mementoes of celebrities went over to the corner in which Edward and Julie were standing and asked the Prince for a lock of his hair. "You must be mistaken, ma'am," said Edward. "I am only the Duke of Kent." The girl made a moue of disappointment and rustled off in search of more illustrious game. An onlooker saw Edward and Julie laugh.

But many times that evening the sight of Wellington must have filled them with sadness. During the Iron Duke's attack on Badajoz young Edward de Salaberry, their godson, had fallen. News of his death was followed quickly by casualty lists from India which anounced that his two brothers, Maurice and Chevalier, had died on active service of tropical disease. It was months before Julie dared to send a message of sympathy to their parents, Louis and Catherine de Salaberry, in Quebec City. Finally, on September 28, 1814, she picked up her pen.

"I ought not to be reproached for my silence," she wrote. "Alas, I had a great desire to write but I felt I could not do so without exposing my afflicted friend *La Souris* to a blow that might be fatal. It was necessary to act with prudence and I have waited until the time would arrive when I might write without increasing her grief. I hope that her health, which is so precious, will be completely restored to her, and that religion, in giving her the consoling hope that she will again see her children in a better world, will relieve the anguish of her heart." Julie went on to say: "My memory will always recall Quebec and Beauport and a friendship which has triumphed over twenty years of absence."

She concluded with a reference to the oldest soldier son, Colonel Charles de Salaberry, now a hero of the War of 1812. In 1813 he had commanded at Chateaugay, on the border between New York State and Quebec, about six hundred Canadian Fencibles who soundly defeated an invading force of five thousand Americans. "All the public papers here are full of his great deeds," wrote Julie, "and you can easily fancy how I feel. I am as proud as if he were my own brother and I do not fail to say to all who speak to me: 'The young man whom you saw here is *the* Mr. de Salaberry who has conducted himself with such heroism.' It gives great pleasure to repeat this. I wish you to give him a thousand remembrances from me and to thank him for having given my name to his first-born."

Edward expressed a professional opinion that must have gratified the military hearts of the de Salaberry father and son. He wrote to Louis de Salaberry: "I do not hesitate to declare that you have reason to be proud of the victory gained by my protégé over forces so superior in number. He displayed talent and judgment rarely to be found unless in veterans, both in making his dispositions and during the battle."

During the War of 1812 Edward stumped up and down the country making speeches about the valour of the Canadians in the border skirmishes that erupted all along the St. Lawrence River and the Great Lakes. He also inaugurated a charity that raised ten thousand pounds for the relief of British residents in the United States who had been forced to flee to Canada.

The Hundred Days came in 1815, and once more Edward tried to get a command under Wellington. Even if the Regent and the Duke of York had relented to the extent of agreeing in principle, it is doubtful whether Wellington would have accepted Edward. The haughty, reactionary old warrior despised the liberal theories which Edward was now expounding on both military and civil affairs.

After the Battle of Waterloo, Edward knew that his major aspiration was hopeless. As an anodyne for his disappointment, he devoted most of his time to the arts and sciences, and to charities. Among the scores of new societies to which he lent his name were the Theatrical Charitable Fund, the Literary Fund, the Royal Society of Musicians, the Incorporated Society in Scotland for Propagating Christian Knowledge, the Freemason's Charity, the National Benevolent Society, and St. George's Hospital. In 1815 he presided at more than fifty meetings, and in his speeches revealed himself as a zealot for reform. At a meeting of the Literary Fund he said: "England, which has Chelsea and Greenwich for decayed soldiers and sailors, might with propriety provide some peaceful asylum for the aged and worn out writer."

Politically he was a Whig and far in advance of contemporary thought on economy. At one meeting of the National Benevolent Society he said that individual generosity was an inadequate remedy for poverty. "No charitable provision or establishment," he said, "could remedy the evil of a depressed working class."

Edward's radical views were regarded as disreputable by most aristocrats, yet neither the arguments nor the reproaches of his family and friends could shake them. At a meeting of the St. Patrick's Charitable Society in 1815, Edward said: "My politics are no secret nor am I ashamed to avow them." Once Edward was asked if he did not think that the new socialism then being preached was rather dangerous and levelling. He replied: "I foresee results. I know that there will be a much more just equality of our race, and an equality that will give much more security and happiness to all than does the present system. It is for this reason I so much approve and give it my support."

Edward was influenced strongly by Robert Owen, the eccentric father of British socialism. Owen, a wealthy cotton manufacturer, established in New Lanark, on the banks of the Clyde in Scotland, a company town. The mill workers lived in clean, roomy homes provided by the company and received a measure of education at company expense. In an effort to achieve what he regarded as a healthful balance between the old agricultural and the new industrial economy, Owen set aside a number of hours in each employee's day for work in the fields that surrounded the factory, and made the community partly self-supporting.

Owen's community, in which theft, drunkenness, immorality, and malnutrition were rare, was the wonder of visitors from all over the world. Owen reviled the cotton magnates of Lancashire and Yorkshire for their sweating of labour, employment of children, and callous indifference to the living conditions of the operatives. Improve a man's environment, he said, and you improve his character.

Edward sent his physician, Doctor H. Grey MacNab, up to Scotland to prepare a first-hand account of Owen's farm-factory settlement. After studying MacNab's report, Edward wrote to Owen: "I acknowledge myself to be a full and devoted convert to your philosophy, spirit and practice. But we must act with prudence and foresight. The English are emphatically a practical people."

With a brother, the Duke of Sussex, Edward visited one day Owen's London home in Bedford Square to inspect a pyramid of cubes which represented the proportions of England's different degrees of society. At the bottom was an enormous cube representing the working classes, and at the top a tiny cube representing royalty, peers, and prelates. The Duke of Sussex was so astonished at the minute dimensions of his class that impulsively he pushed his elbow into his brother's side and gasped: "Edward! Do you see that?" Edward nodded with the superior air of a man who was already well aware of the cube's significance.

When Owen became a spiritualist he lost the interest and approval of many influential men, as deviation from Church of England precepts at that time was regarded as execrable. Edward, however, continued to visit Owen and to defend him in conversation. In consequence he was looked upon by his family as a crank.

In matters of faith, Edward was, for his day, remarkably impartial. In the House of Lords, for example, he risked much of his growing popularity in the North by speaking warmly in favour of the Catholic Emancipation Bill. About the same time he earned a rebuke from the Archbishop of Canterbury for his energetic support of a body with Methodist leanings. This was the British or Lancastrian System for the Education of the Labouring and Manufacturing Classes of Society of Every Religious Persuasion, an organization that eventually became the British and Foreign Schools Society. Its function was to promote the educational methods devised by Joseph Lancaster, a London-born scholar whose theories were widely adopted in the United Kingdom, Holland, France, Germany, and many Latin American states.

Lancaster made a lecture tour of Canada and the United States, and educators in these countries, too, put into practice many of his principles. The central idea was to make cheap schooling available to the working classes by employing older students to assist in the teaching of younger students. Through Edward's influence, Lancaster's system was introduced into many British regiments, and did much to diminish the high illiteracy rate of the troops. But because it was tinged with dissent, it was frowned upon by the Church of England.

Indeed the Church of England, already in a panic at the spread of Methodism in the industrial North, established its own society to counter the influence of Lancaster. This was the National Society for Promoting the Education of the Poor in the Principles of the Established Church, and it founded the Anglican National Schools. The Queen and the Royal Princesses, with laudible impartiality, subscribed to both bodies. But Edward, who regarded the Church of England as being far too tardy in its efforts to enlighten the poor, confined his subscriptions to the pioneering Lancastrians.

By 1815, Edward was giving more than a thousand pounds a year to charity. Yet the Princess Lieven, brilliant wife of the Russian Ambassador to England, was not impressed. In a letter to her lover, the Austrian diplomat Prince Von Metternich, she described Edward as "false, hard and greedy". She added: "His good qualities are only for show." This rather cruel condemnation was probably based upon Edward's notorious importunity in matters connected with his personal finances.

So far as his own income was concerned, Edward was grasping, and frequently he stooped to flattery, bluster, and whining in his attempts to pry more money out of the Government. There was a spot of conceit in his make-up which blinded him to the fact that his debts, now up to a staggering total of two hundred thousand pounds, were the result of his own vanity. Ever since his Geneva days his homes, horses, servants, equipments, libraries, cellars, entertainments, and charities had been, if not unduly princely, wholly out of step with his pay. Edward's claim that he had been stinted far more than his brothers was valid but this hardly excused the extent to which he had lived beyond his means. Long after he was dead his daughter Victoria was paying off the innumerable debts he had incurred.

Some of the blame for Edward's predicament probably lay with John Conroy, his principal financial adviser. Conroy was a lickspittle who contrived to hold his position in the Kent household long after Victoria came to the throne. Queen Victoria detested him, partly for his supple knees and partly because she believed he had seduced her widowed mother. Had Conroy shown firmness with

Edward in financial matters, the Prince's plight might well have been less severe. As things were, whenever Edward was short of cash, he borrowed large and small sums indiscriminately. Many of his borrowings were highly indiscreet. Even the commoner Robert Owen, who was inclined to chatter, was touched for various sums ranging between one hundred and five hundred pounds.

Since 1806, Edward's parliamentary grant had been £18,000 a year. His pay as Ranger of Hampton Court and as Governor of Gibraltar—the latter an office to which he had clung out of financial necessity and with an increasing sense of guilt—augmented his annual income to £24,000. He would have been able to struggle along in his four costly homes if his creditors in Gibraltar, Canada and London had been content with the interest on their loans. But in 1815, many of them were beginning to clamour for repayment of the capital. The pressure was so great that Edward was at his wits' end.

The depths of his despair may be measured in the servility and diffusion with which he wrote, in June of 1815, begging the Regent to influence the Government to help him out. The letter read in part:

My Dear Brother:

The recollection of those habits of unreserved confidence in which it was my good fortune to live with you in former days, and of the innumerable marks of friendship and affection which I almost daily received at your hands, added to that warm attachment I must ever feel for you to the latest hour of my existence, as ever having been my steadiest friend in many of the most trying moments of my life, renders it impossible for me to reconcile it to my feelings to leave it to your ministers to be the first to acquaint you with my having addressed through them an official appeal to your justice for relief at a moment when, overwhelmed with embarrassments, I could no longer refrain from taking that step. . . . I am sure . . . that you will judge my claim from your own upright, just mind and good heart, as then I can not doubt of the result being favourable to my interest. With every sentiment of warmest devotion and attachment I remain, my dearest brother,
Your faithful and affectionate Edward

The Regent read Edward's pitiable letter with a curl of the lip. Instead of replying personally, he handed it over to Prime Minister the Earl of Liverpool. Liverpool wrote to Edward saying that nothing could be done. He reminded him that his parliamentary grant had been raised from twelve to eighteen thousand pounds a year in 1806, and that in this respect he stood on the same footing as all his brothers save the Regent.

Edward then wrote to Home Secretary Lord Sidmouth, who had been Prime Minister during his second tour of service at Gibraltar. He advanced as grounds for financial assistance his restoration of military morale on the Rock. No more forlorn argument could have been presented to Sidmouth, who officially had endorsed the view that Edward's measures had been too severe.

Ironically enough, Sidmouth was later to get a taste of Edward's own medicine. He was execrated in 1819, for precipitating "The Battle of Peterloo", an occasion on which he ordered out mounted troops to repress a peaceful demonstration of cotton operatives on Peter's Field, Manchester. Several fatalities and many injuries resulted from the troopers' use of swords. Perhaps at this later period Sidmouth looked back on Edward's problem at Gibraltar with more sympathy. Meanwhile, however, he wrote to the debt-ridden Prince regretting that he could be of no service.

Edward's last attempt to obtain extra money from the Government took the form of many letters to the War Office pointing out that as the result of accidents, wrecks and enemy gunfire he had lost on active service half a dozen general officers' equipments, valued in total at more than thirty thousand pounds. The War Office replied that there was no clause in army regulations under which he could be reimbursed.

To help Edward through a couple of tight spots, in which the shadow of the bankruptcy court loomed chillingly close, Lord Fitzwilliam and Lord Dundas lent him money. But it was Robert Owen who early in 1815 visited Edward and suggested that he should seek a cure for his trouble rather than a succession of palliatives. After the interview Edward appointed as his trustees William Allen, one of Owen's partners, and Joseph Hume, the radical. To them he handed over seventeen thousand pounds a year of his income, for regular repayment of his debts by instalments. On the remaining seven thousand he would try to live. Julie, who had been receiving an allowance of one thousand pounds a year, insisted on Edward's reducing it to four hundred. For a year Edward and Julie lived in conditions of relative frugality. They cut down their entertaining to a minimum, gave up their box at Drury Lane, and closed all their homes but Castle Hill Lodge. Edward kept only one saddle horse, his favourite charger.

During this period of retrenchment Edward was tempted to risk once again the displeasure of the Regent. The Princess Charlotte, daughter of the Regent and of Caroline, Princess of Wales, and second in the line of succession to the throne, enlisted his help in her love affair with Prince Leopold of Saxe-Saalfeld-Coburg. Charlotte would have been a siren had not her beauty been marred slightly by a stutter and a lop-sided stance—afflictions contracted, perhaps, as the result of being born into a broken and profligate home. She was high-strung, headstrong, and romantic, yet capable of candour, good humour, and affection. In her late teens she had arrested, with her freshness and sunny disposition, a considerable decline in the popularity of the Throne. Crowds cheered her when they recognized her driving or riding in Hyde Park. They saw in her, as a future Queen Regnant, hopes of a better monarchy to come.

Prince Leopold of Saxe-Saalfeld-Cobourg was an ambitious younger son of a tiny German duchy, and the thoughtful, abstemious, rather pedantic pupil of that formidable Baron Stockmar who was to have such influence later on Queen Victoria's life. Leopold fell in love with Charlotte during a visit to England, but thought twice about marrying her, because of the bizarre environment in which she had been reared by the Princess of Wales, and the contemptible character of her father the Regent. The shock any Coburg must have experienced on admission to the House of Hanover was explained succinctly by Pierre Berton in his book *The Royal Family*. Berton wrote:

> The Coburgs were everything the Hanovers were not. The Coburgs were sparse, dry men; the Hanovers were gross giants. The Coburgs' prevailing uniform was black; the Hanovers wore loud and often vulgar clothing. The Coburgs sheltered their carefully controlled emotions behind graven faces; the Hanovers wore their hearts and temperaments on their brocaded sleeve. The Coburgs followed the chill light of their intellect; the Hanovers

were slaves to the hot dictatorship of their blood. The Coburgs were discreet, taciturn, upright and frugal; the Hanovers were tactless, outspoken, lusty and prodigal.

Edward, however, was the exception to the Hanoverian rule. Although he was utterly Hanoverian in physique, he had more in common temperamentally with the Coburgs. On visiting Edward and Julie at Castle Hill Lodge, Leopold found to his relief that at least one Hanoverian knew how to live in decency and tranquility. Edward became much attached to young Leopold and convinced him that a marriage to the Princess Charlotte would not be beyond the bounds of Coburg prudence.

For many months, of course, the Regent, who had never shown much love for his daughter, displayed violent and capricious objections to the marriage. His attitude was so hostile that he kept Charlotte in conditions that amounted almost to imprisonment at Windsor Castle, and practically ordered Leopold to return to Germany. But Edward kept the two lovers in touch by employing one of his equerries to travel back and forth between Coburg and Windsor with their letters. Fortunately for Edward, the Regent never discovered his services as an intermediary. Had he done so he would probably never have relented, as he did in the end, and consented to the betrothal of Charlotte and Leopold.

Charlotte's gratitude to Edward showed itself in a most curious and brash suggestion. Wouldn't it be a good idea, she said, late in 1815, if Edward got rid of Julie and married Leopold's sister, the Princess Victoria of Saxe-Saalfeld-Coburg, a most comely widow of thirty. Edward dismissed the suggestion with a frown and reproached Charlotte for her boldness.

It was Julie alone who was making his life tolerable at Castle Hill Lodge during this painful economy wave. Edward's increasingly heavy sense of persecution, his dense bouts of self-pity, his depressing exhibitions of censoriousness, and his ponderous social bearing were leavened by the yeast of Julie's laughter, the sparkle of her conversation, the lilt of her little French songs at the spinet, and the flavour of her delicate cuisine.

That she sustained Edward with tenderness, ardour, affectionate teasing, and encouragement during this bleak year, is indubitable. On one of those rare occasions on which Edward permitted an outsider a glimpse of his feelings for Julie, he wrote to de Salaberry: "I am sure you will be pleased to know that what our life was when we were beside you, so it has continued during twenty years since we left Canada, and I love to think that twenty years hence it may be the same."

Poor Edward, poor Julie!

Chapter XI

DURING the aftermath of Waterloo shopkeepers filled their windows with coloured cartoons lampooning the times. One of the most derisive consisted of four frames entitled "John Bull's Progress". In the first frame a plump John Bull, with a tankard of ale in his hand, was shown sitting contentedly by a cosy fireplace after a hard day in the fields. In the background his wife worked happily at her spinning-wheel, a buxom daughter could be seen entering the room with a churn full of butter, and two well-clad younger children chattered merrily with a caged parrot. In the second frame John Bull was shown in soldier's uniform, marching proudly off, to drum, fife and trumpet, to battle against the French. Frame three depicted the wife and children in the act of entering a pawnshop, carrying the spinning-wheel, the butter churn, the caged parrot, and the bread-winner's spades, hoes and rakes. The last frame showed the mother and children, ragged and emaciated, crouching on the floor in a hovel, and staring in horror at the father, who was returning from the war—a gaunt hulk of a man now, with sunken cheeks, a patch over one eye, and a missing leg; on crutches and with his uniform in tatters.

For the poor the five years that followed Waterloo were lean. The industrial North was wracked by bouts of unemployment as the ever improving machinery eliminated labour, as demobilization of the army reduced demand for cloth and steel, and as the reopening of markets in Europe and North America proved a slow and uncertain business. The agricultural South, which had been committed during the war to intensive production of corn, had a glut on its hands. Unemployment spread as old sources of grain in Europe and North America became available once more.

But neither factory workers nor field labourers were able to benefit from the lower corn prices that should have resulted from bursting bins. In 1815 an iniquitous Corn Law was introduced to protect the interests of the English landowners. It raised the price of European and American corn by excessive import duties, and so sustained the price of domestic corn at a level that was far above the poor man's pocket. In the North, factory workers rioted and smashed many of the new machines that had deprived them of jobs. In the South the farm labourers jeered at the passing gentry, and engaged in the risky game of poaching in order to eat.

The landless poor tended to become poorer, and to espouse the the radical, republican, nonconformist sentiments voiced by an increasing number of orators and journalists. Meanwhile the landed rich, waxing fat on their ground rents, tended to become more and more reactionary and repressive, and by appropriating the monarchy and the Established Church for their figurehead and mast did more to sully these institutions than the peevish, arrogant, and degenerate Regent himself.

Life in the middle classes was an intolerable gamble. The violent fluctuations of supply and demand made millionaires overnight of some merchants, manufacturers and farmers. But many more were bankrupted because they were overstocked with manufactured goods that were no longer needed, or with foodstuffs that the people could not afford to buy. According to their unpredictable fortunes the middle classes divided into a lower and an upper bracket, the lower siding generally with the multitude, the upper with the nobility.

In the rising conflict between the rich and the poor, a conflict rendered ever more acrimonious by the vacillation of the fast-expanding but highly unstable middle class, one fragment of society pursued a serene and steady course. It was a course that eventually filled with cement the void between the warring factions and produced the solid nation of the Victorian age. This fragment was known as "the steam-intellect society". Its members were the engineering products of the mechanics' institutes, a movement of intelligent, self-educated workmen who banded together at night for the study of machines and ways of improving them. They became the *élite* of the Industrial Revolution, and were to be found throughout the land at the head of huge nomadic gangs of labourers. They dug mines and canals, built bridges, locks and factories, bored tunnels, laid macadam highways, and pored over maps seeking suitable routes for the railroads that they knew were bound to come.

It was the scientific genius of these men that invested the middle class with a political importance it had never known before. Their expanding and irrevocable influence on political economy eventually forced the passage, in 1832, of the first Reform Bill, which tripled the electorate and opened the safety valve on a boiler that was about to explode into a republican revolution. Meanwhile, in 1815, England was riven by class warfare. In one sense it was a war between the England of Mr. Pickwick and the England of Oliver Twist.

Foreign visitors were still entranced as they bowled rapidly along the new hard roads in fast, comfortable scarlet coaches; past fields of fat cattle, ducks, geese and chickens; past gracious country homes with Palladian columns and ornamental gardens; past picturesque cottages with thatched roofs and mullioned windows; and into the crooked little towns, where grinning ostlers unhitched the steaming horses, and a manservant called "Boots" carried their bags into cosy inns that shone with brassware and polished oak and smelled of sizzling beef, foaming ale, and sweet wood smoke.

On certain evenings the visitors might look out of their bedroom windows, over the romantic old sign of the inn, and see in the dusk a gang of harvesters, flush for once with money, dancing into town behind a fiddler. Or they might watch a procession of gigs, post-chaises, wagons, and mounted men taking off on an all-night journey to the great boxing match that was to be staged next day in a field twenty-five miles away. Or they might find their thoughts taken back to bloodier times as a regiment of infantry veterans, in tall shakos, red coats and narrow white trousers, tramped by, to the time-shouting of sergeants, on its long northward march to a new station in Scotland.

In such colourful moments it was easy to forget the village idiot who drooled down an adjacent back alley, the thin, white-faced children who fought for a potato in some dank and mouldering nearby cottage, and the half-starved poacher who waited in agony, with his legs in the steel teeth of a man-trap, for the gamekeeper, who would bring him up next day before the magistrate.

Nor was it likely that the visitors would bother to press so far north as Manchester, where skinny infants crawled under the clattering looms for twelve hours a day, sweeping up cotton fluff in factories reeking of hot oil and human sweat; where women, naked to the waist, panted on their hands and knees along the lower workings of mines, with a leather collar around their necks, and with a pull-chain running down between their breasts and out between their legs to a train of railway trolleys loaded with coal; where men like scarecrows tottered over the bleak moors from one valley to another, seeking work in vain, and returning at night to sleep in a slum, on a bare, lice-infested floor, among the exhausted bodies of wives and children who had toiled all day without earning for the family the price of one meat meal.

For some England was still the land of roast beef, beer, and pints of imported claret. But for many more it was the land of weak tea and unbuttered bread.

In the peoples' clothing, a new-born utilitarianism and materialism obliterated all but a few faint traces of the gorgeous eighteenth century. Women still wore dresses cut low over the bosom—so low, in fact, as to be gross and repellent in many cases. But the filmy draped finery of earlier days had given place to full thick skirts, with apron fronts and heavy flounces, to poke bonnets and ugly high-buttoned boots. A few men still wore knee breeches, but most wore trousers with heel straps that held the cuffs tight around the ankles, weighty tweed coats in sombre colours, high stiff collars with a stock or a cravat, and tall fuzzy top hats with a curling brim.

Even the Duke of York, who disliked innovations intensely, had taken to trousers, probably as a heaven-sent concealment for his scrawny legs. It was rumoured that while morbidly studying his demented father through a peep-hole he had caught the strap of his left trouser leg in the spur on his right heel, and in this ankle-locked predicament had fallen over backward, with a sickening crash, and stunned himself. Such stories were told with glee, for the House of Hanover, in its continued debauchery, and its chronic blindness to the extent of the hardship among the nation's sixteen million people, was fast becoming an object of mockery and hate.

Edward, who could do little to retrieve his family's waning popularity, found England a depressing place—and, with only seven thousand pounds a year to live on, highly expensive. Julie, too, who had once just stopped short of calling London "a hole", felt in need of a change. The Continent, so long closed to Englishmen by war, began to beckon. Scores of English families with modest private incomes had moved to Brussels, where the cost of living was lower.

Prince Leopold, now the Princess Charlotte's husband, advised Edward to follow their example.

In March, 1816, Edward crossed to Brussels and rented for a year, at a fee of three hundred pounds, a home belonging to the Flemish Count de Maldegham. During the war it had deteriorated, and Edward, much to the consternation of his trustees, borrowed more money to renovate it. According to a Mr. Pryse Gordon, a former army officer who took up residence in Brussels and left a memoir of the occasion, Edward repainted the house inside and out, replanted the garden with "the choicest flowers and rarest shrubs available", and repaired the crumbling stables.

For transport he shipped from England his favourite vehicle, which he had bought in Canada twenty years before and had preserved ever since with loving care and economy. It was a curricle, a light, hooded, two-wheeled carriage drawn by a pair of horses harnessed side by side. As he showed it off to the Count de Maldegham he said: "I was never spilt out of it but once, near the falls of Niagara, over a concealed stump in a wood just cleared." The Allied armies were selling mounts off cheaply, and Edward bought two carriage horses and two saddle horses. He also shipped from England his charger, a fine stallion, and decided to make a little extra money by putting it at stud.

Alongside the house was a quarter of an acre of waste ground which had been used as a garbage dump and was an offence to the eyes and nose. Edward approached the Brussels City Council and asked them to clear it up. But the Council said that there were no municipal funds available for the job, and that in any event the land was to be used, in a year or so, for the laying of a new street.

Edward felt he could not bring Julie to Brussels while this eyesore remained, so he secured the permission of the Council to improve the site himself. He cleaned it up and covered it with neatly sanded serpentine walks, bowers of rambler roses, rockeries, clumps of flowering shrubs, and sweeps of lawn. Pryse Gordon said that the whole area was "enclosed with a trellis-work of willow with the bark on, which saved the expense of painting". The Flemings came from miles around to view Edward's handiwork; and, in the words of Pryse Gordon, the young Count de Maldegham "could hardly recognize his late abode".

In choosing his Brussels staff Edward was almost unbearably

meticulous. When a man applied to him for a post as groom he wrote six letters to the applicant's late master, enquiring into the most minute details of his family, education and character. In a seventh letter he enquired if the man had a wife. On learning that he had, Edward rejected him, explaining that he did not employ married men.

In July, 1816, Edward was satisfied that the Brussels house was sufficiently attractive for Julie, and he returned to England for the purpose of escorting her back across the Channel. When they were reunited at Castle Hill Lodge, Julie asked a favour of him: before settling in Brussels, she said, she would like to go to Paris to visit her sister, the Comtesse de Jensac, whom she had not seen since the French Revolution. Edward readily agreed, and decided that while Julie visited Paris he would make a tour of all those parts of northern Europe from which Englishmen had been debarred for so long by the war.

They crossed the Channel together. At Calais they parted, Julie heading south to Paris, and Edward north for Brussels. What happened next is best told in Edward's own words to Mrs. Fitzherbert. This well-known letter, written from Brussels on December 20, 1816, was first quoted by W. H. Wilkins in his *Mrs. Fitzherbert and George IV*. Edward wrote in part:

My Dearest Mrs. Fitzherbert:

It is now four months since I left England, and rather more than that since I took my leave of **you**. During the first half of that time I have been a great traveller, and little able to write to anyone. And during the last two months I have been so taken up with the necessary details to make myself comfortable that I have been only just able to reply to those of my correspondents who have written to me here.

I shall now give you a hasty sketch of my proceedings. I left dear Castle Hill at 3 o'clock on the 19th of August. I was detained here in Brussels till 12th of September owing to the non-arrival of my servants, equipage, and baggage. But it was well I stayed, for after I turned my back very little was done to this old mansion I occupy, all the workmen being called off to prepare for the court, who were to arrive about the third week in October.

On the 12th September, however, I set out accompanied by Lieut.-Colonel Muller of my regiment, in my travelling barouche, with my valet, and one footman on the box and another in the corner. Passing through Liége, Aix-la-Chapelle, Cologne, Coblenz and Mayence, I reached Frankfort on the 15th. There I stayed three days on account of meeting my old Uncle, the *then* reigning Duke of Mecklenburg-Strelitz (since dead), and went in company with him to visit the Landgrave of Hesse-Homburg, whose eldest son was an old German friend of mine. There was a fine-ish young woman, a Princess of Anhalt-Dessau, granddaughter of the old people, who is talked of as my brother Adolphus's future bride, but perhaps with as little foundation as that odious Princess Amalia of Baden, whom I find the papers have thought fit to give to *me!*

From Frankfort I went to Darmstadt, where I passed an evening with my old acquaintances the Grand-Duke and Duchess (formerly a celebrated beauty), by whom I was most hospitably received. The next day I went to Karlsruhe, where I saw the *old Madam* above alluded to (Princess Amalia), who is twin sister of the Queen of Bavaria, sister of the Empress of Russia, of the ex-Queen of Sweden, and of the Hereditary Grand Duchess of Hesse-Darmstadt. But from her being the *only one* of the six sisters left on hand at the age of forty-one, and the eldest *too,* you may judge how little *desirable* she is.

I must, however, say that I was most hospitably and magnificently entertained by the Landgravine, her mother, and was compensated for the ennui of her company by becoming acquainted with that most lively, fascinating little creature, Stéphanie de Beauharnais, now Grand Duchess of Baden, her sister-in-law.

On the night of the 21st I left Karlsruhe, after a *séjour* there not exceeding thirty hours, and reached Stuttgart to breakfast on the 22nd, when you will easily imagine the pleasure my sister and myself experienced after a separation of more than one-and-thirty years. I remained *with her* till the third of October, I *may* say *comblé de politesses et d'attentions* from her husband and with many proofs of affection from herself.

I had then intended going by way of Strasburg and Luxemburg straight to Cambrai, the original intention of the Duke of

Wellington having been to hold his grand review on the 11th or 12th. But the lateness of the harvest obliging him to postpone it till the 21st, I found that I had just time to run over to Paris. And so, proceeding first to Wurtzburg to pay a visit to the Prince Royal of Bavaria, who married a cousin of ours, a very sweet woman, I pushed on by the route of Mannheim, Metz, and Verdun to Paris, which I reached on the 8th of October. The only incident that I met with worth noticing at Wurzburg was my becoming acquainted there with the Empress of Austria, one of the plainest, yet one of the most pleasing, mannerly women, I have ever met with. . . .

I was most kindly received in Paris by all the royal family. I had two audiences of the King, and dined with him once. I also dined once with Duchess-Dowager of Orléans, once with the English Ambassador, and once with the Hanoverian Minister, and all the other days at home. My evenings I generally went to the theatre in a private box, and the morning I devoted to seeing those objects that I considered most deserving of attention, accompanied by —, a very intelligent young man. I had thus the good fortune to be able to inspect everything with great comfort, being perfectly *incog.* except at Versailles, St. Cloud and Les Invalides, where I was, of course, obliged to appear with some one from the court to attend me. In short the day was never long enough for all I had to do, and I left a great deal to see for another time.

I left Paris on the 19th, for Cambrai, taking on my way Chantilly and Compiégne. At the former place I saw old Prince Condé, much broke, yet apparently happy and resigned. Not withstanding the dreadful state of the weather and the ground on the morning of the 23rd, at 6 o'clock we separated, he being bound for Paris and I to Brussels. Here I have remained ever since except going once, on November 2nd, to take my Birthday dinner with the officers of my own Corps *at their request,* and upon which occasion the Duke of Wellington and Lord Hill came over from Cambrai to meet me. . . .

The Court was already arrived here on my return from my journey. I was received by the King, Queen, Prince of Orange and his young wife, and Prince Frederick his brother, with every possible mark of politeness and good-humour. I am asked to dine, or sup, with them whenever they have any public party, but this is rare as the court lives uncommonly retired by choice, perhaps more so than is good for the sake of establishing a degree of popularity in the new capital. Otherwise I accept no invitations, as there is such a mixture of company of all countries and politics in this place that it would be quite impossible to discriminate. And I only occasionally invite four, but oftener two, friends to dinner, to have my rubber of whist at what evenings we don't go to the theatre, where, by-the-by, the performance is very passable.

I continue to be an early riser, but not so early as I was at home, for I now rise at half past six, or a quarter before seven, instead of at five as I used to do; and I am seldom out of bed after eleven, the theatre rarely being over after ten, and all parties, except amongst *our* countrymen, breaking up about the same hour. Thus you see I am living most quietly, and I trust contentedly, in the full spirit of my plan of economy and retrenchment. My house, though old, thanks to painting, papering, whitewashing, carpeting, and putting up a number of stoves, is very tolerably comfortable, totally *isolé* from any other, not overlooked, and with a fine flower garden and small shrubbery, a good deal of fruit on the wall and on standards, and I have the advantage of having all my horses, equipages, and stablemen within my own yard.

I had intended running over to England for about three weeks at the end of October, or the beginning of November . . . but now I look forward to the *probability,* though not to the *certainty* of paying you a visit in the spring. But whether I do so or not (after my presuming to bore you with so long a letter about myself, which nothing could warrant my doing but my confidence in your regard for me) do not doubt the sincerity of that lasting and warm attachment, with which I am, my dearest Mrs. Fitzherbert, ever your most faithful, devoted and affectionate

Edward

Edward was prompted by discretion, even in letters to so good a friend as Mrs. Fitzherbert, to refrain from mentioning Julie by name. Mrs. Fitzherbert, of course, took it as read that he stayed in

Paris with Julie's relatives. The "intelligent young man" who accompanied Edward on a sight-seeing tour, and whose name he left blank, was one of Julie's nephews, a son of the Comtesse de Jensac.

For a year Edward and Julie led an idyllic life in Brussels. They were now both forty-nine, yet their visitors marvelled at the warmth of the affection they displayed for one another. By day Edward kept himself occupied in visits to his old regiment, the Royal Fusiliers, which was stationed on the outskirts of the city; with the running of the stable, where his stallion serviced brood mares from miles around; and with letter-writing to the scores of social-welfare institutions in England of which he was still a patron. Couriers from the British Embassy staggered up to his home with an average of one hundred and fifty letters a week. When his new military secretary, Captain Bessel Harvey of the Royal Scots, complained that he could not keep up with the volume of work, Edward paid two sergeants from the Royal Fusiliers to give part-time help.

Julie renewed her acquaintance with many French and Belgian nobles she had known before the Revolution, entertained the numerous relatives of Louis Philippe who visited Brussels, and once went with Edward to call on Mrs. Fitzherbert, who was spending a holiday at the nearby Hôtel d'Angleterre.

With their small dinner-parties, music, whist, and occasional visits to the theatre, Edward and Julie were content. Edward's seven thousand pounds a year sufficed for their needs; the knowledge that his creditors were being steadily paid off was heartening; the Gallic air of Brussels proved a tonic to their spirits; and the assurance of a long peace seemed to promise them a restful middle age. Indeed Edward and Julie might have spent the remainder of their days in Brussels but for a calamity that, in the moment of their greatest bliss, tore them cruelly apart.

On Saturday, November 6, 1817, Princess Charlotte, heir presumptive to the throne, died in childbirth. The nation went into mourning, and the widower, Prince Leopold, was prostrated by grief. For a few weeks the United Kingdom was so stunned that the press refrained from comment on the fact that no other legal children of Princess Charlotte's generation stood in line of succession. Thus the Duke of York was now heir presumptive, with the Duke of Clarence second in the line of succession, and Edward third.

Caroline, Princess of Wales, was now too old and too dissipated to be looked to for another child. That the Duke of York was sterile, or the Duchess of York was barren, had been patent for years, so no heir could be expected of them. But the Duke of Clarence, in his relationship with Mrs. Jordan, had proved himself immensely fertile. And by now Clarence was a most eligible bachelor. He had thrown Mrs. Jordan out of his home in 1811, and in 1816 she had died in poverty in Paris. Clarence had no encumbrances save his ten natural children by Mrs. Jordan, who still lived with him at Bushey Park. It seemed certain, therefore, that Clarence would now have to marry for the sake of begetting an heir to the throne. If Edward considered the possibility of himself having to marry, he did not mention it at this time to Julie, for she showed no anxiety for her own position.

One Sunday a few weeks after Princess Charlotte's death, Julie returned from Mass to find Edward at the breakfast table. A pale winter sun and a crackling log fire enriched the glow of the Persian carpets and glittered in the candelabra and silverware. A servant entered, placed Julie's coffee and rolls on the table, and removed the plate off which Edward had just eaten his customary bacon and eggs. When the servant left the room Julie kissed Edward lightly on the forehead and for a moment he put his hand in hers. Then, while she ate, Edward began to open his giant mail.

For fifteen minutes or so there prevailed the kind of silence that envelops in a congenial communion couples who have been so long together as to be almost one body and one spirit. As Julie finished her breakfast, she asked Edward to pass across to her the previous day's copy of the *London Morning Chronicle*. He did so, and went on reading a report of the annual meeting of the St. Patrick's Charitable Association.

Edward recalled later to Thomas Creevey, a Member of Parliament and inveterate gossip and diarist, that his attention was called suddenly to "an extraordinary noise and a strong convulsive movement in Madame de St. Laurent's throat". Julie fell to the floor in a swoon. Edward told Creevey that on running around the table to her aid he "entertained serious apprehensions for her safety". With the help of servants he revived Julie and asked her what had happened.

She pointed to an editorial in the influential *Morning Chronicle* which expressed the view that all the sons of George III who had not already contracted a valid marriage should do so at the earliest possible moment in order to beget a series of young and indisputable heirs. Edward's name appeared to be uppermost in the editorial writer's mind. Edward did his best to comfort Julie by arguing that the onus to marry was on Clarence alone, and that their own relationship was not in jeopardy. Julie smiled wanly and retired to her room. Edward called for another cup of coffee.

For a few days Edward and Julie each pretended to the other that all would be well; but on pondering the significance of the *Morning Chronicle* editorial, both must have reached the agonizing conclusion that the parting of their ways was near.

On December 11, 1817, Thomas Creevey was passing through Brussels on his way back to London after a visit to the Duke of Wellington. This Liverpool-born M.P. was then famous as an intermediary through whom important people communicated their opinions and desires, with diplomatic indirection, to quarters where they wished them to be known. In other words, Creevey served as a sort of itinerant kite-flyer. Edward saw no objection to using him as a means of informing the royal family in London that while it distressed him, he was facing up to the problem of a new heir in a business-like way. He summoned Creevey to the house for an interview, which the diarist recorded in these words:

The Duke began, to my great surprise, a conversation upon the death of Princess Charlotte, and to the best of my recollection, and I would almost say word for word, spoke to me as follows:

"My opinion is the Regent will not attempt a divorce. I know persons in the Cabinet who will never consent to such a measure. Then, was he to attempt it, his conduct would be exposed to such recrimination as to make him unpopular beyond all measure, throughout the country. No: he never will attempt it. Besides, the crime of adultery on her part must be proved in an English court of justice; and if found guilty she must be executed for high treason. No: the Regent will never try for a divorce.

"As for the Duke of York, at his time of life and that of the Duchess, all issue, of course, is out of the question. The Duke of Clarence, I have no doubt, will marry if he can; but the terms he asks from the Ministers are such as they can never comply with. Besides a settlement such as is proper for a Prince who marries expressly for a succession to the Throne, the Duke of Clarence demands the payment of all his debts, which are very great, and a handsome provision for each of his ten natural children. These are terms that no Ministers can accede to. Should the Duke of Clarence not marry, the next prince in succession is myself; and altho' I trust I shall be at all times ready to obey any call my country may make upon me God only knows the sacrifice it will be whenever I shall think it my duty to become a married man.

"It is now seven-and-twenty years that Madame de St. Laurent and I have lived together. We are of the same age and have been in all climates, and in all difficulties together: and you may well imagine, Mr. Creevey, the pang it will occasion me with to part with her. I put it to your own feeling—in the event of any separation between you and Mrs. Creevey. As for Madame de St. Laurent herself, I protest I don't know what is to become of her if a marriage is to be forced on me. Her feelings are already so agitated upon the subject. You saw, no doubt, that unfortunate paragraph in the *Morning Chronicle,* which appeared after the Princess Charlotte's death. From that day to this I am compelled to be in the practice of daily dissimulation with Madame de St. Laurent to keep this subject from her thoughts.

"I am, fortunately, acquainted with the gentlemen in Brussels who conduct the *Liberal* and *Oracle* newspapers. They have promised me to keep all articles upon the subject of my marriage out of their papers, and I hope my friends in England will be equally prudent. My brother the Duke of Clarence is the elder brother, and has certainly the right to marry if he chooses, and I would not interfere with him on any account. If he wishes to be King—to be married and have children poor man—God help him! Let him do so! For myself I am a man of no ambition, and wish only to remain as I am.

"Easter, as you know, falls very early this year—the 22nd of March. If the Duke of Clarence does not take any step before that time, I must find some pretext to reconcile Madame de St. Laurent to my going to England for a short time. St. George's Day is the day now fixed for keeping the birthday, and my paying my respects to the Regent on that day will be a sufficient excuse for my appearance in England. When once there, it will be easy for me to consult with my friends as to the proper steps to be taken.

Should the Duke of Clarence do nothing before that time as to marrying it will become my duty, no doubt, to take some measures upon the subject myself.

"You have heard the names of the Princess of Baden and the Princess of Saxe-Coburg mentioned. The latter connection would perhaps be the better of the two, from the circumstance of Prince Leopold being so popular with the nation. But before anything is proceeded with in this matter, I shall hope and expect to see justice done by the Nation and the Ministers to Madame de St. Laurent. She is of very good family and has never been an actress, and I am the first and only person who ever lived with her *(sic)*. Her disinterestedness, too, has been equal to her fidelity. When she first came to me it was upon £100 a year. That sum was afterwards raised to £400, and finally to £1,000: but when my debts made it necessary for me to sacrifice a great part of my income, Madame de St. Laurent insisted upon again returning to her income of £400 a year.

"If Madame de St. Laurent is to return to live among her friends, it must be in such a state of independence as to command their respect. I shall not require very much, but a certain number of servants and a carriage are essentials. Whatever the Ministers agree to give for such purposes must be put out of all doubt as to its continuance. I shall name Mr. Brougham, yourself and two other people on behalf of Madame de St. Laurent for this object.

"As for my own settlement, as I shall marry (if I marry at all) for the succession, I shall expect the Duke of York's marriage to be considered the precedent. That was a marriage for the succession, and £25,000 for income was settled, in addition to all his other income, purely on that account. I shall be contented with the same arrangement, without making any demands grounded on the difference of the value of money in 1792 and at present. As for the payment of my debts, I don't call them great. The nation, on the contrary, is greatly my debtor."

Here a clock striking in the room where we were seemed to remind the Duke he was exceeding his time, and he came to a conclusion almost instantly, and I retired.

The sincerity of Edward's grief at the prospects of parting from Julie was evident in the emotional nature of a letter he wrote early in December, 1817, to Mrs. Fitzherbert:

My heart is half broke when I look upon my poor companion. I think we may perhaps ere long be forced, by my duties to my family and to my country, to part. The thought quite distresses me and from morning to night I hardly have a dry eye. But I strive to think that an all wise providence will direct all eventually for the best. . . . It will be for me to wait and see if I am thought of not by the Public Voice [the press], for that we know matters little, but by my eldest brother and his government. If it comes to that I hope I shall have the energy to do my duty, but the sacrifice will be dreadful. . . . Even that case can only be thought of if the means are afforded me . . . to provide for the honourable and comfortable independence of that individual who has been my sole comfort and companion during many dreary years which I passed, one might say, almost beyond the pale of society. You see how openly I speak to you, but I know that you enter into my feelings.

Christmas in Brussels in 1817 was, for Edward and Julie, a poignant holiday. They knew that the festival would be their last together, and they spent it entirely alone. In Edward's desk were letters from the Regent and Prime Minister Lord Liverpool informing him that the Government expected him, as well as the Dukes of Clarence, Cambridge, and Sussex, to marry at the earliest possible moment for dynastic reasons. All through January, 1818, Edward lingered in Brussels with Julie, putting off from day to day the dreaded discussion of a separation. Some idea of his anguish may be gathered from a letter he wrote on January 18, 1818, to August Vasserot, Baron de Vincy, that Swiss friend in whose home, twenty-eight years before, he had first met Julie. The letter read:

Dear Vincy:
    If I have delayed in thanking you for your letter of November 10th, which I received on November 25th, I beg you to believe that it is entirely due to the complete desolation which I have felt since this cruel catastrophe the death of the Princess Charlotte, which has taken from me all initiative either for correspondence or any other occupation. I have, in fact, been living for more than two months in complete seclusion. I have only left the house for the air and exercise that health dictates, and I have hardly seen a living soul. All that you tell me concerning the good opinion which my fellow-countrymen have of me is certainly very flatter-

ing. But at the moment it is precisely this which causes me great regret, because I see already that this kindly feeling on their part could compel me to make sacrifices that will cost me dear and will greatly affect the happiness of the peaceful life which I have been leading since my retirement from active service in 1803.

I do not know if you understand to what I refer, but I imagine you do, and in any case the uncertainty of the post forbids me to enlarge upon so delicate a matter. So I shall limit myself to saying that I place all my confidence in divine providence to guide me, and give me the necessary firmness, should that terrible moment which I fear arrive, to do that which my duty to my country and my family may exact from me, despite all that I may have to suffer personally. My faithful companion, to whom I have read the paragraph of your letter which concerns her, is very alive to all those pleasant and complimentary remarks which you make in regard to her. She is, thank God, in good health, although she has profoundly shared all my grief during these last two months of seclusion. Just as she has been before this in America, in Canada, in Gibraltar, my one and only companion, she has also become dearer to me, if such a thing were possible, by her conduct during this wretched time.

Edward, Duke of Kent

Edward's later letters suggest that it was Julie who took the initiative in precipitating the final separation. Despite the scantiness of the records of Julie's life, they reveal an unmistakable nobility of character, and we may be sure she approached the parting with dignity. There would be no tears, no clutching of Edward's lapels, no subsiding to the floor and hugging of her lover's knees. Rather would she stand before him, a little wistfully perhaps, but calmly, and with gratitude outshining the regret in her brilliant sloe eyes. One can imagine her reminding him that they had been fortunate to spend the best years of their lives together, and that, now that the time had come to face the inevitable, she proposed to free him, for the sake of England's future.

In toying too long with sentimental theories, however, we encroach upon the bastard craft of the historical novelist. It is our task to cleave to the records, which indicate only that some time early in 1818 Julie made a suggestion to Edward. She offered to remove herself from his orbit by retreating to a convent in Paris. Edward assented. Then, in spite of Edward's protests, Julie refused to accept his offer of a continued annual allowance. Finally the parting took place.

The tribulation suffered by Edward and Julie left the British press unmoved. The spirit in which the newspapers anticipated the imminent marriage of four royal dukes was distilled in a verse by the satirist Peter Pindar, who wrote:

> Yoics! the Royal sport's begun
> I'faith but it is glorious fun
> For hot and hard each Royal pair
> Are at it hunting for the heir.

In March, 1818, Edward returned to London alone and learned that the Regent and Prime Minister Lord Liverpool had selected as his bride the German princess whom Princess Charlotte had urged him to marry and whose name he had mentioned himself to Thomas Creevey as being the most suitable: Victoria Maria Louisa, the thirty-two-year-old daughter of the Duke of Saxe-Saalfeld-Coburg, widow of Charles, Prince of Leiningen-Dachsburg-Hadenburgh, and a sister of the recently bereaved Prince Leopold.

Victoria was a handsome, buxom young woman, with dark hair, dark brown eyes, a rosy complexion, and a generous red mouth. The *Ladies' Monthly Museum,* a fashionable English periodical, eulogized her as "majestic, with plastic and expressive features". The writer of the article added: "The bright, almost high colour in her cheeks makes her resemble the lovely princess of the Irish legend whose beauty was compounded of ravens' plumes, blood and snow. With the fine eyes characteristic of the family she has been fortunate enough not to inherit the hooked Coburg nose." In her manner Victoria was talkative, bustling, efficient, and often a little censorious. She dressed in elaborate rustling silks, draped velvet, and waving feathers, and she moved with such celerity and purpose that after she passed one of her guests in a corridor one day he remarked: "I almost lost my wig to the gale."

Although Victoria led a disciplined life, and outwardly observed a stern Lutheran code of morals, it was noticed that the sight of a well-built man could set her bosom heaving. Years later when she was in her fifties, her daughter Queen Victoria caught her in the passionate embrace of the Kent family comptroller John Conroy, and disliked her ever afterwards. As a girl, back in 1802, when the French armies had marched and counter-marched across her father's domains, the sixteen-year-old Princess Victoria had looked into Napoleon's eyes with such promise that he had sent agents to inquire if she would care to replace Josephine. But the agents were too late.

In 1803, when she was seventeen, Victoria married the Prince of Leiningen, a widower, nearly thirty years her senior. He had sought refuge at the Court of Coburg after his Principality of Leiningen, on the banks of the Moselle, had been siezed by the French. He was a hard drinker, and given to fits of depression and cruel wit, but he was sophisticated and good-looking in the slightly weary, rather dissipated manner that appeals to many women, and well practised in the art of courtship. He had no difficulty winning the hot-blooded young daughter of his host.

Eventually Napoleon granted Leiningen, in compensation for his lost territories on the Moselle, the tiny territory of Amorbach in Lower Franconia, and thither Victoria went as his chatelaine. German and French armies advanced and retreated across Amorbach until the end of the Napoleonic Wars, and the territory was reduced to poverty by looting and requisitioning. In the stress of these bloody, hungry days the young bride revealed an invincible spirit and developed what Lytton Strachey, in his *Queen Victoria,* describes as "an independence of character and tenacity of purpose which were to prove useful in very different circumstances".

At Amorbach it was not the Prince of Leiningen, but Victoria, who went out onto the terrace to order away with imperious gestures the French and German soldiers who strayed onto the estate in the hope of stealing a pig or a chicken. With equal firmness, but with more compassion, she rounded up the wounded and typhus-ridden stragglers of both armies and sent one of her menservants to guide the battered little column to the nearest field hospital. Often she went out herself, with a party of gardeners, to bury the dead left by both sides in the endless thrusts and counter-thrusts across her husband's lands. Nearly all the family linen was requisitioned by army surgeons for bandages.

Shell-fire ignited their valuable pine woods and reduced them to a waste of ashes. Tenant farmers, unable to work their fields in the constantly shifting no man's land, failed to pay their rents, and Victoria and her husband were wracked by money problems. But Victoria never yielded to despair. She would win a fierce argument with military requisitioners, dismiss them, and then, smiling triumphantly, enter the room where her husband sat drinking and pull him down into her arms.

The elderly Prince of Leiningen survived only eleven years of Victoria's conjugal rapacity and domestic regimentation. Once the Princess Lieven made the significant comment that Victoria "kills all her husbands". After the Prince of Leiningen's death in 1814, Victoria—who was left with two children, Prince Charles and Princess Feodore—was declared Regent of Amorbach until the boy's coming of age. And she was discharging this duty, with her usual asperity, diligence and success, when the rulers of the United Kingdom took to appraising her as a possible bride for Edward.

According to the diary of Victoria's mother, the Dowager Duchess of Saxe-Saalfeld-Coburg, Edward was considering marriage to her daughter as early as October, 1816, a year in advance of the Princess Charlotte's death. She wrote that Edward had "voiced his intention quite openly" to engage himself at that time, but that Victoria "could not make up her mind". If this was true, then Edward was guilty of treating Julie with an odious duplicity, and the story that he married for purely dynastic reasons crashes in ruins. Since nobody has ever corroborated the Dowager Duchess's testimony on this important point, it is only fair to Edward to argue that her statement might well have stemmed from wishful speculation in Princess Charlotte's letters, and from a mother's natural desire to protect her daughter from the moral stigma that was attached to so brazen a marriage of convenience.

Victoria was certainly not vacillating before the prospects of the marriage when early in May, 1818, after four years of celibate life, she joined her mother at the Schloss Ehrenburg, the Coburg family seat, for the purpose of receiving Edward. The Prince's mounted emissaries, Colonel Bessel Harvey, Mr. Brook Taylor, Mr. Knatchbull and Mr. Barnard, arrived first. They clattered under the portcullis of the ancient castle at four o'clock, several hours before they were expected, and caught the large Coburg family at "dinner". The Dowager Duchess recalled that the table was hastily cleared away as the emissaries entered to produce the formal proposal of marriage, and to announce that Edward would follow them two hours later.

In her diary the Duchess wrote: "We waited with strained curiosity and Victoria with beating heart: she had seen him only once before." When the strapping Edward was announced, it was clear from the gleam in Victoria's eye that she found his physique and his importance equally congenial. "Kent," wrote the Dowager, "was a little shy, however much he is a man of the world, dropping thus, like a bomb, into such a large family. He is a good looking man for his age, a very taking face, pleasant, and a very attractive expression of good nature about his mouth. His tall figure has something noble about it: and the simple plain manner of the hero, combined with delicate good breeding, makes his conversation very agreeable."

The betrothal was announced on May 27th, and two days later the wedding took place at the Schloss Ehrenburg. If its turrets and battlements gave the Schloss a bleak and forbidding exterior, its interior offered a rich, warm, and wholly agreeable setting for the ceremony. The high vaulted ceilings were supported on pillars of shining marble; the walls were hung with draperies in pink, green and gold; passage from one salon to another was yielded by massive doors of polished, inlaid wood; guests walked over acres of white carpets woven with patterns of pink roses, and admired the fine collection of paintings and elegant gilt furniture.

At half past nine in the evening Edward waited before the altar in the Hall of Giants, whose high, richly painted ceiling was supported on the shoulders of massive sculptured figures drawn from the brooding mists of Teutonic legend. He stood beneath a crimson velvet canopy in the full dress uniform of a field marshal, with enormous epaulettes and, in the words of the Dowager Duchess, "an incredible cocked hat". When Victoria entered to the Bridal March, her proud mother thought that she "looked most attractive in a dress of white silk lace trimmed with white roses and orange blossom". The Lutheran ceremony proceeded, and soon the ancient cannon on the battlements barked twenty-one times to announce that the Houses of Hanover and Coburg, so recently riven by the Princess Charlotte's death, were now united once more.

It was a union destined to produce the greatest monarch in British history, a woman who bridged the turbulent divide between medieval feudalism and modern capitalism, carried the nation unshaken through a maelstrom of scientific upheaval, and left a crown she picked up from the muck and reek of lechery securely ensconced in a new, durable, and highly venerated royal code.

For state reasons Edward and Victoria had to be remarried according to Church of England rites in the United Kingdom. So they left the Schloss Ehrenburg shortly after the Lutheran ceremony and made a honeymoon journey toward the channel. Edward was flattered and surprised by Victoria's ardour. There can be no doubt that she fell deeply in love with him, and that her youth commanded no mean measure of response. He made no attempt to hide from her the story of his life with Julie, and he admired the composure and understanding with which she heard it.

During the journey they stayed for a few days in Brussels, and Edward pointed out to Victoria the house of the Duke de Maldegham where, with Julie, he had spent such a happy year. The sight of the house set him worrying about Julie's fortunes, and he excused himself from Victoria on the evening of June 22, 1818, to write this letter to the Baron de Vincy:

My Dear de Vincy:

I shall not conceal from you that to fulfil this duty to my country and my family my separation from my excellent and faithful companion of almost twenty-eight years cost me a far greater sacrifice than it would ever be possible for me to express to you. But I hope that the manner in which we quitted each other will render it certain for life that the friendship produced by so long an intimacy will never diminish and that nothing can alter the sentiments we mutually entertain for each other, and which can in no wise influence the new duties which it is incumbent upon me to fulfil.

Therefore, in future, when any of my friends is within easy reach of this excellent and estimable woman, I desire that they consider as the strongest proof of attachment that they can give to me any mark of attention which they can show to her, and above all, if they are married men, let them remember that she is a woman of virtue, my connection with whom, by virtue of my position, can only have been respectable, and consequently that, by taking their wives to call on her, they cannot be accused of doing that which is incorrect, whilst, as for me personally, they will be doing that which will be particularly agreeable and flattering to me.

Edward

A few days after this letter was mailed, Edward and Victoria reached London and stayed in his old bachelor apartments at Kensington Palace. On July 11, 1818, they were married according to the Anglican rite, before the Regent and Queen Charlotte, in the Queen's drawing-room at Kew Palace. The ceremony was a double wedding. At the same time the obese and heavily powdered Duke of Clarence, now fifty-four, was married to the twenty-six-year-old Princess Adelaide of Saxe-Meiningen.

Victoria, dark eyed, blooming, and gorgeously dressed, almost eclipsed the gentle, plain, evangelical, and rather frightened Adelaide. At the family party which followed, however, both Victoria and Adelaide were outshone by the beautiful, slender, vivacious, twenty-year-old Princess Augusta of Hesse-Cassel, who, two months before, had married the Duke of Cambridge, at forty-five years of age the youngest of the royal brothers, and the only one to share with the Regent a continuing addiction to the wig.

The celebrations were not particularly enjoyable for the three brides, because all were aware of the embarrassing importance the House of Hanover set upon their fertility, and of the excited speculation about which of them would be first to produce a child. The position of the forty-six-year-old Duke of Sussex, who wore a small black cap because he believed he was suffering from an acute malformation of the skull, intensified the atmosphere of the racecourse at the start of a race. Sussex had been scratched from the event at the last moment because his marriage to Lady Augusta ("Goosy") Murray, in 1793, while officially invalid, was now deemed morally inimical to a second wedding.

The favourite in the race was Cambridge, because of the youth of his bride; next was Edward, because of his health and vigour; and the outsider was Clarence, because of his debility. But, as Peter Pindar wrote:

Agog are all, both old and young
Warm'd with desire to be prolific
And prompt with resolution strong
To fight in Hymen's war terrific.

Edward and Victoria settled in Kensington Palace and tried to live on the seven thousand pounds a year that still was Edward's sole income. They had only one cook, and a few serving-girls; butlers and footmen were beyond their means. Edward made repeated appeals to the Regent for financial aid, but without success.

The Regent, who had never cared much for the Princess Charlotte when she was alive, now felt her death keenly. Blessed with a lively spirit, good looks and a handsome young husband whose sobriety had appealed strongly to the people, Charlotte had captured the heart of the nation; and the Regent, as her father, had enjoyed a measure of reflected popularity. Now that Charlotte was gone, the Regent realized that all the remaining monarchist sentiment and hope in the country was focussed on his recently wedded brothers, and that he stood in danger of being forgotten.

There was neither youth nor beauty in the Regent's household. He had not realized until recently how important are these elements to the glamour that must invest an enduring throne. When he heard, for example, that Princess Augusta of Hesse-Cassel, the Duke of Cambridge's lovely bride, a complete new-comer to the English scene, had been followed by wildly cheering crowds in Hyde Park, the Regent was astonished—and then dismayed. If this was what the people wanted, then he had nothing to give. The thought rankled. He begrudged his brothers their new status and the bright future it seemed to promise them. And Edward, of course, the brother he had always detested, was to suffer most from his malevolence.

The shrewish hostility that Victoria, Duchess of Kent, displayed in later years toward George IV and William IV was incubated during this summer of 1818, when she realized that she was married to the most unwanted man in the royal family. And it was not out of selfishness that her rancour grew. It was not because she resented having to share Edward's exclusion from favour and ceremony—Victoria didn't care a damn for state occasions. It was the sheer injustice of the matter that aroused her ire. Here was Edward, by far the most meritorious of George III's sons, treated like a pariah. Victoria now loved Edward dearly; and one day, with her infant daughter to fortify her importance, she would avenge him.

Meanwhile she pleased Edward hugely by exhibiting a surprising enthusiasm for his odd interests and curious friends. She accompanied him to prize-giving day at the British and Foreign Schools

Society, and consented to become head of the Ladies' Committee. She drove all over London with him, to Sunday schools, bazaars, charity whist drives, orphanages, hospitals, and stone-laying ceremonies. When dull dogs like Robert Owen, William Allen, and Joseph Hume came to tea, she listened to their high-flown notions on how to charm away the troubles of the world with all the bug-eyed admiration of that new breed of women who were already known as "bluestockings".

Edward and Victoria passed the summer of 1818 in England. Outwardly, at least, they were very models of sobriety, virtue, civility, and frugality. The Princess Lieven, detecting—perhaps with envy—the lustier intervals of which Victoria was capable behind closed doors, but condemning with superior satisfaction Victoria's patently limited intellect, wrote to her lover Metternich: "Victoria would cut an interesting figure now if she had it in her to do so; but whatever you may say she is the most mediocre person it would be possible to meet."

If the royal family found Edward and Victoria equally tedious and middle class, it was because their ideas were as out of date as their reputation among the population at large was low. As Hector Bolitho says in his *The Reign of Queen Victoria:* "The age of princely insolence was over and the day of princely service was beginning. The Duke and Duchess of Kent were heralding a new monarchy of which their daughter was to be the real founder."

But still Edward yearned on occasion for those lighter feminine touches with which Julie had released him so often from his partly inherited, partly self-built, prison of pomposity. In these moments of nostalgia he would pick up his pen and urge his friends to rally around Julie in Paris and ameliorate with their society the loneliness into which she had been plunged by the exigencies of his rank. On July 31, 1818, he wrote once more to the Baron de Vincy:

I appreciate as I should the assurance that you gave me upon a point to which I attach the greatest interest in consequence of that which I feel for the amiable and excellent person of whom I wrote to you in my letter of June 22nd, and to whom I owe so much, because of her perfect behaviour towards me, during so many consecutive years, and above all in this last crisis. Were I to live to the age of Methusaleh, I should never be able to discharge my debt.

Already all my friends, who at different times have been my familiar companions and who are aware of all the attachment that I must feel for her, have promised to go to visit her with their wives, as soon as opportunity arises, to prove that they were capable of appreciating the respectability of her character, and particularly her noble behaviour, when my public duties, towards my Country and my Family forced me to terminate a connection which, on either side, we wished not to see end but with life itself.

I believe that I should call to your attention that with His Most Christian Majesty's approbation, she has resumed her family name and is now styled Comtesse de Montgenet, and that she resides at present in the Hôtel de Ste. Aldegonde, 116 rue de Grenelle, Faubourg St. Germain, Paris. She had made all arrangements to take up her residence with her elder sister the Comtesse de Jensac, and things were just beginning to get settled a little and she to feel comfortable, when her poor sister fell ill and after an illness of four days' duration died in her arms.

Consider what an increase of misfortune this is and what energy she will need to struggle with this additional grief. But I flatter myself that with the strength of character which I know her to possess she will successfully overcome it and that she will in the end regain the calm and tranquillity which are so essential to tranquilize my fears for her health, and that by the help of my friends, and above all of their wives, she will succeed in gathering together a small and respectable society, of which I dare to predict she will be the delight.

It will be then that, learning from the lips and the letters of one and another of my friends that she is at least tranquil and contented, I shall at last begin to taste, in my new union, the happiness which the perfect character of the amiable Princess to whom I am now linked for life is calculated to produce. Certainly she seems entirely worthy of my attachment, the more so since she is not ignorant of my previous connection, and gives me every reason to believe that she respects it.

Your very affectionate and devoted,

Edward Duke of Kent

In the autumn of 1818 Edward and Victoria decided to winter at Amorbach. They travelled economically, Edward accompanied by an orderly and Victoria by a German lady-in-waiting. On the way through Belgium they called on the Duke of Wellington, whose headquarters were then in Valenciennes. Wellington's ramrod frame was now so stiff with pride and his chin so elevated with conceit that he was incapable of looking upon anything, animal, vegetable or mineral, except down the line of his goose-beak nose. The man who could utter such a hidebound inanity as "the Battle of Waterloo was won on the playing fields of Eton" obviously had no time for a royal duke who worried about the problem of where poor women could find a decent lying-in.

Much as he disliked Edward, however, Wellington hid his true feelings from the Prince. Instead he contented himself with sarcastic comments, behind Edward's back, particularly to the toady Thomas Creevey. As he invited Edward and Victoria to dinner Wellington noticed, with a wrinkling of his overworked proboscis, that the Duchess's lady-in-waiting was old and ugly. Thomas Creevey recorded that as soon as the Kents were out of earshot Wellington went stamping among his staff bleating: "Who the devil is to take in the maid of honour?" Hearing no volunteers, he cried, "Dammit, Freemantle, find out the mayor and let him do it." The mayor, according to Creevey, was dutiful.

The next day Edward attended a review by Wellington of Saxon and Danish troops. Creevey, who was also there, wrote: "The Duke of Kent's appearance was atrocious. He was dressed in the jacket and cap of his regiment [The Royals] and but for his blue ribbon and star he might well have passed for an orderly sergeant. The Duke of Wellington's appearance was, as it always is on such occasions, perfect. I have never seen anyone to be compared with him." That same evening Edward and Victoria dined with Wellington once more, and after the meal there was dancing. Creevey says: "The Duchess of Kent waltzed a little and the Duke of Kent put his hand on her cheek to feel if she was not too hot."

This display of bourgeois tenderness on Edward's part made the Duke of Wellington turn suddenly to Creevey, saying: "Well Creevey, and what has passed between you and *the corporal* since you have met this time?" Creevey told Wellington that Edward had mentioned the fact that Queen Charlotte was ill and that on this account Edward had had some misgivings about leaving England. Upon which Wellington laid hold of Creevey's button and said: "God dammit! Ye know what his sisters call him? By God! They call him *Joseph Surface.*" Wellington then ventilated one of his "roaring laughs" which "made everyone turn about to the right and left to see what was the matter".

Creevey explains: "The Duke of Wellington's constant joking with me about the Duke of Kent was owing to the curious conversation I had had with him in the autumn of 1817, the particulars of which had always amused the Duke very much." He was referring, of course, to the conversation in which Edward had acknowledged that it was necessary for him to leave Julie and to marry for dynastic reasons.

A few days later Edward and Victoria accompanied Wellington and the indefatigable Creevey to breakfast with the Count Woronzow, commander of a Prussian corps. Before sitting down to eat, however, Woronzow invited them to inspect his military school, where five hundred privates were learning reading, writing and arithmetic under the Lancaster plan. "Nothing could be nicer than the room or more perfect than the establishment," wrote Creevey. "This education takes eight months and the whole army goes through it in turn."

Edward naturally was delighted at seeing the educational system he had done so much to promote now employed in Allied armies, and while the Duke of Wellington hummed and hawed and kicked his heels he lingered to chat with the soldier students. Then came another visit to another school, where the Prussian privates were taught shoemaking, tailoring, blacksmithing, and other trades that would benefit them on their discharge.

Creevey complained: "As the Duke of Kent was to the last degree tiresome, in examining all the details of this establishment, and asked questions without end, I expressed some impatience to get at my breakfast upon which the Duke of Wellington, who heard me, was much amused and said: 'I recommend you whenever you start out with any of the Royal Family in the morning, and particularly with *the corporal,* always to breakfast first.'"

Wellington had learned much on the playing fields of Eton, but neither manners nor compassion—an omission for which he was to pay, years later, when he was reduced to the indignity of ducking stones that were hurled through his windows by a London mob. Edward was not so insensitive as he sometimes appeared, and he must have heard the snorts, sneers and sniggers that mysteriously made the air sibilant whenever he turned his back on the Iron Duke. At all events Edward and Victoria departed suddenly one morning for Amorbach and a winter among the sparkling hills that sweep down to the Rhine.

Amorbach was a pleasant place, with a Benedictine abbey and a ferruginous spring. The castle that the Duchess of Kent's son Prince Charles would inherit when he came of age looked like an illustration from a book of fairy-tales. Within its walls Goethe had composed *Hermann und Dorothea* and Schiller had written *Wallenstein*. But it was still riddled with the cannon-ball holes of the Napoleonic wars and was therefore drafty and damp. Edward borrowed ten thousand pounds for its renovation. All through the winter of 1818-19 imported English workmen engaged in repairs. Edward and Victoria engaged in their duty to England, and before Christmas the Duchess was sure she was pregnant.

About the same time it was announced that the Duchesses of Clarence and Cambridge were also in this happy condition, and that each had decided to bear her child in Hanover. Edward was fearful of his child being born in Amorbach, because of the remote location and the risk of "the thousand and one rumours that might hereafter be raised relative to its identity". In other words, he suspected that the Regent might denounce his child as a "warming-pan baby" if its birth were not witnessed, according to royal custom, by British or Hanoverian statesmen.

He therefore informed the Regent by mail, in March of 1819, that he was bringing Victoria to England for the *accouchement*. He asked for the use in Kensington Palace of an apartment that had once belonged to a Mrs. Meynell, a lady-in-waiting, "and the loan of the kitchen and its appertaining offices". He asked that the royal yacht should meet him at Calais on the morning of April 19, 1819, to transport his *entourage* across the Channel. And he begged the Regent to send him a little money to cover the costs of the journey.

Grudgingly the Regent agreed to Edward's use of the Kensington Palace apartment and the royal yacht, but declined to send money. Edward then appealed for funds to his wife's brother, Prince Leopold, who was still drawing the fifty thousand pounds a year he had been voted by the British Parliament on his marriage to the late Princess Charlotte. Leopold knew that the Regent did not want Edward and Victoria to come to England. So, despite all that Edward had done in earlier days to help him achieve his wealth and rank, Leopold decided he was not going to risk the Regent's displeasure by paying for the trip. Resorting to typical Coburg guile, he pleaded a temporary financial embarrassment and kept his hands in his pockets.

When Edward tried to borrow money from his sisters, they refused on the pretence of being shocked at the idea of exposing the pregnant Duchess of Kent to the fatigues and joltings of a long journey. "I am outrageous with Edward," wrote the Princess Augusta. "He is behaving like a fool and a madman." Eventually it was Edward's much despised commoner friends who made it possible for the future Queen to be born on British soil. By holding back one of the instalments due on his debts, his trustees William Allen and Joseph Hume were able to send Edward a small draft on a bank in Frankfort. It was so small, in fact, that it compelled him to travel like a merchant or an engineer. He hired a heavy coach that was nearly a hundred years old, and two dray horses, and set off in what an English observer described as "an unbelievably odd caravan".

On the driver's box, with whip and reins, sat Edward, looking most plebeian in his ulster and a private's forage cap. Inside rode the Duchess of Kent, with Feodore, the daughter of her first marriage; a nurse, a lady's maid, two lap-dogs, and several cages of canaries. By night they stopped at wayside inns, many of which still bore the scars of shell-fire. Sometimes the roads were so rough and so steep that all save the Duchess had to dismount and walk to lighten the load of the slipping, panting nags. Several times the horses, unused to long journeys, balked and caused hours of delay. But after two weeks of whipping, bumping and swaying the coach clattered into Calais, where, to his great relief, Edward found the royal yacht awaiting them. Wearily the travel-stained party staggered up the gangplank, and then for many hours were tossed about the Channel by a gale.

On reaching Kensington Palace, about the middle of April, Edward wrote to a friend a letter quoted in Roger Fulford's *Royal Dukes*. "I trust," he said, "that my countrymen will duly appreciate

187

the great sacrifice and exertion made by the Duchess in travelling at a period drawing so near her confinement." Edward then made a reference to the reactions of the Regent. "With regard to congratulations from a certain quarter to which you allude," he wrote, "I could say a great deal, but as harmony and peace is my object I would much rather the world should think that everything was most cordial between us than the reverse."

The Duchess of Kent proved as secure in her carriage of the child as she had been enthusiastic in its conception, and on May 24, 1819, went into labour. The Regent appointed Home Secretary George Canning, the Archbishop of Canterbury, and the Duke of Wellington to observe the birth. Just as the gipsy of Gibraltar had predicted, the child, delivered by Frau Siebold, the midwife of the Saxe-Saalfeld-Coburg family, was a girl; and the Duke of Wellington noted, from behind his twitching nostrils, that she was "as plump as a partridge".

Edward denied that he would have preferred a son. He wrote to a friend: "As to the circumstances of the child not proving to be a son instead of a daughter I feel it due to myself to declare that such sentiments are not in unison with my own; for I am decidedly of the opinion that the decrees of Providence are at all times wisest and best."

The Duke of Clarence's child lived for only a few hours, so the baby Princess of Kent stood fourth in the line of succession. The very thought of a successor sprung from the loins of his despised brother filled the Regent with resentment. His anger was intensified by Edward's choice of the Tsar of Russia, a man the Regent disliked, for one of the godparents. Edward's reason for this odd selection was the Tsar's interest in the Lancastrian system of education. Such an interest, of course, merely strengthened the Regent's conviction that the Tsar was as eccentric as Edward.

As the date of the christening approached, Edward made several attempts to get the Regent to approve a name for the baby. He submitted a list including the names Elizabeth, Georgiana, and Augusta; but the Regent brusquely rejected them and dismissed Edward with curt insults. On the eve of the christening the Regent was still hesitating over the choice of a name, and Edward and the Duchess of Kent were panic-stricken by the lateness of the hour. Edward was driven to seeking the counsel of the Duke of York, who

KENT HOUSE
the Duke's residence in Quebec, then as now, 25 rue St-Louis.

Quebec Historical Service,
Samuel de Champlain National Society.

Government House, Gibraltar

THE CONVENT
a Franciscan monastery, circa 1480, used as Government House
in Gibraltor after the British occupation.

Picture Collection,
Toronto Public Libraries.

PRINCESS VICTORIA
with her mother, the Duchess of Kent,
from a painting by Sir William Beechey, R.A., 1821.

Hector Bolitho Victoriana Collection,
Toronto Public Libraries.

advised him to leave the matter until the very moment of baptism.

There followed, of course, a famous scene. On June 24, 1819, the royal family gathered for the christening ceremony around the gold font in the Grand Salon at Kensington Palace. As Manners Sutton, the Archbishop of Canterbury, began the service there were muttered conferences, anxious glances and deprecatory coughs, for everyone knew that the Regent, puffy-eyed and liverish from the previous night's wine, was still debating in his befuddled mind the problem of the child's name.

When Manners Sutton took the child in his arms and said to the godparents, "Name this child," the unfortunate people looked around wildly and spluttered in helpless ignorance of what to say. Edward spoke from the congregation, venturing again the name Elizabeth. The Regent said loudly, "On no account." Somebody else said "Charlotte." And the Regent's voice rang out in the words: "Certainly not!" The archbishop then asked the Regent what name he *should* give to the child; and the Regent, after considerable delay, said "Alexandrina." The Duke of York then piped up, saying that surely one name was not sufficient. He suggested Victoria. Then there was a long, embarrassed pause, during which the Princesses Augusta and Mary clucked reproachfully. "Very well," said the Regent, "call her after her mother. But Alexandrina must come first."

So the infant was christened with the most un-English names Alexandrina Victoria. Her father stared ahead in stony rumination over his rejected wishes, and her mother, who had never been consulted at all, collapsed in tears.

Meanwhile Frau Siebold, the busy Coburg midwife, had returned to Germany, travelling night and day in a coach driven by hard-riding relays of postillions. On June 21, 1819, three days before the christening of Victoria, she had delivered one of the many first cousins of that illustrious infant. Officially he was the second son of the young Duke of Saxe-Saalfeld-Coburg, the Duchess of Kent's brother. According to rumour he was the son of a Jewish courtier with whom Luise, the pretty young Duchess of Saxe-Saalfeld-Coburg, was suspected of relieving the tedium of her husband's long absences on hunting trips.

That highly descriptive diarist, the Dowager Duchess of Saxe-Saalfeld-Coburg, described this little boy as being as "quick as a weasel". She added that her son the Duke "wishes to give him the old Saxon name of Albert". Thus, in the space of one month, the foundations of the Victoria and Albert epoch were laid.

But many years were to pass before olive-skinned Albert the Good of Coburg, with his lips firmly sealed against indiscretion, presumption, or humour; with his eyes on the chess-board, the royal accounts, and plans for the Crystal Palace; and with his ears ever open to the counsel of Baron Stockmar, his sombre, Teutonic "grey eminence", would wipe off the throne of England the last gaudy stains of Hanoverian lust, recklessness, foppery, and arrogance.

In the meantime Edward, the only Hanoverian with a hint of Coburg sobriety in his make-up, was entering upon the last year of his life. It was to be an empty year. Edward's romance had been crushed by duty, his valour had been strangled by jealousy, his idealism had been ridiculed by ignorance, and there was no time left for him to soften those harsh outlines of the martinet, malcontent, hypocrite and prig which so many writers have used when sketching him into biographies of more memorable people.

While the infant Victoria became the centre of public attention, Edward enjoyed little reflected glory. Indeed, in his attitude toward the child he appeared to many as a rather foolish middle-aged man, showing more of the mawkish sentiments of a grandparent than the restrained pride of a father. He wrote, for instance, letters revealing a most unbecoming interest in the more intimate functions of motherhood. Proud that the Duchess was able to breast-feed Victoria herself, he wrote sententiously to friends of the child's "maternal nutriment on the soil of England". On hearing that the mothers of England approved of the Duchess's nursing, he wrote to say he was glad "that an office most interesting in its nature had met with the wishes of society". Later, referring to the weaning of the child, he wrote that "we do not expect, at the earliest, to be able to get over that arduous charge until the second week in November."

There was one occasion, however, when Edward displayed for his daughter more majestic sentiments, sentiments that reflected his awareness of the child's great destiny. When Victoria was only three months old he took her to a grand review of troops on Hounslow Heath. She lay in a little wicker basket, on the seat of the old, high-wheeled Canadian curricle, within a few feet of the charger on which her father, in field marshal's uniform, sternly watched the march past.

It was not until after he had taken the salute that the Regent turned around and noticed the odd presence of a curricle amid the mounted brass hats behind him. With bulging eyes he studied it for a moment and then, in a fit of wrath, he spluttered in front of all his state officers: "What business has that infant here?" Edward made no reply. As he stared fixedly ahead, observers noticed a tiny smile flicker across his lips, as if he were saying under his breath: "Brother, you know well enough. Her business is with the troops who will soon be her own."

As a reminder that his days were numbered, the baby Victoria was a constant irritant to the swollen, dropsical, baleful "Prinny". He was particularly affronted by the way Edward and the Duchess took Victoria with them on visits to philanthropic meetings and public institutions, and thus won for themselves the plaudits of aldermen, shopkeepers, mechanics, accountants, and others belonging to that despised class whose rising power frightened and bewildered him. Had Edward and the Duchess refrained from parading the child so frequently, the Regent might well have softened and found means of providing his brother with more money. As things were, Edward still had to struggle along on seven thousand pounds a year.

By September of 1819, Edward was knee-deep once more in financial difficulties. "I am satisfied," he wrote to a friend, "that to continue to live in England, even in the quiet way we are going on, without splendour and without show, nothing short of doubling the seven thousand will do, reduction being impossible in an establishment like ours where there is not a servant idle from morning to night."

In the autumn of 1819 Edward was seized with a most fantastic brain-wave for solving his money problems. In a letter to his old friend Sir Alexander Mackenzie, the great Canadian explorer, he said that he had gathered around him a "committee of friends" for the purpose of organizing the sale of Castle Hill Lodge "by way of Tontine, or raffle, upon the propriety of which I am quite delighted to find that you so perfectly concur with me". Posters appeared throughout London inviting citizens to buy a ticket in the raffle, and informing them that all money subscribed in excess of one hundred thousand pounds—a fair price for the house—would go to charity. Members of Parliament were shocked at the idea of a prince seeking money by such undignified means, and the matter was raised in the House of Commons. A Commons committee failed to share Alexander Mackenzie's indulgence toward the scheme, and Edward was ordered to drop it.

With winter coming on, the Duchess of Kent felt in need of a holiday. But there wasn't a penny in the bank to pay for it. The kindly Robert Owen invited the Duke and Duchess to accept his hospitality at New Lanark. Edward excused himself on the grounds of the long journey involved:

With respect to myself, be assured that I consider the trouble and fatigue of the journey as nothing: nor would the Duchess, but for the critical moment of her health which, immediately after nursing, requires so much attention. With regard to the "plain and simple accommodation" you will have to offer us I speak equally her feelings and my own when I say it is what we should prefer to any other, accompanied by the sincerity of that welcome which Mrs. Owen and yourself would give us. For my own part I am amply convinced that what I should see on the spot would amply repay me for any little trouble and expense the journey might occasion me.

Edward's old tutor, "The Kingfisher", now Bishop of Salisbury, suggested a holiday at Sidmouth in Devonshire, and the idea appealed to Edward. On November 1, 1819, he wrote to Sir Alexander Mackenzie:

I ran over to Devonshire last week to look for a house that might suit the Duchess to pass the next four months in, near the sea, to enjoy the benefit of the mild air of that part of the coast, and of the tepid seabaths, and I trust we shall be able to manage our remove thither in the course of this month. In the meanwhile I know it will give you pleasure to learn that she is getting over the effects of weaning her infant as well as I could possibly expect, and that our little child does not appear to thrive the less for the change. Sincerely hoping that Lady Alexander will get over her own *accouchment* with every possible comfort, and with every sentiment of the warmest friendship and regard for yourself, I remain ever, my dear Sir Alexander,

Yours most faithfully,
Edward

That was one of the last letters Edward wrote from London. One of the last letters he received there contained a welcome cheque. It came from Prince Leopold, who, knowing that the Regent would be only too glad to see the Kents depart from the capital, decided that there was no risk attached this time to footing the costs of the trip.

At the beginning of December Edward set out with his family in a big coach and headed west. They were accompanied by two people who were to have a major share in shaping the character of the young Queen Victoria—Comptroller John Conroy and Governess Luize Lehzen. The latter had been summoned from Amorbach to tutor the Princess Feodore. They drove in easy stages, stopping one night at Windsor Castle, where Edward's spinster sisters expressed delight with "the beautiful fat baby and the excellent, good little wife who has made Edward so happy". They stayed another night in Salisbury with The Kingfisher, and paraded Victoria before an admiring gathering of Cathedral clergy and choir-boys. A third night was spent at an inn. And then, on an unseasonably mild day, they drove into the cluster of small, white, pebble-dashed houses that constituted the resort of Sidmouth.

Edward directed the coachmen to an insignificant two-storey house named Woolbrook Glen. It stood on the hillside, about a quarter of a mile above the beach. Its furnishings were old and ugly and much worn, and its atmosphere had the mustiness of all houses that are regularly rented furnished and stand empty for long intervals between tenants. A cook, a couple of housemaids, and a valet, who had been sent ahead, had struggled hard to give the place a cheerful air, but the Duchess found it "dank and gloomy". One dark omen of the disaster ahead happened the first night. A small boy, potting sparrows with a catapult on the road outside, accidentally shot a stone through the nursery window and narrowly missed hitting the baby Victoria. Edward attempted to relieve the depression at dinner by making a joke about his daughter withstanding fire in a manner becoming a soldier's child.

Christmas came and went under a blanket of mist through which

193

the pallid rays of the sun pushed an uncomfortable warmth. It was humid, windless, oppressive weather; and even the sea, plashing listlessly on the beach, failed to give off any of the invigorating ozone for which Edward had hoped. Every day he pushed Victoria in a perambulator down to the tiny esplanade, sweating heavily in his winter clothes and then dallying dangerously to show his baby off to the little groups of other visitors who were invariably waiting to meet him.

Early in the new year, Edward tried to keep up his sagging spirits by assuring his household that the holiday was doing him a lot of good. He spoke one night of his brothers, and said: "I shall outlive them all." The next day, to prove the extent of his energy, he climbed Peak Hill to observe the view across the waters of Torbay.

It was a muggy, reeking day, following a night of light drizzle. His underclothing became soaked with sweat and his feet and legs became sopping as he slashed through the long, wet grass. Yet when he got home he tarried in his soaked clothes over Victoria's cot, playing with her, and summoning the Duchess to watch her smiles. His valet reproached him for not changing and tried to get him to take a potion of calomel; but Edward, convinced that years of soldiering in foreign climes had given him the constitution of an ox, waved the man away. By the time he decided to change for dinner his clothes had dried on him. The next morning he had such a bad fever that he could not raise his head from the pillow.

A local physician was summoned. He diagnosed a severe chill in the lungs and said he did not wish to shoulder alone the responsibility of caring for so important a patient. Signals were sent to London by military telegraph, and Edward's own surgeon drove down non-stop in less than two days. Hard behind the surgeon drove Prince Leopold—moved, no doubt, by anxiety for his sister, remorse over his shabby treatment of Edward at Amorbach, and a sharp Coburg awareness of the increasing importance of his baby niece Victoria.

Couriers sent down by the Regent galloped back to London with daily dispatches of Edward's worsening condition. At Windsor Castle the Princess Augusta took some consolation in the fact that his health was in the hands of "a very discreet and very bold physician". The physician's boldness lent itself to a therapy of blisters, cuppings, bleedings and leeches, and Edward lost a hundred and twenty ounces of blood.

During these anxious days the Duchess of Kent proved to her household that her love for Edward, despite the expedient nature of their marriage, was deep and abiding. For five days and nights she sat by her husband's bed without once leaving the room long enough to change her dress On the landing outside his door servants listened anxiously to Edward's uneven breathing, and when he broke one day into a racking fit of hiccups they raised their hands and rolled back their eyes in despair.

None knew what was going on under the sweat that welled up among the grey roots of Edward's now thin and streaky dyed hair, but it is probable that in the swirling mists of his fever he saw a momentary image of the seductive face of La Dulaque at Geneva; the lovely face of Julie on the night of the farewell ball at Gibraltar; the ashen face of Private Draper, marching behind his own coffin in Quebec; the shocked face of de Fortisson, picked up from the shambles at Fort Royal; and those two faces he had almost forgotten because he had turned from them in secret shame—the faces of his hardly known sons, Robert Wood and Jean de Mestre. Shakily he held out his hand to the Duchess, and as she graspsed it Edward murmured: "May God have mercy on my wife and child, and forgive my sins."

And then perhaps he saw the brooding, censorious, half-daft face of his father, infuriated at a small boy's breakage of an old clock; the lean, sensuous, foxy face of his brother the Duke of York, indefatigably plotting against him; the silly horse-faces of his sisters as they jeeringly called him Joseph Surface; the insolent donkey-face of Wellington, hee-hawing behind his back and daring to dub a royal field marshal with the nickname "corporal"; and the monstrous purple balloon-face on that indignantly quivering mound of flesh known as the Regent. But Edward knew now that the time for recriminations had gone by. Still holding his wife's fingers, he breathed the Regent's name and said: "If I could now shake hands with him I should die in peace."

It is possible, too, that he saw the lights of the candles in every window in Quebec City as those French people who adored him celebrated his birthday; and the House of Commons passing by acclamation a vote of thanks to him for his part in the victorious

West Indian campaign; and the telegraph, and the great fortifications which had daunted the enemy off Halifax; and the meeting of the Irish Charitable Society where he had joined in the songs and first learned the rudiments of princely service to others.

"Do not," he said, clutching his wife's hand, "do not forget me."

Then on January 23, 1820, as a breath of breeze came at last off the glassy sea, and stirred the wet brown leaves on the road outside, His Royal Highness Prince Edward, Duke of Kent, died at the age of fifty-two.

The Reverend Isaac Sloper wrote this brief eulogy:

His excellent understanding, liberality of sentiment, and benevolence of heart, endeared him to all classes, and rendered him an able advocate and useful patron of numerous societies which distinguish the present age by the Christian principles on which they are constructed. His death deprived the world of a living example of moral worth and public spirit, undiminished by the efforts of bigotry and intolerence, and never obscured by the splendour of a court.

But few people read it. As Edward's coffin, more than seven feet long and over a ton in weight, lumbered on a gun-carriage up to the royal catacombs of Windsor, through Bridport, Blandford, Salisbury and Basingstoke, old George III suddenly tired of life himself, and expired. His inconsiderateness in choosing this time to die thwarted his son's dying wish to be remembered. While Edward's body was being entombed, the newspapers were so full of laments for George III and so full of hails for George IV that there was hardly a line of type left with which to record Edward's funeral service.

Though once or twice Victoria mentioned her father proudly, she encouraged the nation to forget him. After learning of his long association with Julie de St. Laurent, and the existence of her half-brothers overseas, Victoria was embarrassed at mention of her father's name. For nearly a century it was politely pretended by the court that Julie de St. Laurent had never existed; and biographers felt bound to limit themselves, when introducing Edward to their

196

readers, to those very few aspects of his life in which Julie had no part.

Nobody understood Victoria's feelings better than the sweet Julie herself. After Edward's death she sent to Maria Fitzherbert all the correspondence she had exchanged with the Prince. Mrs. Fitzherbert kept the letters in a safe until she died too. When the safe was opened the letters were handed over to Queen Victoria, and what she did with them has not yet been discovered.

Julie's long survival after Edward's death makes a piquant and hitherto unpublished story. She spent a few years recovering from her grief in the Paris convent on the Rue de Grenelle, and then one day in her mid-fifties decided that mourning was a doleful bore. Quietly she slipped out into the world and brightened it once more with her sunny smile, her light-hearted affection, and her hospitality.

Charles X, the last of the Bourbon kings, restored to her a family estate at St. Laurent-sur-Mer, and her title in her own right of Comtesse de Montgenet. This gave her a respectable income and a dignified place in French society. She was still gregarious, but no longer dominant in the salon. It was her custom to gather about her a group of older, quieter guests and to enjoy herself unobtrusively. If English royalty or nobility were present at the many receptions she attended, she kept out of their way and so saved them from an embarrassing memory of her earlier associations.

Men found her slender figure, delicate features, and lively mind still attractive, and among several widowers who paid her court was Prince Prospero Colonna, a member of the Russian branch of the illustrious Italian family. They had family interests in common. Colonna was the father of two sons who lived in New Orleans, and Julie was the mother by de Fortisson of Mélanie Levison, wife of a New Orleans engineer. After a brief betrothal Julie was married quietly to Colonna, and they sailed together to Louisiana to visit their children. Later the couple travelled to Quebec City, where Julie was reunited with Robert Wood, her son by Edward, and her beloved de Salaberry friends.

Robert Wood had been christened at Christ Church Anglican Cathedral in Quebec City; and according to the Montreal historian Luis Carrier, a note regarding his royal ancestry was torn out of the register soon after Queen Victoria came to the throne. By the time Julie arrived in Quebec City, Robert Wood was married to

197

Charlotte Gray, whose father was employed in the Royal Navy commissariat at Kingston, Ontario. Wood lived the life of a small-propertied gentleman on funds that had been supplied by Edward and were later augmented by Queen Victoria. Meanwhile Jean de Mestre, Julie's younger son by Edward, had gone out to Australia as a member of the French consular corps. There he eventually settled. He inherited de Fortisson lands in France, but became a British subject and prospered on Crown lands granted him in Australia by Queen Victoria.

Julie enjoyed Quebec City so much that she persuaded Prince Prospero Colonna to settle down for a prolonged stay. After about three years of happily married life, Colonna embarked on a trip to Russia. His ship foundered at sea, and Julie was widowed again. According to Joan E. Morgan's *Castle of Quebec,* she "lived out her days alone at Montmorency House, Edward's old summer home, on the beautiful Falls, and though surrounded by friends, many of whom had been personal friends of His Royal Highness, she remained in dignified retirement, emerging only on rare occasions."

But Julie kept in close touch with her family. It became a tradition for the male descendants of both her sons by Edward to enter the Imperial Army, and several of them lost their lives in the field. Once, about the year 1845, Julie was visited by two grandsons from Australia. In Canada and Australia there are today distinguished descendants of her association with Edward. She lived until 1872, five years after the Confederation of Canada and the elevation of the nation from colonial to Dominion status. She had reached the magnificent age of one hundred and six.

The twilight of Julie de St. Laurent's life must have been rendered golden by the thought that through her noble sacrifice of Edward there reigned, across the Atlantic, the greatest monarch the British Empire had ever known.

BIBLIOGRAPHY

Anderson, W. J., *Life of the Duke of Kent*

Annual Register

Berton, Pierre, *The Royal Family*

Bolitho, Hector, *The Reign of Queen Victoria*

Bolitho, Hector, *A Biographer's Notebook*

Bradley, A. G., *Lord Dorchester*

Le Bulletin des Recherches Historique (Quebec)

Cobbett, William, *An Autobiography*

Cole, G. D. H., *Life of Robert Owen*

Cole, Margaret, *Robert Owen of New Lanark*

Coleridge, E. H., *Life of Thomas Coutts*

Crabites, Pierre, *Victoria's Guardian Angel*

Creston, Dormer, *The Youthful Queen Victoria*

Davis, Blodwen, *Storied Streets of Quebec*

Dictionary of National Biography

Dufebvre, B., *Cinq Femmes et Nous*

Duff, David, *Edward of Kent*

The Encyclopaedia Britannica

Fenety, G. E., *Life and Times of the Hon. Joseph Howe*

Fortescue, J. W., *A History of the British Army*

Fulford, Roger, *George the Fourth*

Fulford, Roger, *Royal Dukes*

Garratt, G. T., *Gibraltar and the Mediterranean*

The Gentleman's Magazine

Greenwood, Alice Drayton, *Hanoverian Queens of England*

Hasted, Jane-Eliza, *Unsuccessful Ladies*

Kalm, Peter, *Travels in North America*

Kenyon, E. R., *Gibraltar*

Lessert, Gaston de, *Le Chateau et Seigneurie de Vincy*

Ludwig, Emile, *Napoleon*

Maxwell, Sir Herbert, *The Creevey Papers*

Morgan, Joan E., *Castle of Quebec*

Neale, Erskine, *Life of the Duke of Kent*

Owen, Robert, *An Autobiography*

Podmore, Frank, *Robert Owen*

Potvin, Damase, *La Dame Française du Duc de Kent*

Raddall, Thomas H., *Halifax: Warden of the North*

Raymond, W. O., *The Winslow Papers*

Robertson, John Ross, *Diary of Mrs. Simcoe*

Scott, Duncan Campbell, *John Graves Simcoe*

Sitwell, Edith, *Victoria of England*

Smith, Edward, *Life of William Cobbett*

Southey, Thomas, *Chronological History of the West Indies*

Strachey, Lytton, *Queen Victoria*

Stuart, D. M., *Daughter of England*

Stuart, D. M., *Mother of Victoria*

Trevelyan, G. M., *English Social History*

Wade, M. S., *Mackenzie of Canada*

Wilkins, W. H., *Mrs. Fitzherbert and George IV*

Wilson, R. M., *Josephine*

Wood, William, *The Father of British Canada*

INDEX

203